Family Business and Social Capital

T0327588

Family Business and Social Capital

Edited by

Ritch L. Sorenson

University of St. Thomas, Minnesota, USA

Edward Elgar

Cheltenham, UK • Northampton, MA, USA

Published by
Edward Elgar Publishing Limited
The Lypiatts
15 Lansdown Road
Cheltenham
Glos GL50 2JA
UK

Edward Elgar Publishing, Inc.
William Pratt House
9 Dewey Court
Northampton
Massachusetts 01060
USA

A catalogue record for this book
is available from the British Library

Library of Congress Control Number: 2011929462

ISBN 978 1 84980 737 1 (cased)
ISBN 978 1 78254 444 9 (paperback)

Typeset by Servis Filmsetting Ltd, Stockport, Cheshire
Printed and bound by CPI Group (UK) Ltd, Croydon, CR0 4YY

Contents

v

Figures

Tables

Contributors

Carol J. Bruess, PhD Professor Carol Bruess has been teaching for over ten years at the University of St. Thomas, Minnesota in the Communication and Journalism department and has recently become Director of Family Studies. Professor Bruess is committed to the understanding of the communication patterns of couples and families through her research on family and couple ritual and construction of family co-culture through language and ritual. As an active researcher in the area of family communication, Professor Bruess has presented her work at dozens of national, regional, and international conferences and has published in national and international journals and professional books. Some of her co-authored works include *Contemporary Issues in Interpersonal Communication* (with Mark P. Orbe), *What Happy Couples Do*, *What Happy Parents Do*, and *What Happy Women Do* (all with Anna Kudak). In addition, she has been quoted and interviewed in a variety of national media outlets, including PBS, *The Chronicle of Higher Education*, *American Health*, *Cosmopolitan*, the *Early Show*, and a local CBS affiliate.

Jon C. Carr, PhD Dr. Jon Carr is currently an Assistant Professor of Management at the Neeley School of Business, Texas Christian University. His research interests include workplace attitudes and entrepreneurial cognition and their impact on well-being and performance. In 2001, he was a NASA-ASEE Faculty Fellow, where he worked on projects related to technology transfer, remote sensing applications, and organizational development. Dr. Carr has published research on entrepreneurship, family business, and organizational behavior in numerous journals including the *Academy of Management Journal*, *Organizational Behavior and Human Decision Processes*, *Journal of Management*, *Entrepreneurship Theory & Practice*, and the *Journal of Business Research*.

Margaret A.T. Cronin, JD Margaret Cronin obtained her Bachelor of Arts with high honors from the University of Notre Dame, Indiana and her Juris Doctor from the University of Minnesota, magna cum laude. Currently, Margaret is an attorney specializing in the representation of families of wealth, closely-held businesses, and entrepreneurs. Specifically, her practice focuses on business planning, estate and charitable planning, and cabin succession planning. Many of her clients are family enterprises, including closely-held businesses and private charitable foundations. She works with these family enterprises at various stages of growth, from formation, partnership development, trademarks and branding to succession planning. Margaret is a qualified neutral under Rule 114 of the Minnesota General Rules of Practice for the District Courts. She is also a member of many professional organizations including the American Bar Association (Probate and Real Property, Tax Sections), the Minnesota State Bar Association (Estate Planning and Real Property Sections), the Hennepin County Bar Association and the Family Firm Institute. In addition, Margaret is presently enrolled in the Family Firm Institute's educational program to obtain Certificates in Family Business Advising and Family Wealth Advising. She is a founding member of the Board of Directors of Women Entrepreneurs of Minnesota, a member of the Board of Advisors of the University of St. Thomas Family Business Center, and a member of the University of St. Thomas Family Business Advisors Network. She is also chair of the Minnesota ND Women Connect chapter through the University of Notre Dame Alumni Association.

Sharon M. Danes, PhD Dr. Sharon Danes is a Professor in the Family Social Science Department at the University of Minnesota. In 2004, she was the Juran Faculty Scholar in the Juran Center for Leadership in Quality in the Carlson School of Management at the University of Minnesota. She has authored numerous refereed research articles, book chapters, and outreach publications emphasizing the intersection of economic and social decision-making, including at the family/business interface of family businesses. She has received over a million dollars of research and educational grants, including a recent one from the National Science Foundation. She is one of the developers of the Sustainable Family Business Theory. Short audio-streamed PowerPoint presentations and assessments of her family business work can be accessed on the Rural Minnesota Life website: www.ruralmn.umn.edu.

Kimberly Eddleston, PhD Professor Kimberly Eddleston is an Associate Professor of Entrepreneurship and Innovation at Northeastern University, Boston, where she holds the Tarica-Edwards Research Fellowship. She received her PhD from the University of Connecticut and her Master's Degree from Cornell University/Groupe ESSEC (IMHI). Professor Eddleston's research focuses on family businesses and the careers of entrepreneurs and managers. She has won multiple awards for her research including the Family Owned Business Institute Research Scholar Award, Journal of Small Business Management Best Paper Award, Emerald Citation of Excellence Award, Sage Best Dissertation Award and the Cason Hall and Publishers Best Paper Award. Her research has appeared in journals such as the *Academy of Management Journal, Journal of Applied Psychology, Academy of Management Perspectives, Journal of Business Venturing, Entrepreneurship Theory & Practice, Journal of Vocational Behavior*, and *Journal of Management Studies.*

Kenneth E. Goodpaster, PhD Professor Kenneth Goodpaster earned his AB in Mathematics from the University of Notre Dame, Indiana and his AM and PhD in Philosophy from the University of Michigan. Professor Goodpaster taught graduate and undergraduate Philosophy at the University of Notre Dame throughout the 1970s before joining the Harvard Business School faculty in 1980. Currently, he is the David and Barbara Koch Endowed Chair in Business Ethics at the University of St. Thomas, Minnesota, where he has taught since 1989. He has published articles in a wide variety of professional journals, including the *Journal of Philosophy, Ethics, Environmental Ethics*, the *Journal of Business Ethics, Thought, Business Ethics Quarterly*, and the *Harvard Business Review*. His latest book is *Conscience and Corporate Culture.*

Katherine Hayes Katherine Hayes graduated from Carleton College, Minnesota in 1992 with a BA in Studio Art and is currently enrolled in the University of St. Thomas Minnesota Evening MBA program. She is a fifth-generation member of the Andersen Windows family. In 1996 Katherine's family formed an independent family office called HRK Group Inc., and in 1997 the members of HRK Group Inc. sold their ownership of Andersen Windows. HRK is a full-service family office comprising an investment partnership, a private trust company, and a private foundation. Katherine has served as the Portfolio Manager since 1998, participating in oversight of investment managers, tracking and rebalancing the portfolio, and long-range financial and estate planning for HRK clients. Katherine also serves as the HRK Trust Company Board chair. Before joining the staff at HRK, she worked as a metalsmith and jewelry designer. Katherine has served on numerous boards including the HRK Foundation Board, the Artspace Projects Board, and the Merce Cunningham Dance Foundation Board.

Tom Hubler Tom Hubler began his family business consulting practice in 1980. He integrates the notion of spirit in his work with family businesses and assists family business clients with succession planning, leadership development, business planning, board development, and wealth preparation planning. In addition to consulting, Tom has served as a professional in residence at the University of St. Thomas, Minnesota and served on the advisory board for the Family Business Center at the University of St. Thomas for ten years. Tom has worked as an adjunct instructor at the

University of St. Thomas where he co-taught a class on Family Business Management for ten years. He is also a founding member and Fellow of the Family Firm Institute (FFI) in Boston. Additionally, he serves as a member of the editorial board of the *Family Business Review*, and has authored articles on success strategies for family-owned businesses and has been widely quoted in publications such as *The New York Times, The Wall Street Journal, Business Week, Corporate Report, Nation's Business, Inc*, and the *Minneapolis Star Tribune*. Tom is a frequent guest on the *NBC Weekend Today Show* and a periodic participant on Minnesota Public Radio's *Midmorning* and *Midday* programs. Tom also writes a bi-monthly column that appears in *Minnesota Business Magazine* and is the founder of the Minnesota Family Business of the Year Award, now in its third year of celebrating family business.

Terri McEnaney Terri McEnaney is the President of Bailey Nurseries, Inc., a family business started in 1905. Currently there are seven fourth-generation family members active in the business and two third-generation members act in advisory roles leading the Board of Directors. After graduating from the University of St. Thomas, Minnesota she worked for over eight years at 3M in accounting. The remainder of her career has been spent at her family's business in management positions. She has served as President since 2001.

William (Bill) Monson Bill Monson is the president of iManage, a consulting practice helping executive and owner teams manage alignment in their corporate strategies, structures, systems, and execution. iManage clarifies and speeds up how corporate leaders help each other learn to reinvent their management processes to improve the performance of their organization as a whole. Bill is also a member of the Board of Directors for Family Enterprise USA. Previously, Bill was the director of the Family Business Center at the University of St. Thomas. His job was to take innovative ideas in family enterprise and translate them into practice. Before leading the Family Business Center, Bill directed the university's Executive MBA program for 16 years. The distinctive positioning of that program was to help mid-life, experienced managers hone their capabilities to run an organization and to optimize the whole system rather than their function. He was also Associate Dean of Graduate Programs in Management at the College of St. Thomas during the start-up phase of its evening MBA program and Manager of Corporate Management Development at Medtronic.

Allison W. Pearson, PhD Dr. Allison Pearson is a Giles Professor of Management in the College of Business at Mississippi State University. She is also a Grisham Master Teacher and received the MSU Alumni

Association Graduate Level Teaching Award. She received her PhD in Organizational Behavior from Auburn University, Alabama. Dr. Pearson utilizes her background in organizational behavior to research team dynamics and individual differences in business organizations. Her research has been published in a variety of scholarly outlets including *Journal of Applied Psychology, Journal of Management, Decision Sciences, Entrepreneurship Theory & Practice, Journal of Organizational Behavior, Journal of Business Venturing, Journal of Business Research,* and *Family Business Review.* Her work has also been featured in *Worth Magazine* and on the NBC *Today Show.* She currently serves on the editorial board of four journals, including *Family Business Review* and *Entrepreneurship Theory & Practice.* She was selected as Entrepreneurship Research Exemplars by The Academy of Management and The Connecticut Center for Entrepreneurship & Innovation in 2009. She received the 2009 Best Reviewer award for *Entrepreneurship Theory & Practice.* She was named the Richard C. Adkerson Notable Scholar in the College of Business in 2009. In addition, she serves at the Vice-President for the Family Enterprise Research Conference (FERC), a global organization designed to bring together researchers to share research ideas to advance family firms. In 2009, Dr. Pearson was award the FERC Distinguished Service Award. She also serves on the MSU Entrepreneurship Center advisory board and is a founding fellow of MSU's Center of Family Enterprise Research.

Angela Pritchard Angela Pritchard serves as the Business Manager in the Fleet Division of Pritchard Family Auto Stores, representing the fifth generation of her family's owned and operated company. Upon joining her family's tradition in the automotive industry, Angela's personal goal was to expand a division within the company in order to diversify, and ultimately strengthen, the foundation on which the company stands. The company has always generated a steady amount of sales within the Fleet Division, and Angela was directed to capitalize on the opportunities available within their market. Since joining the family business full-time in 2007, she has assisted in landing and maintaining their largest fleet account. She has also diversified the services provided within their Fleet Division to include not only Fleet Sales, but also Fleet Management. Angela has also participated in obtaining the company's inaugural government contract through the General Services Administration in Washington, DC to further their national government presence.

Teresa J. Rothausen, PhD Dr. Rothausen holds a PhD in Human Resources and Industrial Relations with specialties in staffing, training, and development and organizational behavior/organization theory from the University of Minnesota; a BA in Economics from St. Olaf College,

Minnesota; and a CPA. She is Professor of Management at the Opus College of Business at the University of St. Thomas, Minnesota. She is the founding director of the full-time MBA program and currently has primary responsibility as Leader Development Professor in this program. She teaches, conducts research, and consults on leadership; job satisfaction; retention; human resource management; and diversity, cross-cultural, and career management with Fortune 100 companies, small- and mid-sized businesses, and not-for-profit organizations. Prior to joining UST in 1998, she was an Assistant Professor of Management at Texas A&M University and worked at Arthur Andersen & Co. She is the author of several articles and book chapters, one of which was nominated for the Rosabeth Moss Kanter International Award for Excellence in Work–Family Research given by Purdue University and Boston College, and another of which was runner-up for best article of 2009 in *Family Business Review*. In addition to scholarship, she writes guest columns for the *Minneapolis Star Tribune* and articles for practitioner journals.

Sylvia Shepard Sylvia Shepard is a fifth-generation member of the Smith family, which has owned Menasha Corporation, a Wisconsin-based manufacturing company, for 160 years. While serving on the Menasha Corporation Foundation board she was introduced to the idea of family governance. Over the past ten years Sylvia has been the driving force behind the development of family governance within the Smith family, beginning with the founding of a family council seven years ago. She is still active on the Smith family council, presently serving as its chair. Sylvia recently completed her MBA from Babson where she studied family entrepreneurship with Tim Habbershon, and in October, was awarded her certification as a family business advisor from the Family Firm Institute. Sylvia also holds a Master's in Psychiatric Occupational Therapy from Columbia University, New York and a BA from Smith College, Massachusetts. She spent 25 years in college textbook publishing as an editor at McGraw-Hill and then in a freelance capacity. She is the executive director of the Jane and Tad Shepard Family Foundation.

Trina S. Smith, PhD Trina Smith currently works as the research manager for the Family Business Center at the University of St. Thomas, Minnesota. She completed her PhD in Sociology at the University of Minnesota and her BA in Sociology and Psychology at the University of Nebraska. Her dissertation assessed how international non-governmental organizations work on gender and family issues. Trina and co-authors have published a chapter titled, "The rise of the child as an individual in global society," in the book, *Youth, Globalization, and the Law*. She worked as a site leader in the Twin Cities for the University of Minnesota's American Mosaic

Project examining neighborhood organizations and diversity issues. She has presented her research at numerous local and national conferences. She has taught sociology courses at the University of Minnesota, Hamline University, Inver Hills Community College, and St. Olaf, Minnesota and had her teaching materials published in two American Sociological Association teaching guides. Most recently, Trina worked as an ethnographer and qualitative analyst for the market research company Smart Revenue and as an enumerator in Minneapolis for the 2010 US Census. She is also an active member of Sociologists for Women in Society, the American Sociological Association, and the Midwest Sociological Society.

Ritch L. Sorenson, PhD Dr. Ritch Sorenson is a Full Professor, the Opus Endowed Chair of Family Business at the University of St. Thomas, Minnesota and the Director for the Family Business Center. Before joining St. Thomas, Dr. Sorenson was the Trinity Company Professor of Management at Texas Tech University, where he was recognized for excellence in teaching, served as Area Coordinator for Management (Department Chair) and directed the Centers for Entrepreneurship and Family Business and Managerial Communication. Dr. Sorenson was an early pioneer in establishing a family business education. He continues to develop new courses and established a new undergraduate major in family business at the University of St. Thomas. Dr. Sorenson is an associate editor for *Family Business Review*, the premier journal in family business, and he publishes research in top management journals including *Family Business Review, Entrepreneurship Theory & Practice, Journal of Business Venturing, Group and Organization Studies, The Leadership Quarterly*, and *Academy of Management Executive*. In 2008 he developed a unique series of conferences at the University of St. Thomas about "family capital" in family business. In addition to his duties at the university, he is an active participant in many professional organizations including the Family Firm Institute, the United States Association for Small Business and Entrepreneurship, and the Academy of Management.

Kathryn Stafford, PhD Dr. Kathryn Stafford is an Associate Professor at The Ohio State University in the Department of Consumer Sciences. She teaches graduate and undergraduate courses in management theory, family business management, and quantitative methods. She has studied economic analyses of employed wives' use of resources, managerial decisions of home-based workers, and managerial practices of family business owners. For over a decade she has collaborated with members of the Family Business Research Group to collect the first panel data from a national sample of family business owners and their families. From the results, they have proposed the first holistic model of family firms, obtained reliable estimates of economic impact of family firms, and have begun to distinguish between beneficial practices for family firms in the short and long run. Currently, she and her colleagues are analyzing the effects of natural disasters and disaster policy on the survival and success of family firms in a study funded by the National Science Foundation. She has published in professional journals and her research has been featured in the *Wall Street Journal*, *Time*, and *Newsweek*.

An appreciation

Ritch L. Sorenson, PhD, the Editor

Ritch L. Sorenson and his family were third-generation owners of a bank. When the family patriarch and only family member employed at the bank passed away, the family decided to sell the business. During this time of transition in the family business, Ritch had just completed his PhD at Purdue University, Indiana and was an Assistant Professor in Organizational Communication at Iowa State University.

Currently, Ritch is Full Professor and the Opus Endowed Chair of Family Business at the University of St. Thomas, Minnesota, where he is the Director for the Family Business Center. Before joining St. Thomas, Ritch was the Trinity Company Professor of Management at Texas Tech University, where he was recognized for excellence in teaching, served as Area Coordinator for Management (Department Chair) and directed the Center for Managerial Communication and the Center for Entrepreneurship and Family Business. At Texas Tech, Ritch was an early mover in establishing a family business emphasis in management. At the University of St. Thomas, he developed a major in family business.

Ritch is an active researcher in family business and former associate editor for *Family Business Review*. He has conducted two national surveys in family business. His research interests include family business, leadership, conflict management, entrepreneurship, and organizational communication. His research has been published in journals such as *Family Business Review, Entrepreneurship Theory & Practice, Journal of Business Venturing, Group and Organization Studies, The Leadership Quarterly, Academy of Management Learning and Education,* and *Academy of Management Executive.* Ritch has received research awards and recognitions from the Academy of Management, Family Firm Institute, United States Association for Small Business and Entrepreneurship, and Western Academy of Management.

Ritch has served as the Program Chair and Chair for the Family Business Interest Group of the United States Association for Small Business and Entrepreneurship. He was Chair of a research symposium and editor for proceedings at the Family Firm Institute. Ritch has also served in various service capacities for a variety of professional organizations including the Academy of Management.

In October of 2008, Ritch orchestrated the development of the first multi-stakeholder conference at the University of St. Thomas. The focus of that conference was Family Capital, Family Business, and Free Enterprise. Papers from that conference appeared in the fall 2009 issue of *Family Business Review*. This book contains papers and proceedings of the second multi-stakeholder conference focused on Social Capital in Family Business.

Trina Smith, PhD, Managing Editor
Trina Smith has a PhD in sociology and editing experience, which helped prepare her to be the Managing Editor for this book. As a Managing Editor, she corresponded with authors, organized and arranged content, obtained and edited biographies, consulted with the Editor about organization and development of the book, edited and organized endnotes, and interacted with the publisher. Trina's academic training enabled her to provide editorial feedback and guidance to help develop practitioner papers, to provide developmental feedback to the editor, to develop helpful summaries of transcripts from conference dialogues and breakout groups, and to write introductions for sections in the book. She has done all of these things with diligence and care, and deserves much credit for the completion of this book.

Preface

Family capital distinguishes family from other forms of business. Family capital includes human, financial, and social capital. Together, these three forms of capital account for a significant portion of family firm performance.[1] "Of the three types of family capital, family social capital best distinguishes family from non-family businesses . . . family social capital cannot be hired or imported; it exists within family relationships."[2] Any firm can secure financial and human resources outside the family. However, family social capital is available only in the family.

These comments were written in the introduction to a special issue of *Family Business Review* devoted to family capital. The source of the special issue was the first Conference on Family Capital, Family Business, and Free Enterprise sponsored by the Family Business Center at the University of St. Thomas, Minnesota.

In that conference and associated publications, it became clear that social relationships in families can be a form of capital or a liability to a business. When families have trust and work together well, relationships can be an asset. When they distrust one another and have considerable contention, family relationships can be a liability. The purpose of the second conference and this book is to examine business families through the lens of social capital to better understand how they build trusting, cooperative relationships that can be a source of capital for the business.

Thus, this second multi-stakeholder conference sponsored by the St. Thomas Family Business Center examined social capital in family business. The stakeholders who participated in the structured dialogue were family business scholars, family business owners, and advisors to family businesses.

The purpose of this book is to increase our understanding of social capital as it relates to business families in ways that can be understood and applied by practitioners. A structured dialogue process was used in developing the content of this book. As a result of the conference, scholars better understand whether and how social capital concepts apply to family businesses. They can ground theory, research, and teaching in the experience and perspectives of family business owners and advisors. Owners and advisors develop a working understanding of social capital language and concepts that can be helpful in their practice. As a result of common understanding that is developed, scholars, owners, and advisors in different occupations and disciplines better understand one another.

Structured dialogue has been used in a variety of contexts to help multiple stakeholders understand and act on complex issues and problems. The rationale, foundation, and approach for the structured dialogue process used in the conference are described in more detail in Appendix B. Briefly, the process is described below.

First, scholars from a variety of disciplines were asked to write papers and give short presentations summarizing their papers at a multi-stakeholder conference. To provide a diversity of perspectives, scholars from a variety of disciplines were invited to participate, including family business, family communication, family social science, entrepreneurship, management, ethics, organizational behavior, human resources, and consumer sciences.

Second, family business owners and advisors from a variety of backgrounds were invited to read the papers, attend the conference, listen to presentations, and join in dialogue with the scholars about the elements of social capital. Family business owners represented a variety of industries including construction, manufacturing, agriculture, financial investment, sales, and service. Advisors had expertise in law, family systems, family office, and team development. Because their input was so important to this book, their biographies are included in Appendix A.

Third, the structured dialogue occurred in three two-hour sessions. At the beginning of each session, scholars gave two short presentations about social capital in family business. Following the presentations all participants joined in dialogue. The dialogue was structured so that all had an opportunity to participate. Each individual was given a block of wood with their name attached. To make a comment, the individual placed the block of wood on its end. A facilitator called on individuals for comment following the order in which blocks were set upright. An exception to the order could be made if someone had a comment relevant to the comment made by someone else.

Fourth, because each two-hour session was focused on a topic related to family social capital, participants developed a common body of knowledge about social capital. Before the second and third forum sessions started, participants were given a summary of the previous session.

Fifth, following the conference, selected practitioners at the conference were invited to write a commentary that applied social capital concepts from selected conference papers to their family firm or practice. This gave them the opportunity to look at their business or practice through the lens of social capital. These papers add contextual richness to our understanding of social capital in family business.

Sixth, the dialogue that occurred during the conference was recorded. Transcripts of the conference audiotapes were made. Summaries organized around common themes were written from the transcripts, including quotations from individuals.

Seventh, an extended introductory paper was written, illustrating social capital concepts. The illustrations were drawn from the papers or comments made by conference participants. This paper titled "Social capital in family business" appears as Chapter 1 after a brief introduction to the book.

The summary and conclusion for the book (Chapter 18) reviews the basic elements of social capital that were discussed during the conference and suggests how these concepts apply to business families, which provides insights into the nature of *family* social capital. Finally, recommendations (Chapter 19) were drawn from a discussion led by a facilitator that synthesized what had been said during the conference and final comments given by the stakeholders at the conference.

NOTES

1. Danes et al. (2009a).
2. Sorenson and Bierman (2009, p. 193).

Introduction and overview

In the fall of 2009, family business owners, advisors, and researchers met in dialogue to explore the relationship between social capital and family business. The conference provided a triangulation of perspectives. Owners were embedded and intimately involved in their own family businesses; they helped determine whether the social capital concepts were applicable within their business families. Advisors had observed and helped multiple families in business; they helped assess whether and how social capital concepts applied to a broader set of business families.

Researchers typically gathered observations from a broad set of families and businesses, and developed concepts and language that apply to broad population. However, researchers were also furthest removed from family businesses, and did not, therefore, have the benefit of the rich family business context available to owners and advisors. In dialogue, the three stakeholders informed one another. Owners and advisors learned new concepts and language. Researchers gained information informing them about the validity of social capital concepts.

This volume contains three kinds of writing. First, researchers provide papers describing social capital concepts, which were written before the conference and then revised following the conference. Second, following the conference, family business owners and advisors wrote articles that applied social capital concepts to their family firms or practices. Third, the book includes summaries of conference dialogue. Dialogues were recorded and transcribed. Then comments were organized into categories and summarized. The summaries of dialogue represent the perspectives about social capital from the three stakeholder groups and how these perspectives apply to their experiences.

A paper titled "Social capital and family business" (Chapter 1) follows this introduction and serves as an extended introduction illustrating how elements of social capital apply to family business by quoting liberally from the papers and dialogue summaries included in this volume. It helps place the articles in this volume within the context of social capital.

The contents of the book are divided into three main parts, which parallel the three two-hour forums in the conference, and a final concluding part. The first three parts begin with a short introduction that provides an overview of papers. Then, papers written by researchers and practitioners are included. These are followed by a summary of the dialogue that occurred during the relevant forum session. Reading an entire part will provide a full sense of the combined perspectives of the three stakeholder groups. The summary of the dialogue at end of each part helps to integrate the three perspectives.

Part I is titled "Understanding the elements of family social capital." Combined, the papers in this part provide an overview of the elements of social capital, illustrate how these elements contribute to "resilient trust," and provide insights about how trust in business families is developed.

Part II is titled "Co-constructing family-business social capital." Together, the papers in this part illustrate how elements of social capital, such as communication and conflict management patterns, can build resilience and sustainability within the business families.

Part III is titled "Complementing social capital in family and business." Collectively these papers provide insights about the relevance, importance, and processes of developing a family-business identity. They suggest that both the family and the business can benefit from having a shared identity.

Helpful concluding materials are provided at the end of the book in Part IV. First, the "Summary and conclusion" defines the nature of *family* social capital. That is, it defines elements of social capital and summarizes how they uniquely apply to business families.

Second, "Recommendations for building family social capital" are provided. At the conclusion of the conference, a facilitator provided an overall review of the three sessions and led participants in dialogue about what they had learned about how social capital applies to family business. Recommendations were drawn from the transcripts of dialogue and summarized in this paper.

Finally, the book also contains three appendices. Since all conference participants contributed to this book, Appendix A provides their biographies.[1] Appendix B describes the structured dialogue process used during the conference. Lastly, Appendix C summarizes the stakeholder groups' thoughts and recommendations on social capital as discussed in the conference and its meaning for their practice.

NOTE

1. Biographies for conference participants who wrote chapters for the book can be found in the list of contributors at the beginning of the book.

1. Social capital and family business

Ritch L. Sorenson

Social capital[1] refers to trusting, cooperative relationships that enable collective action. The notion of social capital emerged from sociological research within communities that found that networks of civic engagement based on existing interpersonal relationships enabled individuals to work together on community projects. The combined labels "social and capital" suggest that networks of trusting relationships are assets that enable individuals to work together for the common good.

Armed with this knowledge, community development specialists drew upon existing social capital within church groups and civic organizations to accomplish community projects. In addition, they developed social capital among previously disconnected individuals and institutions by opening communication channels, focusing attention on common values and goals, and promoting relationships of trust that enabled people to work together for community improvement.

Family social capital refers to trusting, cooperative relationships in a family that enables it to engage in collective action. This book represents an application of social capital concepts to families in business in a conference at the University of St. Thomas in October of 2009. A multi-stakeholder group consisting of family business owners and advisors met to engage in dialogue about social capital in families that own businesses. Scholars introduced and explained social capital concepts. Then, all 27 conference participants, who sat at tables in a large circle, engaged in a structured dialogue about social capital in family business. The dialogue was structured so that all participants were equals and could discuss social capital from their point of view (see the preface for a full description). This volume contains papers that were presented by scholars at the conference, the papers written by practitioners following the conference, and summaries of dialogue that occurred during the conference.

The purpose of the structured dialogue was to create a common understanding among conference participants about that nature of family social capital. The conference represented three different kinds of groups. First, family business owners represented those who were embedded within family social activities, which are often taken for granted. If meaningful, social capital concepts could help owners see daily taken-for-granted activities through new eyes. Second, family business advisors represent those who work closely with families, but from an external and relatively objective point of view. As a group, family business owners and advisors are in the best position to determine the extent to which social capital concepts meaningfully apply to families in business. Third, scholars represent those who more broadly and objectively examine family business. They formulate concepts in the form of principles, hypotheses, and theories, and determine whether and how those concepts apply broadly to family firms.

By convening scholars and practitioners in dialogue, our hope was to determine which, if any, social capital concepts are relevant to families in business. After participating in the conference, reading and editing papers, and compiling summaries of conversations, I wrote this paper on social capital and family business. Because it is intended for a broad audience, an attempt was made to use language and examples that are broadly understood. This paper is organized into sections that address the components of social capital described in the literature: communication, identity, and trust. Because it serves as an introduction to the remainder of the book, I liberally quote from the papers, commentaries, and summaries of dialogue included in this volume to show how the concepts within the papers relate to social capital.

SOCIAL CAPITAL IN FAMILIES

Based on the social capital literature, family business scholars suggest that the relationships of trust within families give them an immediate form of social capital, called here family social capital. A family can draw upon family social capital for the good of a business. Danes and Stafford, in Chapter 7, describe it this way:

> [F]amily social capital is goodwill among family members and between owning family members and their communities that can be infused within the owning family and their business to facilitate action. (Chapter 7, p. 79)

Pearson and Carr, in Chapter 2, suggest that family social capital can provide an advantage for family businesses because, like existing church or civic groups, social capital already exists in families. Thus, family social capital provides an advantage for family businesses:

[G]roups with strong social capital can operate more efficiently and with lower direct and indirect costs. Since these costs take time, energy, and resources, they can slow down efficient operations. In short, organizations with low social capital need formal, legal requirements and are thus less efficient than those organizations that can rely on their strong and vibrant social capital to get things done. (Chapter 2, p. 35)

Pearson and Carr further suggest that non-family businesses also develop social capital. However, the process of building interpersonal trust likely takes longer. And the nature of trust in non-family businesses will not be the same as it is in family firms:

Social capital in non-family firms is not easily attainable and must be developed gradually over time. Even so, it may never have the power of relationships that exist in families and subsequently in family firms. (Chapter 2, p. 41)

Not all families, however, have the relationships of trust that provide a strong and vibrant form of social capital. In fact, some family relationships are filled with distrust and hostility that are an all-consuming liability. And there are families that have reasonably good relationships, but their combined attention has not been aligned in ways that can help a business. If these families align themselves around common values and goals, they have the potential to develop a strong and vibrant family social capital and to employ it for business purposes. Family social capital consists of three basic elements: communication, identity, and trust.

COMMUNICATION

Communication provides the basis for establishing and maintaining social capital. Communication channels provide opportunity for individuals and institutions to share information and establish relationships. Over time repetitive patterns of communication occur, relationships are developed, and collective trust emerges.

Communication Channels

When communication channels are established, people can interact and share information. *Formal* channels of communication are developed within and across institutions to share information, coordinate, and organize. Both families and businesses use meetings and information networks as formal channels of communication.

Informal channels of communication also emerge when people in close proximity or in a social context have opportunities to interact. Family members who live in the same household have much opportunity to communicate, as do employees in a business. Most of the information within families and business is communicated through informal channels.

Because of proximity and opportunity, it is relatively easy within families and within businesses to engage in both formal and informal communication. Even when family members work in a business, both formal and informal channels help maintain communication between the family and the business. Formal communication could be in the form of meetings between family and business to discuss strategy, policies, and plans, and to agree on values and goals that align the business with the family. Informal communication opportunities occur throughout the workday and at social events outside of work.

Relationships of trust are more readily built when communication channels are open. *Open* communication includes honest and frank statements of feelings, conscience, and perspective. Openness enables individuals to uncover and communicate relevant facts and bring all concerns into the open. Goodpaster, in Chapter 4, notes that frank and honest communication in families can help keep business owners from becoming too fixated on the business at the expense of the family. One conference participant described the frankness that can exist in families this way, "If your butt looks too big in those jeans, they will tell you" (Chapter 6, p. 74). Goodpaster describes open communication as the following:

> This kind of *honesty* comes alive in candid conversations with trusted friends and workplace colleagues. It is alive in company cultures that encourage constructive self-criticism rather than blind allegiance. (Chapter 4, p. 58)

Another part of open communication is *transparency*. In a business, transparency means that reporting procedures within a business make performance, financial and other business activities clear to relevant stakeholders, including the owning family and board members. In a family, transparency means that information about the business is made available to all family stakeholders.

Thus, open communication and transparency in both formal and informal channels of communication provide a foundation for establishing trusting relationships and for social capital in family and in business. Levels of openness and transparency are influenced by informal communication rules.

Communication Rules

When communication channels are available, individuals within any group or institution, such as a family or a business, develop both formal and informal rules for communication. Bruess, in Chapter 9, indicates that three kinds of rules are formed:

> What can be talked about? How can it be talked about? To whom can it be talked about? (Chapter 9, p. 117)

These rules prevail within both formal and informal communication channels. In formal communication, the rules may be explicit. For example, newsletters for either families or businesses may have formal guidelines for content.

However, most communication occurs in informal conversations. For example, in families, parents often establish an open communication about issues that are not discussed with children. Similarly, children often develop close communication ties and may discuss things that are not shared with parents. Informal rules guide what is discussed within and across these informal boundaries.

Similarly, in businesses both formal and informal communication rules are established. Formally in business, the rules are expressed in terms of an organizational hierarchy and responsibilities associated with assigned roles. Managers, for example, have the right to direct; they determine content of meetings under their control. Informal communication networks also are prominent in businesses, sometimes called the grapevine, which have their own set of rules for inclusion and about sharing information.

Communication rules also apply to the family-business relationship. Formal and informal rules establish both boundaries and connections between the business and the family. Formal rules, for example, stipulate who can attend board meetings and the nature of participation. Sometimes rules dictate that family members who do not sit on the board may attend board meetings, but they are not allowed to participate in the discussion. Families sometimes create formal rules that establish boundaries. This is illustrated by the following comments from a family business owner at the conference:

> My mother, the chief emotional officer, made a rule of no more talk about the business on holidays. It's not a board meeting . . . in the family. (Chapter 11, p. 150)

Informal rules based on family history and norms also maintain boundaries. For example, Rothausen and Sorenson, in Chapter 12, describe an incident that occurred while attending a family business seminar:

> During a breakfast conversation with the wife of one of the family business owners attending the seminar, she explained that she planned to shop while her husband attended the seminar. The author suggested that if she attended the seminar, she would better understand the family business and as a result might learn how she could contribute her talents to the business or how to develop her young sons to participate in the business. However, when she suggested the idea to the owner, he reacted negatively. The owner apparently wanted to maintain . . . separate systems. (Chapter 12, p. 168).

Over time, as communication with the same individuals is repeated, patterns emerge that are guided by formal and informal rules and that influence the nature of relationships.

Communication Patterns and Relationships

When communication channels and rules are used repeatedly, over time communication patterns and interpersonal relationships are formed. In business, communication patterns develop around formal business roles and informal relationships. Because they are based largely around organizational structures and roles, business patterns and relationships are relatively easy to understand.

On the other hand, family patterns and relationships have an emotional basis and a long-term history. To an outsider who is not privy to family history, patterns of communication and relationships are difficult to understand.

When a couple forms a marriage relationship, much interaction is required to establish common understanding and acceptable patterns of communication. For example, Sorenson and his co-authors, in Chapter 10, provide a case study about the formation of a marriage relationship between a family-business-owning couple. The couple, who formed their relationship in the late 1940s, had a collection of over 380 letters written while courting that described daily activities, feelings about one another and their lives, and personal aspirations and hopes. Through these communications, the couple developed a common understanding and strong emotional bonds that a casual outside observer would not understand.

Communication patterns and relationships emerge that are unique to each family. Bruess, in Chapter 9, refers to some of these patterns as rituals – repetitive communication patterns that are guided by informal rules.

Bruess indicates that communication patterns help define family relationships. She cites research showing that patterns of positive communication strengthen relationships, while patterns of negative or hostile communication weaken or destroy relationships.

Thus, while family patterns may seem mundane, they define and reinforce relationships, and they also can provide relational stability. Bruess summarizes research indicating that alcoholism introduces instability in family relationships. However, in families that have a history of alcoholism, family rituals and communication patterns, such as a regular dinnertime, can help break the cycle of alcoholism.

Family Business Communication Patterns and Relationships

When members of the family and of the business work closely together, they both may adopt some of the communication and relational patterns of the other. The extent to which family communication patterns become a part of the business likely depends on the number of family members that work in the business. When two or more family members work in the business, they reinforce the use of family communication patterns at work. For example, when a wife and husband or two siblings run a business, they likely rely on communication patterns to which they have become accustomed in their families.

If only one family member, the owner, works in the business, communication patterns in the business may be more bureaucratic, reflecting business norms common among non-related individuals. This is especially true when the owner chooses to keep the business totally separate from the family.

However, a sole employee/owner may also choose to adopt family-like communication patterns in the business. For example, Sorenson and his co-authors, in Chapter 10, describe how one business owner found ways to create family-like communication patterns, similar to a family dinner, even when he was the only family member who worked in the business:

> During the formative years at work, George gathered all the employees together, no matter their position, to have brown bag lunches together. Brown bags gave way to a communal kitchen in which employees took turns preparing meals for one another. The family history indicates that one employee indicated that communication during lunch was more important than the meal; it made them all feel very close. (Chapter 10, p. 135)

When family is tightly associated with the business, and family communication patterns and relationships are adopted in the business, the strengths and liabilities associated with those patterns also become a part of the business. One way to characterize family communication and relationship patterns is that families are more or less "functional."

Based on research from a national database of family businesses, Danes and her colleagues developed a theory of sustainable family business. Their research indicates that family functional integrity helps develop sustainable family businesses. The integrity of family functionality helps families to handle tension associated with change and other challenges associated with family business. They describe a measure of functional family integrity, discussed in Chapter 7, which is an indication of stocks of family social capital available in the family. Danes and Stafford describe the effect of functional integrity:

> The functional integrity of the owning family is critical to navigating the conflict environment. When tensions arise, families with higher levels of functional integrity have a greater store to draw upon to manage these tensions and to creatively turn them into change needed to sustain the business over time. When there is sustained tension, the family can buffer the impact on the business. However, if its functional integrity is weak, the family can become further stressed when experiencing effects of tension created by the business. The more stressful events families experience, the less capacity they have to lessen the consequences of the tensions created by the business. (Chapter 7, p. 96)

Families that have dysfunctional communication patterns may bring more social liabilities than capital to a business. As one owner put it, being in business doesn't necessarily make families more functional:

> I question that family involvement in the business necessarily leads to a happier family. Families that are already more functional may stay involved with the business, so they look happier. But it's not necessarily because they are in the business. They are involved in the business because they are a functional family – that's why they are in the business. In the model where family is separate from the business, the family may not have the family skills to be involved. (Chapter 7, p. 213)

On the other hand, family participation in business may improve some communication patterns and relationships in the family. For example, businesses provide training in communication and relationship skills. These skills often carry over to the family. One participant at the conference described the impact of business development on family:

> One of the gifts and one of the challenges of a family business is that the business itself adds another developmental dimension to the family. The business calls on the family to develop as it develops . . . Skills learned in the business can carry over to the family. So, being a family in business provides additional opportunities to develop relationship skills. (Chapter 11, p. 147)

Bruess in Chapter 9 indicates that a purposeful change in communication patterns or rituals can change relationships. For example, family communication patterns may include a child's deference to parents or traditional gender roles that exclude women from business discussions. However, new communication patterns are required of family members as employees or owners in the business. Next-generation family members who become business managers develop new patterns of communication related to their role. New patterns of communication also develop as they work together in and on the business.

Siblings who become equal shareholders may learn new patterns of interaction as they participate in shareholder meetings and family councils. One participant in the conference observed:

> One family business owner I know moved here to work with five adult siblings in the family business. She had a psychology background, so she immediately started working to improve family relationships. She said her efforts went nowhere; her siblings weren't interested. But they started working together on the business and found that they weren't working very well together. This then gave them a reason and permission to work on sibling relationships. *Some people may build good relationships to accomplish a purpose.* (Chapter 11, p. 147)

Thus, when family members engage in new communication patterns for business purposes, those patterns may also transfer to the family. Some businesses, for example, provide training in active listening. Active listening can work as well in the family as it does in business.

In summary, the formal and informal channels of communication within and between the family and the business provide the platform on which family-business social capital may be established. In general, more open and transparent communication is desirable. Communication rules, rituals, and patterns help define relationships, which may be an asset or a liability to a business, or possibly both. In addition, communication patterns become a part of and help develop identities for the family and for the business.

IDENTITY

Family businesses may have four types of identities: (1) individual – a belief about who "I" am; (2) family – a consensual belief about the "we" of family; (3) business – a consensual belief about the "we" of the business; and (4) family-business – consensual belief about what the family and the business have in common. An identity includes a belief about an "I" or a "we." It also includes a consensual belief about "them" – other people or institutions, and how "we" or "I" relate to "them." An important part of individual identity is what "I" will or won't do. An important part of a family, business, or family-business identity is what "we" will or won't do as a group.

Family Identity

Family identity is deeply rooted. Each of us is born or adopted into a family that has already formed an identity sustained by family communication patterns and rituals. Each family plays a role in these rituals. For many years throughout childhood, family patterns reinforce family and individual identity. In Chapter 9 Bruess summarizes how rituals and mundane patterns of family life help to sustain identity:

> Rituals are pivotal yet often mundane acts of family identity, unveiling themselves through cues both big and small, each a kind of "moral commentary about what is valued, or an expressive hope for what could be."[2] Knowingly or not, families use rituals to create and recreate family identity, consciously and unconsciously relying on them through both the spectacular and the banal events of every family's life. (Chapter 9, p. 121)

Bruess also indicates that communication rules play a role in establishing identity:

> One of the primary ways that families develop their sense of identity is through shared rules. As shared understandings of what communication means and what is expected behavior in certain situations, rules are central to family functioning and even more so for families sharing a business. (Chapter 9, p. 117)

Everyday family communication rules and patterns are so much a part of family life that, like a fish out of water, they aren't noticed unless attention is drawn to them. Outsiders may notice patterns more than the family does. Communication patterns become so ingrained and "natural" that when individuals rejoin the family as adults, they often find themselves reverting back to roles and patterns established within the family in their youth.

Family-business Identity

In each family, the extent to which family identity is associated with the business varies. By nature the two institutions are quite different. Families seek to nurture and sustain family members and relationships. Businesses seek business performance and financial success. As noted earlier, even though some businesses may be categorized as family firms, some owners prefer to keep family and business separate. Families and firms in these businesses likely have very different identities.

Then there are family firms in which most family members are owners and also work in the business. Family and business identities are intertwined and they have a family-business identity. They may refer to themselves as a "business family." Having a family-business identity, they feel a strong investment in the business. Family vision, values and norms become associated with the business vision, values, and norms. In Chapter 15, Kimberly Eddleston describes the nature of a family-business identity:

> While some leaders choose to separate their family from the business, others choose to integrate their family and business roles to create a family-firm identity. Behavioral expectations drawn from the family role center on nurturing, caregiving, commitment, and loyalty to family members, and reflect a collectivistic orientation. In contrast, behavioral expectations derived from the business role center on devotion to the business, pursuit of business success, and legitimacy in the marketplace. Leaders who define their business as a "family business" therefore aim to integrate their family and business roles, viewing the family as a key component of the business. When the family is central to the firm's identity, the family's values provide a foundation for decision-making and contribute to a culture of identification and shared identity. (Chapter 15, p. 189)

When a family has a family-business identity, it is likely to commit its time and resources to the business. Eddleston indicates that a family-business identity provides a motivation to help the business prosper:

> When family businesses integrate the family into the firm's identity they may provide the business with an important source of competitive advantage that others cannot imitate . . . As a matter of fact, research indicates that the most successful family firms are those with loyal, interdependent, committed and altruistic family members. When family members are deeply committed to the business and members believe that they have a common family responsibility to see the business prosper, they are highly motivated to fulfill organizational goals and maximize firm performance . . . Therefore, a strong family-firm identity can create a sense of oneness and shared destiny among family members that lead them to work toward organizational goals and to uphold the values of the family firm. (Chapter 15, pp. 189)

Values that are common to both the family and the business are an important part of a family-business identity. Common values provide a platform for developing the family and business relationship – a mutual basis on which to build working relationships. These values that become embedded into both the family and the business become an asset. Values help connect the family to the business and provide fundamental guidelines for behavior in both the business and the family. Pearson and Carr, in Chapter 2, describe the advantage of shared values in a family firm:

> Research suggests that groups with strong social capital are effective because they operate on the basis of shared values, rather than on extensive contracts or legal regulations that are necessary when trust and voluntary obligations are non-existent. (Chapter 2, p. 35)

Developing and Maintaining a Family-business Identity

There are families that initially had a family-business identity. But as the firms prospered, family members in succeeding generations became more independent, and few, if any, family members worked in the firm. The family-business identity was lost. Large families in the third, fourth, or fifth generation may find it difficult to retain an identity as a family, let alone as a family business. In Chapter 16, Sylvia Shepard, a fifth-generation owner in a family business, describes how through the generations her family lost its family-business identity.

> The centrifugal force of a growing family pushing toward individuation and self-determination necessarily strains the ties between the family members and their connection to the business. (Chapter 16, p. 203)

Other families have experienced a similar problem. A family business advisor and a family business researcher in attendance at the conference made these comments about the family-business identity:

> I work with a lot of families who have wealth and in the third or fourth generation, the adults no longer feel an identity with the business. They're very wealthy . . . Somehow the values have been lost. They didn't grow up in the business. They didn't earn it. There's a lot of entitlement. (Chapter 17, p. 214)

Another participant noted:

> There is disjointed lack of connectivity between legacy and wealth in the families we have studied. The wealth doesn't . . . have same meaning or purpose or identity, especially as it impacts more generations. So over time for more and more wealthy families there is a separation between family and business. (Chapter 17, p. 214)

Furthermore, looking back through her family and business history, Shepard indicates that in each successive generation a different identity emerged. Some generations embraced the family-business identity. Some did not. In thinking through the five generations in her family, Shepard ties a strong family-business identity to a strong family identity:

> [I]t is clear to me that a family-firm identity changes as each generation assumes ownership and leadership roles, with the early generations building the identity, and the later generations modifying, sustaining, or neglecting it. If the family firm identity is to survive over the generations, the family's identity must remain strong. (Chapter 16, p. 198)

Shepard indicates that over time both their family identity and the family-business identity diminished. Because there was little consensus about family and family-firm identity, the family was uncertain about how to act and made poor decisions. In essence, the social capital they once had was gone; the family-business identity was no longer an asset to the business.

So, a fifth-generation family member who served on their business board began developmental efforts to reclaim the family-business identity and to rebuild family social capital. She opened communication channels among family members by organizing annual picnics before annual shareholder meetings. Furthermore, like many other large wealthy families who have lost their family-business identity, Shepard indicates that the family established a family council:

> [T]he gulf widens between people when there is less communication. There are natural communications with the immediate nuclear family, which makes that group more powerful and makes everybody else feel left out. *A family council enables communication with the rest of the family and makes them an insider. It creates shared meaning and connectedness.* (Chapter 11, p. 149)

In addition, Shepard notes that the family began development to restore the family-firm identity. Family members were given copies of the family tree. A family history was written and distributed. Communication channels were opened between the family and the business. Shepard summarizes that the family's effort culminated in the family re-establishing its identity within the business:

> As our family has reclaimed its identity as a business-owning family, we have made an effort to ensure that our family's vision and values are reflected in the company's mission statement and on its website. Aside from actively working to revitalize our family-firm identity, we are convinced that the employees of our company are more likely to identify the firm as a family firm as a result of our renewed commitment, and regular interactions with a variety of family members. Ultimately, as we regain our sense of who we are, we believe that our company is once again finding a consensual view of who they are as an organization. (Chapter 16, p. 207)

A visual representation of the family identity, such as a mission or vision statement on a website, helps focus attention and reinforce the family-business identity. In discussing family identity, Angela Pritchard, a fifth-generation family business member, notes, in Chapter 17, that after a period of growth that placed much emphasis on the business and took family in different directions, her mother, the chief emotional officer, sought a way to restore balance and refocus family attention on family-business identity. Pritchard indicates that one thing her mother did was create a logo for the business that helped reinforce the family-business identity for both the family and employees: a common symbol that provided a common focus:

> [W]e've been family owned and operated since 1913. So it's been passed down from generation to generation . . . our family put our name into the logo just five years ago, when we expanded. My mother developed the logo and now that's actually an identifying characteristic not only for our company, but for us. That is something that we pride ourselves in . . . It is not just an identifying characteristic for our family, but for our employees and for family who aren't even involved with the company. . . The logo represents our family identity. (Chapter 17, p. 212)

In the previous examples, women played a very prominent role in developing family and family-business identity. In Chapter 7, Danes and her colleagues found in a study of dialogue among couples that women may play a prominent role in establishing a family-business identity. After examining conversations of couples about their businesses, Danes and Stafford drew the following conclusions:

> Women frequently used "we" in their communication about their businesses, reflecting key female roles identified in the family business literature: building relationships, negotiating, maintaining multiple simultaneous roles, and providing flexible bonds to hold changing family businesses together. (Chapter 7, p. 99)

Women often take the lead in building family and a family-business identity. For example, they frequently organize family social events and dinners. Family dinner is a powerful ritual that helps define family identity. It provides an enjoyable setting for a family gathering. Dinner conversations reaffirm and define family beliefs. As family members tell about life events, family comments tend to reaffirm its identity – this is "who we are" and "how we do things." Similar kinds of informal conversations occur in smaller private settings and during family social activities.

Frequently, women play the pivotal role in putting "family" into the family-business identity. Danes and Stafford summarize research indicating that women in small family firms focus on the future and on change, while men focus on current tasks:

> This same family business discourse study identified a previously ignored role of women in family business. Women in this study placed much greater emphasis on words about "future" and "change" than did men. Women's more frequent use of those phrases shows that women are more likely to act as springboards for innovation within family businesses. In contrast, men used words related to accomplishing tasks in the present. (Chapter 7, p. 100)

The study reported above suggests that women often provide a leadership role in developing a long-term vision for the business, perhaps thinking of their family across generations. This contribution and others made by women are often overlooked. Perhaps they are overlooked because much of women's influence comes in family patterns and rituals that are taken for granted.

But some male family owners appreciate the insights of women in their families. In Chapter 10, Sorenson and his co-authors report that that one family business owner frequently discussed the family business with his stay-at-home wife:

> One of their children noted that throughout their married lives George relied on Sandra as a sounding board regarding business personnel matters, and that Sandra's insights and judgments were extremely acute. She had a gift for evaluating people. George took Sandra to dinner with prospective employees. On the way home, he sought Sandra's opinion about hiring the person. George also valued Sandra's perspective and guidance in executing promotions. (Chapter 10, p. 135)

Similarly, Pritchard reports that in her family, her father relied on the judgment of her mother in making personnel decisions. It seems that these women had keen insights into people and whether they would be a good fit with the values associated with the family-business identity.

TRUST

Simply put, trust is the capability to rely on another individual or entity. Collective trust is the ability to rely on the group, the family, and/or the business. In families, family members rely on other family members. In business, the family has confidence that the business and its leaders will enact family values, goals, strategies, and deliver a reasonable return on its investment.

In Chapter 2, Pearson and Carr indicate that families tend to have a resilient, long-lasting form of trust. Based on emotional bonds, families have an underlying and enduring commitment to relationships. The same commitment is not available in typical business relationships. Pearson and Carr compare resilient trust based on emotional ties to fragile trust based on contracts:

> Fragile trust is similar to the kinds of transactions we engage in where there are tangible benefits gained from the relationship. In fragile trust relationships, we are motivated by the potential for reward rather than the relationship itself – a sort of extrinsic trust that exists only when those rewards are present. Resilient trust is defined as lasting trust, formed through emotional ties to others and is a stronger form of trust that emerges from relationships rather than from contractual relations. Resilient trust may be able to withstand breaches, as long as that trust is relationship based. (Chapter 2, p. 38)

Resilient trust occurs because family members have an emotional commitment to family relationships. For example, some families are so committed to maintaining family continuity that they settle for lesser levels of business growth or financial performance to maintain family relationships.

Trust in families is built on emotional ties that lead to relational commitment. Relational commitment means that family members rely on one another for varying kinds of support. Each family has its own rules about the kinds of support it provides.

Typically, a nuclear family is formed when two individuals commit to an enduring relationship. The basis for commitment is usually emotional affection. Marriage ceremonies express the nature of relational commitment that emerges from emotional bonds: to support and sustain one another in good times and bad, in sickness and in health, for the rest of their lives. Whether or not a formal marriage occurs, relying on one another to get through trials and difficulty is one hallmark of a family relationship. When there is a strong and positive emotional bond, there is commitment to the relationship. When the emotional bond is weakened, relational commitment is also weakened.

Trust in business has a contractual basis. In business, these contracts are normally between non-related individuals. As individuals fulfill expectations of employment and business agreements, confidence builds that they are able to deliver. If individuals do not fulfill the agreement, trust is damaged and the business relationship may be severed.

As is illustrated in Figure 1.1, when families become involved in business, two bases exist for trust: emotional bonds and commitment to a family-business identity. Highest levels of trust, the kind of trust that can be an advantage to a business, exist when families have strong emotional bonds and are committed to a family-business identity.

If emotional bonds are weak, but family members are committed to the

	Weak emotional bond	Strong emotional bond
Commitment to common identity	High confidence, low relational commitment	High confidence, hight relational commitment
Unclear identity, commitment to personal agenda	Low relational commitment and confidence	High relational commitment, low confidence

Family Business

Weak emotional bond   Strong emotional bond

Family

Source: The author.

Figure 1.1   Trust in family business

family-business identity, there may be a level of trust based on fulfillment of agreements that enables the family to work together. For example, because their emotional bond has weakened, co-preneurs may divorce. But, they may continue to work together because the former spouses are both committed to the family business or at least the business identity.

When a family member is not committed to the family-business identity, but retains strong emotional bonds with the family, they will likely not build trust based on commitment to the family-business identity. However, they will likely remain committed to the family relationship. For example, when a child shows lack of commitment to the family-business identity by failing to perform his/her role as an employee, the parent may love the child and be committed to the family relationship, but at the same time sever the business relationship.

Even when family members have strong emotional bonds, disagreement about the family-business identity may weaken trust. When family members do not agree about identity and have a weak emotional bond, there may be little basis for trust. And, commitment to the business and the family relationship may end. For example, the author personally knows of several businesses in which disagreements over the direction of the business, a fundamental part of a family-business identity, combined with weak family member relationships led to negative emotions and distrust. They hired lawyers and communicated through litigation. Ultimately, family members divided the business assets, severed the business relationship, and family members no longer spoke to one another. Trust had been replaced with distrust. Family relationships that once were an asset had become a liability.

Below, I discuss how emotional bonds and commitment to a family-business identity relate to the three elements of social capital discussed in this paper – communication, identity, and trust. If families have strong emotional bonds and are committed to a common identity, they can have high levels of trust that can be an advantage. However, changes in families and businesses across time and life cycles can erode emotional bonds and lead to a loss of family-business identity. Understanding the nature of social capital may help families build and retain relationships of trust.

Emotional Bonds

Emotional bonds emerge from close, affectionate, interpersonal relationships that are frequently found in families. Emotional bonds tend to be strongest in nuclear families, especially between parents and their children, with the mother typically having the strongest emotional bond with children. Mothers develop a bond with children through close, nurturing, and intimate contact. Breast-feeding a baby is symbolic of the nurturing and intimate contact that creates a strong emotional bond. Without extensive personal contact, this strong bond would not be established. This emotional bond is not limited to mothers. There are many fathers who are primary caregivers of children and who have developed strong emotional bonds with their children.

Because of emotional bonds, family members tend to have a strong commitment to one another. In Chapter 2, Pearson and Carr characterize family ties, some of which are inherited as a birthright, as being timeless and strong. Moreover, in terms of commitment, family ties transcend those of other relationships, especially a typical employment contract. And, family members can typically call upon one another for levels of support and resources not available to others. Below, I summarize some things suggested in this book and from the conference that build or maintain strong emotional bonds.

Care for family
One of the advantages of working in a family business is that the family has the flexibility to focus on both family and business. McEnaney, in Chapter 13, indicates that her family's governance philosophy includes

caring for family as being important to the long-term success of both family and business:

> Family is very important to our business. We believe that time given to caring for children in this generation will yield its fruit in future generations in the business, a key characteristic of the family-enterprise type of family business. Furthermore, the current generation has a traditional family philosophy of having a parent stay at home to be the main caregiver. There is a great deal of respect for our spouses and the important role they play in our work and home lives. Family business can take a tremendous amount of time commitment. To have a supportive home life makes everything come into balance and makes it all worthwhile and rewarding. (Chapter 13, p. 172)

McEnaney also notes that when family needs arise, family members cover work needs for one another so that the family needs can be handled. She says that this attitude pervades their workplace.

In Chapter 12, Rothausen and Sorenson indicate that when firm governance includes both family and business both can prosper. The family can be leveraged for the business and the business can be leveraged for the family. That is, the capabilities of all family members can be employed to benefit the whole enterprise. Based on work–family literature, they offer this observation:

> [W]hen a business organization has a family-supportive culture, its values reflect respect for, and acknowledgment of, the importance of members' families. Having such a culture in a business organization has been shown to positively impact workers' organizational attachment, job satisfaction, organizational commitment, and intentions to stay with the employer. Evidence of a family-supportive work culture may be co-workers who know and take an interest in workers' family members, who are willing to "chip in" when family duties call, and who show appreciation to workers' family members for contributions to the business. (Chapter 12, p. 160)

Making care for the family a priority in family business governance undoubtedly strengthens family emotional bonds. For a *family* business to last, family emotional bonds need to strong. A business that labels itself as a family business and at the same time ignores the family may not retain the emotional bonds that sustain the family side of the business.

Family interaction

Frequent social interaction tends to rekindle a family's emotional bonds. When Sylvia Shepard's family decided to reclaim their family-firm identity, family members felt a need to connect with one another more frequently and intimately. They established family reunions before annual shareholder meetings and published a family newsletter. Tom Hubler, a family business consultant, suggests in Chapter 3 that important elements in building family trust and harmony are family retreats and service projects. Consistent with Hubler's recommendation, McEnaney, in Chapter 13, reports that her family recently had a family retreat. Issues raised in the retreat became a part of bi-weekly family owner meetings that had been established to keep the family engaged.

Nurture family legacy
One way some families rekindle emotional bonds is to help family members focus on and cherish their legacy. In Chapter 16, Shepard indicates that in their effort to re-engage the family in the business, the family arranged for a book to be written about the family history and, in addition, a family member filmed a family documentary. These efforts strengthened emotional bonds:

> The release of the family history book, the showing of the family documentary, and the gathering of the family to celebrate their legacy energized everyone. It made them feel they were not only a part of the family, but also a legacy that involved owning a business together for 150 years. At the end of the film there were tears and hugs. (Chapter 16, p. 205)

Writing family histories and revisiting family strengths reminds families about what they have in common – their common heritage. At family gatherings, the history can be celebrated by revisiting stories about family members' achievements.

Establish positive rituals
Bruess, in Chapter 9, summarizes research showing that patterns of negative communication lead to dissatisfaction and breakdown in the family. Alternately, positive family patterns or rituals can strengthen family bonds and commitment to the family. She summarizes what research suggests about the impact of positive family rituals:

> In families specifically, rituals help create intergenerational bonds and preserve a sense of meaningfulness. They convey family values, attitudes, and beliefs, are related to family strength, provide members with a sense of belonging, bond and promote closeness, help families maintain and perpetuate a paradigm or shared belief system, create and maintain family cohesion, and afford means for maintaining family contact. (Chapter 9, p. 123)

Bruess includes examples of how individuals have changed negative rituals to positive ones. Sorenson and his colleagues (Chapter 10) provide insights into patterns that build family bonds. For example, they report that when courting, a young couple that later became business owners had the habit of cherishing positive memories together. Throughout their married lives at family gatherings, they made it a practice of recollecting happy family memories. Stories about and pictures of family events can rekindle memories and associated emotions.

One common ritual mentioned frequently in the chapters and dialogues is family dinner. Combining food with conversation seems to create good feelings and reinforce emotional bonds. Angela Pritchard provides a vivid description of how a dinnertime ritual created strong emotional bonds in her family:

> One of the most important rituals our CEmO [chief emotional officer] sustained in order to protect the importance of family was dinnertime. Regardless of the situation, dinner was a priority at the Pritchard house. It was a time when business was shut off and we could simply be a family. My mother would coordinate our schedules so that even when we had volleyball or football practice, or if my dad was working late, we would have at least one hour to sit down and be a family. She would not simply have something delivered. Our CEmO would spend her mornings before leaving for the office, or the evenings after coming home to cook and bake a beautiful meal. The dinner was always a reflection of our family's current dynamic; pasta for the older girls because they had a track meet the next evening, but with asparagus because that was my dad's favorite; some carrots for our littlest sister; and a side salad in case my brother was cutting weight for wrestling. Each dish was chosen for a specific reason and made with love. We all made dinner a priority to show our respect for the work that was put into the meal. It was a ritual, a symbolic act, that we unquestionably maintained because of the value it added to our lives. And it was a ritual that was consistently sustained by our CEmO.
>
> During dinner we also had other rituals that facilitated and over time honed our communication techniques. After sitting down together, praying, and dishing up our food, we would go around the table and ask one another about the best part of our day. Even on the nights when we already had an idea what the best part of someone's day may have been, we always made sure the question was asked, and the answer communicated. That one small ritual was like a green light, giving our family the go-ahead to communicate with one another about our lives. It would lead into discussions about school, sports, friends, and anything else we felt like sharing. As the years have progressed, our average dinnertimes have evolved into two- to three-hour-long conversations of telling stories, reflecting on life, sharing goals, and making memories. (Chapter 14, pp. 181)

The preceding discussion suggests that emotional bonds take time, planning, and effort. They don't just automatically occur because individuals are blood relatives. The family has to set aside time for family and engage in patterns of positive interaction that build and sustain bonds.

Commit to Family, Business, and Family-business Identity

Before family members can commit to a family-business identity, they need to agree on the family identity. From a social capital perspective, agreements are based on a common set of beliefs that are expressed as values, goals, norms, and obligations. These beliefs form an identity, a common set of beliefs about "who we are." When family members are committed to the same beliefs, agreement is more likely. When family members are committed to different beliefs, disagreement is more likely. Trust is associated with commitment to the same beliefs; distrust is associated with commitment to differing beliefs.

In family businesses there may be three identities: family, business, and family-business. As mentioned earlier, the business identity may be completely separate from the family identity or it may be closely aligned with family identity. When it is closely aligned with family identity, it might be considered a family-business identity. The family and business identities are intertwined.

From a social capital perspective, the foundation for agreement is a commonly accepted family identity, business identity, and/or family-business identity. All three identities may change across life cycles and generations of families. To maintain commitment, families need to recognize and anticipate changes and put in place new communication patterns that make adjustments in and support the commonly accepted identity so that it is current with family beliefs.

Family identity
Within a young, nuclear family that has much informal interaction, family patterns and rituals may be enough to keep family identity aligned. However, when children become independent adults, each individual may form unique family patterns and beliefs that differ from those of their parents and siblings. As adults, siblings will likely never fully agree on some beliefs. For example, they may differ on business, politics, and religion.

To agree on a family identity, next-generation adults may need to develop new communication patterns and rituals that enable them to re-establish and recommit to a set of common beliefs, which becomes an identity that reflects the values and goals of the current adult generation. Much of the core identity from the preceding generation will likely be retained. But parts of the identity may need to be renegotiated to incorporate change that emerges in adults, which is in part influenced by the larger culture. Agreement on all beliefs is not likely possible. However, families who desire it may find enough common ground to form a common identity.

To renegotiate and sustain a common family identity, new patterns of communication may need to be developed. The parent–child and sibling patterns that emerged in a young family do not work well when children become adults. Among adults, family members need to make decisions more as peers. When several nuclear families are involved, the pattern likely needs to involve formal communication and decision-making structures. In families, formal family meetings or councils may provide opportunities to break out of old communication patterns. Siblings may learn to communicate and make decisions without the mediating role of parents.

Formal communication may help each generation to break out of old patterns and to develop new patterns that allow them to agree on a common identity. When family members have a voice, assumed beliefs and values can be challenged, clarified, and adjusted. The process of coming to an agreement may be more important than the beliefs that are formed. Being involved and having a voice brings agreement, which provides a foundation for trust.

Agreements can be formalized in written documents and adjusted as needed. Through the process of collaborative discussion, family members can create a constitution or charter that summarizes a family's vision, mission, values, and policies. Such documents are living documents; they can be revisited and adjusted over time to accommodate family member concerns. Participation in creating family identity leads to agreement with the identity. Without a commonly accepted identity, it will be more difficult for family members to agree on decisions related to the business.

Business identity

Similar to a family identity, the business identity summarizes beliefs such as: "Who are we as a business organization?"; "What are we trying to accomplish?"; and "How do we treat our employees and customers?" The beliefs that are developed to answer these questions may be completely independent of the family. They may be developed by non-family managers based on professional and industry norms and practices. When this is the case, a family-owned business may be much like public corporations. Beyond receiving dividends, family members may neither feel a connection to the business nor be stewards of its identity. Such was the case in Sylvia Shepard's fifth-generation business. She indicates that the following occurred:

> We were mostly uninvolved with the company, spread out around the country, developing our own careers and occasionally showing up for shareholder meetings. (Chapter 16, p. 205)

However, in the fifth generation, family members reclaimed both their family identity and their family-business identity. The business gave the cousins a reason to reconnect and rebuild a family identity in connection with the family-business identity. The beliefs on which the business was built became a rallying cause for the family. Based on her experience, Shepard suggests that families who assume stewardship for the business have a common focus that can give them a reason to organize and develop a family-business identity.

Family-business identity

When several family members both own and work in the business, family values likely play a major role in developing the business identity. Their values and norms become embedded in the business. Family and business become integrated into their lives, and a family-business identity emerges.

Even when the owner/founder is the only person who works in the business, he or she may treat the business as a family business, and it becomes associated with an extension of the family. Eddleston (Chapter 15) indicates that when owners label their business as a family business, their aim is to integrate family and business roles; thus, when a family views its firm as a family firm, it can have a profound effect on family values and behavior. For example, Sorenson and his colleagues provide the following quotation from a daughter whose father was the only person employed full-time in their business at the time:

> The family and the business have always been entwined. The family values are in the business, and the business values are a part of the family. That has affected our work ethic and the way we treated other people and expected to be treated and how we were expected to do things honestly and fairly. (Chapter 10, p. 140)

When the business is considered a "family business," that is, when the business identity is intertwined with the family identity, family members feel a sense of ownership in the business. For example, a board member for the business described above stated that the spouse of the CEO reminded board members that the identity of the family was tied to the identity of the business:

> One board member indicated that Sandra constantly reminded them that the business, like her relationship with George, was in it for the long haul and that its reputation was to be carefully maintained. (Chapter 10, p. 144)

For many families, the business becomes a canvas on which they can paint their own identity, beliefs about "who we are as a family," and "how we relate to the larger community." A family can clarify its own identity by creating a common view of the business and how the business relates to the larger community.

Social Infrastructure

Both emotional bonds and identity are developed and sustained by social infrastructure. Social infrastructure consists of social networks, interpersonal relationships, and communication patterns. A social infrastructure exists in any family and business. However, the nature of the social infrastructure may sustain neither a common identity nor strong emotional bonds.

Social networks are made up of interpersonal connections among individuals that provide communication and information transfer. Social networks have informal rules about who can be included, the nature of communication, and information that is shared within the network. In family businesses, there may be a family, a business, and a family-business network. The family network is usually made up of blood relatives, although close intimate associates may be included. The business network is made up of business owners, advisors, and employees. The family business network is made of family member shareholders, business board members, advisors, and employees. Upper-level managers are more likely to be included as part of the family business social network than lower-level employees.

To maintain a common identity, members of a social network should be included in activities associated with the network. For example, if members of a family are not invited to family meetings or included in family communications, they may feel disenfranchised. Failure to include individuals in the relevant network will likely weaken both emotional bonds and a common identity, resulting in a loss of trust.

Interpersonal relationships define how participants in networks relate to one another. For example, in some relationships one person may dominate and another person may be subordinate – as might be the case in parent – child or supervisor – employee relationships. Or relationships may be equal – as might be the case with peers or company vice-presidents. And the relationships may be warm and intimate – as they might be with close friends, or the relationships may be distant and cold – as they could be between quarreling and unforgiving siblings. These relationships influence the nature of communication within networks. For example, quarreling siblings may be included in the family gatherings, but refuse to talk with one another or be belligerent.

Relationships within a social network are an important part of identity. If individuals disagree with the nature of relationships, they may withdraw their affiliation with the network. For example, parents who treat their competent adult offspring like children may find that their children prefer to work elsewhere. If relationships do not change over the family's life cycle, family members may have difficulty feeling like they belong. Over a lifetime, the normal progression of relationships is that children become independent and redefine their roles to be contributing adults in the family and the business.

Communication patterns refer to the repetitive flow and exchange of information within a network. As mentioned previously, communication patterns may include rituals such as regular family dinners, annual picnics, or award ceremonies. They could also include regular lunches, e-mails, newsletters, or telephone conversations. The frequency and nature of information exchange is a part of communication patterns.

The social infrastructure of the family has to change throughout the life cycles of the family to sustain a common identity. For adult children, communication patterns that include participation and collaboration can help a family sustain a commonly accepted identity, which unifies the family.

Thus, the communication patterns that existed in a young nuclear family should likely give way to more collaborative patterns among adults. Social activities that emerged naturally among a small nuclear family give way to planned and organized social interaction. Given circumstances in a family, face-to-face communication might be replaced with e-mails, teleconferences, and information exchange on social network sites.

Agreement to a common identity and the development of collective trust is more likely to occur when there is a supportive social infrastructure. Important elements of the social infrastructure are inclusion in relevant social networks, positive interpersonal relationships that fit family life cycles, and frequent and transparent communication. Below, several examples from chapters in this book illustrate the importance of social infrastructure and how it can change over time.

Treating grown children as adults
Treating family members in business meetings as equals and communicating based on business roles may seem very unnatural at first. For that reason, families likely need professional facilitation to help make the transition. Facilitators can help family members adopt new roles and relationships. For example, in Chapter 9 Bruess relates the following experience:

> Frank and Brenda owned a large family farm and hoped their children would
> want to continue working in the family business, raising their own children on

the farm. However, Frank and Brenda's children became discontented as adults when the communication patterns they experienced as kids did not appropriately change as they matured . . . Finally, many of the children were upset enough to either leave the business altogether or state a desire to leave. Frank and Brenda realized they needed some external input and sought help from a family business consultant. The consultant helped the family restructure their ways of interacting and their decision-making patterns. She had the family meet and for the first time engage in open discussion as equals about farm-related issues. As expected, at first the children aired their frustrations. Frank and Brenda felt emotionally torn apart by such open communication; the norms, rules, and roles they had known for so long were radically changing right before their eyes. Over time, they all settled into a new pattern of regular meetings in which the adult children had a role, and everyone participated in discussions. The family also added new rituals of recreation for all members to enjoy together. Children who had left the business came back. All members began to feel like active participants. In the end, the family's identity – as a result of changes in communication patterns, norms, and roles – was dramatically and positively transformed. (Chapter 9, p. 124)

Poor infrastructure leads to different identities

Goodpaster, in Chapter 4, and Hayes, in Chapter 5, provide examples of how a breakdown in common identity and collective trust can occur. Goodpaster indicates that individuals may elevate their own personal interests and fixate on personal goals. As Figure 1.1 suggests, following a personal agenda may be relatively easy when individuals do not agree on identity. It becomes easy to rationalize that because there is no common identity, individuals can actively pursue their own agenda.

For example, one major shareholder, who was also the business CEO in a family that had a weak identity, chose to reinvest profits in the business to promote growth without full disclosure to minority shareholders. In his mind, the urgency of achieving the growth goal justified withholding information from his sisters who were also shareholders. He felt no allegiance to a common identity because he and his sisters had very little contact; they had no infrastructure to maintain emotional bonds and a common identity. The CEO refused to fully disclose information about financial performance. The sisters' distrust increased, they sought relief in court, and won a lawsuit. Unfortunately, the family did not have a social infrastructure in place to discuss the business and to agree on beliefs supportive of business growth, and to avoid the loss of positive emotional bonds and trust.

Katherine Hayes uses a personal example from her family business to illustrate how conflict can escalate when family members fixate on personal goals and when the social infrastructure is not in place to resolve differences. She combines concepts discussed by Goodpaster and Bruess to interpret how conflict in her family quickly escalated. In her experience, fixation and criticism went hand in hand, as did rationalization and defensiveness. Escalating conflict led to stonewalling and defensiveness. However, through a change to more supportive communication patterns, Hayes's family conflict was resolved, even though some negative feelings lingered. Hayes's story brings home the importance of having the social infrastructure in place to manage inevitable conflicts that arise.

Promoting common identity builds trust with clients

Margaret Cronin is a legal advisor who frequently meets with clients on estate and succession issues. In her practice, she found that identifying and adapting to the family's common identity builds trust:

> If the advisor can identify social capital in the form of shared family values, the advisor can explore how these values might translate in each of the family, business, and ownership domains. If the family brings meaning to the transition of the business by seeking to carry on the founder's legacy, the advisor is able to leverage this family social capital in gathering consensus among multiple generations. If the family demonstrates trust with each other, they are more likely to view an advisor with trustful eyes, as a helper or facilitator rather than an outsider. Ultimately, the existence of family social capital can expand the scope of possible outcomes in the advisory relationship. (Chapter 8, p. 113)

In addition, Cronin has found that by including all shareholders in discussions, an advisor can build common identity and strengthen family social capital. Including only some of the shareholders in discussions can be divisive and destructive to family social capital:

> [I]f it is part of the process for the advisor to gather input from each of the family, business, and ownership groups before a significant decision is made, doesn't family social capital become a self-perpetuating asset? On the other side of the coin, if the advisor works with one group to the exclusion of the others, doesn't the lack of family social capital become a self-fulfilling prophecy? (Chapter 8, p. 113)

Moreover, Cronin suggests that for family members to be supportive, the process used in making decisions should both be fair *and* be perceived to be fair.

> "People care as much about the justice of the process through which an outcome is produced as they do about the outcome itself."[3] I have found this to be true. In my experience, when a significant action is taken in a family business without a fair process to support the decision, the complaint is more likely to be, "I wish he/she had just consulted me first before hiring this manager," or "If he/she wanted to change strategic direction, he/she should have run it past the

other owners," than "The manager is not a good hire for our business," or "I don't like this new strategic direction." (Chapter 8, p. 107)

Inclusive support provides common identity and caring bonds

Terri McEnaney is president of a large family nursery that has numerous family-member employees. In Chapter 13, McEnaney describes the social infrastructure that her family has in place to maintain agreement among family member shareholders. All family shareholders are invited to attend regularly scheduled meetings to discuss business strategy and policy. Included in their discussions are social plans, such as season tickets for local sporting events, which help maintain emotional bonds. She also describes a recent family retreat in which family members openly discussed family business issues and policies. The processes her family has in place are inclusive, recognize the importance of family relationships, and provide for open communication. Provision for open discussion and involvement promotes family business agreement and helps to maintain family bonds and the family-business identity.

In the following statement, in Chapter 15, Eddleston supports the case for social infrastructures that include participation, collaboration, and open communication:

> [F]amily firms that implement a participative strategy process are most successful. A participative strategy process enhances family members' identification with the firm, helping them to understand the challenges facing the firm as well as the firm's strengths, weaknesses, resources, and capabilities. Encouraging family members to participate in strategic decision-making may be especially important for family firms because in order to remain competitive, family firms should generate new strategies for each generation that joins the firm. Furthermore, participation in the strategy-making process seems to increase commitment to a course of action and improve the decision-making quality of family firms. Additionally, family firms that encourage participation and collaboration support ethical norms that assist family firm performance through the accumulation of goodwill, loyalty, and social support. (Chapter 15, p. 190)

SUMMARY

Family social capital refers to trusting and cooperative relationships that enable family members to work together as owners and/or in the business. Many assume that because of blood relationships, family members have social capital. And, because of the tendency to develop strong emotional bonds, there is a basis for social capital in families. However, it is obvious that the relationships in some families are a liability. This paper provides an overview of the social elements that contribute to social capital. In most cases, families need at least some development and adjustment across gen-erations to maintain family social capital.

Some families, particularly small nuclear families, may have frequent and open communication, a common identity, and collective trust that create cooperative relationships that are an asset. However, families with multiple adult children, multi-generational families, and even some nuclear families need to purposively establish and maintain a social infrastructure. The infrastructure consists of frequent and open commu-nication within the family network, interpersonal relationships that are consistent with maturation levels and roles, and helpful communication patterns that sustain identity and emotional bonds. When families have a common identity and strong familial bonds, they will have the collective trust that enables the family to be an asset to a business.

NOTES

1. The following works were consulted as sources for discussions about social capital: Coleman (1988); Nahapiet and Ghoshal (1998); Tsai and Ghoshal (1998); Putnam (2000); Hoffman et al. (2006); and Pearson et al. (2008).
2. Baxter and Braithwaite (2006, p. 261).
3. Chan Kim and Mauborgne (2005, pp. 174–5).

PART I

Understanding the elements of family social capital

Part I of the book highlights the infrastructure of family social capital. The papers address questions such as: What is social capital and how does it differ from family social capital? Why is family social capital unique and an asset to family enterprise? How is family social capital maintained? Not only do we learn about these issues from scholarly research; we are also enlightened by both an advisor's and a family business member's application of these issues.

In Chapter 2, Pearson and Carr provide a scholarly overview of the social capital concept, its unique application to family firms, and highlight the importance of trust for social capital. In Chapter 3, from an advisor's point of view, Hubler shows how trust, as a central part of family social capital, is resilient and enduring in families, but that it takes work to maintain this trust.

In Chapter 4, Goodpaster, from a standpoint rooted in philosophy, highlights the morality and ethics tied into family business and trust, giving us a framework to assess hindrances to solving trust in families and tools to rebuild the trust. In Chapter 5, from a family business perspective, Hayes, through a poignant and personal example, shows how a business family can rebuild trust and move forward utilizing Goodpaster's concept of teleopathy or "goal sickness" combined with Gottman's concept of the "four horsemen," which describes patterns of behavior destructive to relationships. Finally, in Chapter 6, Smith presents a summary of the dialogue.

2. The central role of trust in family firm social capital

Allison W. Pearson and Jon C. Carr

> Spontaneous sociability is critical to economic life because virtually all economic activity is carried out by groups rather than individuals. Before wealth can be created, human beings have to learn to work together.
> Fukuyama (1995, p. 47)

> The trust factor is the social glue that binds commitment and promotes action necessary to produce results. Without it, you can't win.
> Bennis and Goldsmith (1997, p. xv)

The concept of social capital originally emerged from work in community studies[1] where city neighborhoods with strong personal relationships that developed over time provided the foundations for strong, trusting, cooperative relationships and collective action that helped sustain the neighborhood. The basic assumption of social capital theory is that when a strong set of relationships exists in a group, these relationships form feelings of gratitude, friendship, and respect, and create a sense of long-lasting obligation to the group. These bonds and ties lead to greater access to information and opportunities than those given to outsiders. Researchers have since expanded the notion that social capital can enhance the successful functioning of a variety of groups, including not only communities, but families and business organizations as well.

Families are composed of a unique combination of interpersonal relationships that includes bonds, ties, and unique information-sharing capabilities. The same is true for business organizations, which are also made up of similar bonds and information-sharing characteristics. Therefore, *family businesses* create a rare opportunity to merge the social capital created in both groups, the family and the organizations they own and work in. The purpose of this chapter is to explore the rich and abundant social capital potential in family firms and examine in more detail the central role of trust in developing and sustaining social capital.

SOCIAL CAPITAL

Personal relationships that exist in a group based on a history of interactions represent an important source of social capital. When personal relationships are based on values such as friendship, respect, or lasting ties, these relationships likely affect individual behavior. The exact nature of the values is less important than the fact that the group *shares* these values. These shared values, in turn, influence behavior.

Social capital suggests that personal and emotional attachments among individuals can shape behavior, both in the family and the workplace. For example, you receive an e-mail at work asking you to buy overpriced cookies that you don't really want. Do you buy the cookies? Your answer may depend partially on the strength of the relationship between you and the person who sent the e-mail. It would seem that the closer the social ties, the more likely you are to buy, regardless of whether you want the cookies! If the solicitation is from your sister, who is also your vice-president of marketing, your answer might be quite different from the one you give the unfamiliar guy in accounting. Thus, social capital theory argues that social connections, including kinship relationships, can create ties, expectations, and durable obligations that can shape and influence our behavior.

Are *all* strong social relationships in groups, and is the behavior they influence always good? Of course not. Remember when your parents asked, "If your friends jumped off a cliff, does that mean you would too?" For some of us the answer was a resounding "Yes!" Strong social relationships can lead to many dysfunctional behaviors (for example, think of the strong social ties that lead to cults, gangs, and drug rings). An abundance of research has explored the conditions where dysfunctional social behaviors can be the result. For example, Janis's work explores the dysfunctional behavior known as *groupthink*, which occurs when a group of people surrender their own individual opinions or judgments to a strong leader who isolates the group from rational outsiders.[2] Under these conditions, the outcomes are usually not good. The point is that social capital can lead to dysfunctional, harmful behaviors through the same mechanisms of strong social ties and obligations.

On the other hand, collective thinking and influential relationships can help us achieve more and do so more efficiently. Individuals embedded in a group often develop short cuts for information and knowledge they share with others, which can help speed up decision-making, innovation, and problem-solving. For example, when you need access quickly to a particular piece of information or person in an organization, what route do you usually follow? Do you pursue the formal organizational chart and policy, or contact the person you know who can create those shortcuts for you?

We tend to take advantage of the social relationships we have with others in our group. These strong social relationships can provide us access to the information we need from a group, whether it is a business or family, and create shortcuts to new knowledge and ideas.

BENEFITS OF SOCIAL CAPITAL

Research suggests that groups with strong social capital are effective because they operate on the basis of shared values, rather than on extensive contracts or legal regulations that are necessary when trust and voluntary obligations are non-existent. Additionally, because social capital is built through relationships, it cannot be simply bought or acquired by others; thus, groups with strong social capital are afforded unique advantages over those groups that do have weak or absent relationships. Finally, groups with strong social capital can operate more efficiently and with lower direct and indirect costs. Since these costs take time, energy, and resources, they can slow down efficient operations. In short, organizations with low social capital need formal, legal requirements and are thus less efficient than those organizations that can rely on their strong and vibrant social capital to get things done.

In exploring what drives these strong, social capital bonds that influence our behavior, we discover that many influences can affect these bonds. While formal ties in both the workplace and family create bonding relationships, it is the strength of these bonds (known as *relational embeddedness*)[3] that really characterizes how well the social capital is being leveraged within the organization. What causes relational bonds to be strong enough to create mutual expectations and obligations, and thus create social capital relationships? A discussion of the central benefits that trust plays within social capital provides some insight into the role of trust in family firms. A brief overview of social capital theory provides some context – and some insights – into the central role and benefits that can be derived from trust.

SOCIAL CAPITAL WITHIN FAMILY FIRMS

Social capital has a strong influence on the flow of information and collective action of groups. Social capital is by definition socially complex and related to the values, cooperation, vision, purpose, and trust that exist in the family firm. Considered a deeply embedded resource within the organization, social capital in the family firm is often difficult for competitors to imitate.[4] We suggest that social capital within family firms has several dimensions, each of which interactively relates to the others to help make a particular family firm unique and ultimately competitive. These dimensions represent the structural, cognitive, and relational aspects of firm social interaction that we, in turn, propose as the specific elements of family business social capital.[5] Family firms have distinctive capabilities resulting from the often unique combination of the structural, cognitive, and relational dimensions of social capital.

The Structural Dimension of Family Firm Social Capital

The structural dimension of family firm social capital is defined as the social interactions, including the patterns and strength of ties, among the members of the family firm. The structural dimension reflects the density and connectivity of social ties, as well as members' ability to use and re-use social networks. In particular, family firms can leverage the benefits associated with the concept of the "appropriable organization" – a term Coleman used to describe how ties among one group could easily be transferred to another.[6] Research suggests that the structural ties of family can and do transfer to the business.[7] It is at this point – the appropriable organization – that family and business social capital merge and create the potential for abundant social capital unique to the family firm.

In contrast, employees in non-family firms often bring few, if any, pre-existing network ties to the workplace. Family firms may then have an advantage over non-family firms in the creation of structural social capital due to prevailing and familiar network ties.

The Cognitive Dimension of Family Firm Social Capital

The cognitive dimension of family business social capital includes "resources providing shared representations, interpretations, and systems of meaning among parties."[8] The cognitive dimension includes the group's shared vision and purpose, as well as unique language, stories, and culture of the family that are commonly known and understood, yet deeply embedded. Shared vision is a bonding mechanism that allows for shared communication and integration of ideas.[9] The vision of the family firm "endows the family enterprise with *meaning* – it conveys a profound explanation for why continuing the business is important to the family."[10] The shared purposes of both the family and the business converge to create the collective understanding necessary for the family to pursue long-term family goals. These cognitive elements of social capital are unique in family firms because they are deeply embedded in the family's history.

The Relational Dimension of Family Firm Social Capital

The relational dimension of family firm social capital represents the third critical component that shapes the social capital within the family firm. How is the relational dimension of social capital unique to the family firm? The very goals of value creation, as opposed to purely economic wealth creation that often exists in family firms, are likely a result of the relational dimension of social capital. Relational social capital is characterized by the norms, obligations, family identity, and trust that are created from the social interactions within the family and the family firm.

Norms are the informal agreement on acceptable actions in the group.[11] Lansberg identifies norms that are often found in the family firm, including norms of behavior regarding profitability, as well as norms of being collaborative, successful families.[12] These norms include egalitarianism, teamwork, and a focus on developing unique values and synergies resulting from the collaboration and integration of the family in the business. Norms in the family firm also serve to influence firm-level decision-making and create unique familial influences that continue in the family firm through the influence of subsequent generations.[13]

In addition to the importance of norms, family and business obligations are also keys to the relational dimension of social capital. Over time, obligations to family create stability in network ties and relationships. The old saying, "you can't fire family," embodies the enduring social ties and obligations often found in many family firms. These enduring ties and obligations are found less often in non-family firms where social relationships are not as committed and long-lasting.

Concerning identification, a key aspect of family members is the degree to which they see themselves as part of the family firm. Strong family-firm identity is a catalyst for information exchange and cooperation.[14] Without strong identification, employees may be far less willing to cooperate, communicate, and coordinate, as well as voluntarily share knowledge and information. Family identity is often a strong, enduring social force. For example, citing a *Wall Street Journal* report, Lansberg describes how approximately 25 percent of family business owners who sold their firms tried to buy them back later on.[15] The motivation to reclaim the family firm arose from the owners' realization, only too late, how closely their identities were tied to the family enterprise.

While norms, obligations, and identity are key elements of the relational dimension of social capital, the central role of trust helps families leverage social capital to their firm. A deeper examination of this central role is provided below.

THE KEY ROLE OF TRUST IN FAMILY FIRM SOCIAL CAPITAL

Trust is often defined as the intention and willingness to be vulnerable to another person.[16] In many ways it is more than that, when we think about what trust means to most people. When we consider the concept of trust, we are often thinking about interpersonal (between-parties) trust. Interpersonal trust arises when both parties believe (1) perceived good intentions exist between parties; (2) reasonable abilities exist to act on those intentions; (3) that the other party will reliably act, and; (4) that there is a high degree of openness between parties. With a high degree of trust, individuals are more willing to participate in social exchange with others – they are more willing to communicate, associate, share ideas, cooperate, and work collectively as a group. Trust in social relationships may also make it easier for individuals to fulfill obligations and expectations, even if they wouldn't do so strictly on their own. In essence, "Where parties trust each other, they are more willing to engage in cooperative activity through which further trust may be generated."[17]

Not all trust relationships can be viewed as having the same level of intensity or strength. We can describe the level of trust as fragile or as resilient.[18] Fragile trust is similar to the kinds of transactions we engage in where there are tangible benefits gained from the relationship. In fragile trust relationships, we are motivated by the potential for reward rather than the relationship itself – a sort of extrinsic trust that exists only when those rewards are present. Resilient trust is defined as lasting trust, formed through emotional ties to others[19] and is a stronger form of trust that emerges from relationships rather than from contractual relations. Resilient trust may be able to withstand breaches, as long as that trust is relationship based. For example, in a family firm, it is almost inevitable that a family member at some point will violate the trust and integrity of the family. However, because that person is a part of the family and the stability of the family relationships are important and lasting, over time the family is likely to re-establish a level of trust with that person. In contrast, in a non-family firm, trust may not be resilient. There may be little beyond the job itself that encourages us to have a deeper relationship with an individual. This type of trust may be shallow and short-lived. Shallow, short-lived trust does not accumulate to create collective action.

In general, interpersonal exchange must occur before either type of trust relationship (be it fragile or resilient) can be built. We develop network ties and relationships gradually over time in any business setting. But each time we enter a new job, we essentially start over. We may maintain ties outside the organization that are useful to us, but inside the new organization, the social relationships begin anew. However, if we are in a family firm, the network ties of the family, both internal and external, are timeless and strong. In fact, we inherit some of these strong ties as a birthright. In family firms, often individual family members can begin a conversation or e-mail with, "Hi, I'm the daughter of XYZ," and gain automatic entry, acceptance, access to information, and assistance simply because of their family kinship bonds.

These types of connections can become critically valuable to business success when they are built on resilient trust; they provide useful information and improve the degree to which knowledge is efficiently developed and shared. In short, these types of strong, durable social ties can form the basis for firm competitive advantage. In such circumstances, the family's resilient trust builds a level of family social capital that can translate into valuable benefits not only to the family, but to the family business itself. As family relationships grow and mature over time, the recurring interactions and resulting interdependences among members build resilient trust.[20] Alternatively, in non-family firms, institutionalized policies, procedures, and rules of reward and exchange may create fragile trust, which supplies a weak link to organizational processes and capabilities as compared to resilient trust.

Family firms do indeed provide fertile ground for resilient trust. For example, for family firms at the start-up or growth point in their business, resilient trust can serve as the powerful glue that binds the business as it struggles to get off the ground or exploit new markets. In such circumstances, family firm members may work above and beyond their prescribed organizational roles with the knowledge that the resilient trust within the family unit is strong. Instead of assuming that their efforts will be rewarded individually based upon an implied trust relationship that is fragile and transactional, employees rely on resilient trust, which lets them know that, deep down, they are part of something bigger. In essence, they are more than employees – they have relational bonds that transcend those of a typical employment contract, and thus provide the family firm with a commitment that is stronger and more vibrant.

GENERATING RESILIENT TRUST IN THE FAMILY FIRM

If resilient trust brings out the wealth of advantages based in social relationships, how can trust be generated in organizations? First, organizations need to begin by taking a baseline measure of the current level of trust in the organization. Firms need to conduct an annual employee survey, including measures of trust. Key trust areas to explore are trust in management, trust in ownership, trust in the direct supervisor, and trust in colleagues and co-workers.

A variety of measurement instruments are available for gauging the level of trust within the organization. Cook and Wall created a simple measure of interpersonal trust at work, with items such as "Most of my workmates can be relied upon to do as they say they will do" to measure trust in colleagues, or "I feel confident that the firm will always try to treat me fairly" as a measure of trust in management.[21] Additionally, Schoorman et al. recommend a concise seven-item measure of trust.[22] Their scale includes items such as, "My supervisor keeps my interests in mind when making decisions," and "If my supervisor asked why a problem occurred, I would speak freely even if I were partly to blame." In addition to measuring trust in the firm, family firms may also want to measure trust in the family. Can the family ownership be trusted to act in the best interest of all employees or just family employees? While these may be painful and uncomfortable questions to ask, family firms can't build valuable social capital through trust if they don't know how trusted and trusting the family firm is.

Once trust levels are identified, generating trust must become a priority of the organization, starting at the top down. If organizational leadership is not trustworthy, there is little hope for trust to develop throughout the ranks of the organization. Family business leaders can create and sustain trust by exemplifying (1) constancy; (2) congruity; (3) reliability; and (4) integrity.[23] For family firms, if effective behavioral practices that generate a high level of family trust are already in place in the family, family firm leadership may want to work on ways to transfer those practices and habits into the business. However, if those trusting practices are granted only to family members, trust will not trickle down through the organization. Extended constancy, reliability, and integrity into all business transactions, for family members and non-family members, create a more trusting workplace for all involved. And, with more trust comes more social capital to create free-flowing information, cooperation, and collective behaviors that can help lead to successful achievement of the family firm's goals.

Development of resilient trust gives family firms a valuable and singular opportunity to succeed. This type of trust positively impacts the three dimensions of social capital within the family firm, which ultimately has important implications for the family firm's value and its performance.

IMPLICATIONS OF FAMILY FIRM SOCIAL CAPITAL FOR FAMILY FIRMS

The presence and strength of all three dimensions of family firm social capital – structural, cognitive, and relational – can lead to favorable organizational processes or capabilities for superior firm performance, and, in particular, to family firm value creation. A key organizational capability enhanced through family firm social capital is the efficient exchange and combination of information. Social relationships and strong social network ties provide the informal channel for efficient information flow. As pointed out by Adler and Kwon, "social capital facilitates access to broader sources of information and improves information quality, relevance, and timeliness."[24] Family firm social capital allows information to bypass the formal boundaries of typical non-family firms.

Family firm social capital can also foster cooperative action. Leana and Van Buren use the term "associability" to refer to the "willingness and ability of participants to subordinate individual goals and associated actions to collective goals and actions."[25] Associability is the result of a high degree of interdependence among members, as well as "general understandings of work organization, implicit norms, and generalized, resilient trust."[26] Lansberg identifies discussion and interaction among employees, both family and non-family, as necessary components for a family firm to develop a cohesive, value-driven purpose.[27] The family firm's special circumstances, creating value for the family, produce greater opportunities for sharing information and working collectively in the family firm.

These integrative social behaviors result in a social environment complete with family habits, shared values, and norms and these integrative behaviors are strong catalysts for resilient trust relationships. Since families are enduring social entities across generations, they have lasting norms, values, and shared understanding. In contrast, business entities, especially new ventures, may be devoid of these collective social habits and norms. Often these non-family businesses seek proxies for family firm social capital, borrowing or attempting to imitate what families (and family firms) may already have. Managers and businesses will often proclaim "we are like family here"; or we treat our employees "like family." These statements attempt to re-create social capital where it may not exist naturally. Social capital in non-family firms is not easily attainable and must be developed gradually over time. Even so, it may never have the power of relationships that exist in families and subsequently in family firms.

LEVERAGING FAMILY SOCIAL CAPITAL WITHIN THE FAMILY FIRM

For those in family business, an important question is, "Can the social capital you develop in one context, such as family, be transferred to another setting, such as the business?" Some researchers argue that family businesses thrive largely because of the long-established social cohesion of the family. For example, Fukuyama suggests that "Because their cohesion is based on the moral and emotional bonds of a preexisting social group, the family enterprise can thrive even in the absence of commercial law or stable structure of property rights."[28] In fact, family bonds appear to be a key source of integrative social behaviors for family firms. Arregle et al. suggest that when the family provides the key resources to the firm, such as capital, labor, management, and innovation, the family has the power to transfer its social capital, including norms and values, to the firm quite readily.[29] Family habits and practices become embedded into the normal, everyday life of the business. For example, an employee says, "If the old man was still here, he would fire me if my truck wasn't clean. He believed in keeping everything clean." The employee, even if not a family member, has a clean truck, notwithstanding the absence of the founder.

To tap into the powerful resource of the social capital of the family, families must first generate and sustain family social capital, and integrate that social capital into the family firm. Four conditions for the successful transfer of valuable family social capital into the firm include (1) the existence of strong social capital in the family, often established by the family business founder; (2) the level of involvement of the family in the business; (3) the functional nature of family social capital; and (4) the family business culture established by the founder or family.

Strong family social capital is often a result of a strong family leader, solid connections between generations, as well as closely-held and practiced family traditions and values. For a family firm to create firm-level social capital, they must first have strong family social capital. On the other hand, family firms with weak social capital in the family are more likely to look and operate like non-family firms. For family social capital to shift to the firm, the family must also be closely involved in the business. If family members are not involved in strategy, policy, and procedures, the family social capital cannot flow into the business. In addition, family social capital must also be functional (as opposed to dysfunctional) to successfully influence the business. Dysfunctional behaviors in the family, such as illegal activities or inappropriate anger, can transfer into the firm just as easily as functional behaviors.

The culture of the business, established by the way the family manages the business, will also impact the flow of family social capital into the business. Dyer categorized family business cultures as (1) paternalistic; (2) laissez-faire; (3) participative; or (4) professional.[30] Paternalistic cultures are closely managed by the founder and/or select family member. In such cultures, family leaders make all the significant business decisions and closely supervise employees – suggesting a lack of trust outside the family, even though the family itself may have high trust.

Laissez-faire cultures also possess strong central leadership by the founder and the family, but the family has consciously decided to trust employees, and as such, both family and non-family employees may contribute to decision-making in the firm. Family members likely control the predominant strategy of the firm, but employees have input on implementation decisions. In a participative culture, group-oriented structures downplay the power and central focus of the family, creating a more egalitarian culture.

Finally, the professional culture is usually found in family firms run by professional managers. These firms are characterized by individualism, competition, and impersonal employee relations. These cultures arise from a strong push to professionalize the family firm and thus minimize the family influence. In sum, trust may thrive more readily in the laissez-faire and participative cultures than the paternalistic or professional cultures, but paternalistic cultures may be more powerful in transferring family social capital because family values are essentially required of employees.

CONCLUSIONS FOR FAMILIES (AND FAMILY FIRMS)

While the problems that often accompany the family firm are well documented, the advantages associated with the family's involvement within the business are also clear. Families have unique characteristics that can be leveraged to improve the creation and growth of family firms. These characteristics at times seem self-evident – families are able to use the strong, powerful bonds of family members to create structural, cognitive, and relational benefits for their firms. Many of these benefits lie with one of the fundamental elements of family relationships – the enduring trust that can be leveraged to the benefit of the family and business. This *resilient* trust is an important part of this equation.

The purpose of this chapter was to give some insights into these important components that affect family businesses. Our intention was to provide an overview of social capital in general, and family firm social capital in particular. The characteristics of trust, and the role that trust plays within the family firm's social capital, were also discussed. As researchers and practitioners develop a deeper understanding of family firm social capital, the benefits of resilient trust will continue to gain prominence for family firms.

NOTES

1. Jacobs (1965).
2. Janis (1982).
3. Nahapiet and Ghoshal (1998).
4. Dess and Shaw (2001).
5. Pearson et al. (2008).
6. Coleman (1988).
7. Arregle et al. (2007).
8. Nahapiet and Ghoshal (1998, p. 244). Ideational reference made by the authors to Cicourel (1973).
9. Tsai and Ghoshal (1998).
10. Lansberg (1999, p. 76, original emphasis).
11. Nahapiet and Ghoshal (1998).
12. Lansberg (1999).
13. Sharma and Manikutty (2005).
14. Nahapiet and Ghoshal (1998).
15. Lansberg (1999).
16. Nahapiet and Ghoshal (1998).
17. Ibid., p. 250. Ideational references made by the authors include: Putnam (1993); Fukuyama (1995); Tyler et al. (1996).
18. Leana and Van Buren (1999).
19. Molm et al. (2009).
20. Arregle et al. (2007).
21. Cook and Wall (1980).
22. Schoorman et al. (2007).
23. Bennis and Goldsmith (1997).
24. Adler and Kwon (2002, p. 29).
25. Leana and Van Buren (1999, p. 541).
26. Ibid., p. 549.
27. Lansberg (1999).
28. Fukuyama (1995, p. 63).
29. Arregle et al. (2007).
30. Dyer (1988).

3.   The trust paradox of family businesses

Tom Hubler

DEFINITIONS OF TRUST

Trust is the central component to the development of a family firm's social capital according to Pearson and Carr's "The central role of trust in family firm social capital" (Chapter 2 in this volume). Their work raises the questions of what trust is and how to sustain it as the family business evolves. Over the past 30 years I have worked with family businesses in the area of transitions, succession planning, and managing what I describe as emotional breakdowns of trust in either business or family relationships. As a result, I believe building trust in the family and in the structure of the business is mutually beneficial to family harmony and a successful family business.

In the family business literature Poza presents a nuanced definition of trust: "Trust is not an article of faith among adults. As adults, trust comes from information, reliability and predictability, accessibility, shared goals, emotional bonds, a sense of fairness and transparency."[1] The definition of trust that I use, based on my experiences working with family business, is that it is a reciprocal relationship premised upon shared reliance, both behaviorally and emotionally. For example, "You are there for me when I need you" demonstrates how trust is defined by many families that I have worked with. Even in dramatic sibling rivalry cases, it is not unusual for the siblings to privately state that they know their sibling would be there if a crisis were to occur.

An example to illustrate the point of being there occurred in a family business where two sons were at odds with each other. The older son had bypassed college to join his father in the family business, assisting him in completing a series of government contracts. He anticipated being the heir, but when his younger brother, who had gone to college and traveled throughout Europe, decided to come into the family business, he was placed at the same level of responsibility and salary. The older brother was miffed and was unable to work out any resolution with his father and younger brother. He left the family business and has since started up as a competitor in a neighboring state.

One winter evening the older brother was acting as a Good Samaritan to help a driver who had gone off the road. Unfortunately, a drunk driver hit the older brother's car when he was standing between his car and the car that had gone off the road. The older son's leg was severely crushed in the accident. He was rushed by helicopter to a regional hospital, and when he awoke, his younger brother was standing there holding his hand. There was not a dry eye in the room, and at a subsequent family meeting when the story was shared, it became the basis for the development of trust in their brotherly relationship.

There are many facets to the building and evolution of trust in a family.[2] First, as the definitions above allude to, trust must be cultivated. For example, deprived of water, nourishment, and sunlight, a houseplant will wither and die. This is an analogy I often use with my clients to discuss trust in families. Trust must be nourished in order for it to survive. Second, trust requires that family members act in expected ways. When this does not happen and a breach of trust occurs, whether it is related to family, business, or financial issues, feelings are hurt and in the context of a business family, strain occurs in the workplace.

Yet, this does not mean that all interactions among family members will be perfect. In other words, it is near impossible for a family "not to inadvertently step on each other's toes occasionally." In those instances when trust is broken and a breach occurs, a family business must move on. For a family to move on, forgiveness must happen.[3]

Maintenance and nurturance of trust in business families requires action and the willingness to contribute to the common good. Ken Kaye, in a recent presentation on trust at the Psychodynamics of Family Business (PDFB) spring 2010 meeting, discussed trust in business families as a function of risk in relation to what you are willing to risk. What are you willing to risk or contribute to the family if there is not guaranteed payback? From my perspective I ask, "What are you willing to risk in order to create a new beginning?" This requires an action on the part of the family to either maintain or rebuild trust.

PROMOTING TRUST IN FAMILY AND IN FAMILY BUSINESS

When I suggest to business families the need to create formality and structure in their family business, many believe that structure is not necessary because they all love each other. I explain that because family members

Table 3.1   Activities to promote trust in family business

	Maintaining Trust		
	Family	Family–Business relationship	Business
Actions	Sustain/build social relationships through family retreats or service projects.	Establish and maintain policies and rules regarding compensation and working in the business	Agree on business strategies and goals
Expert external support	Obtain facilitators and counselors	Establish a board of directors or advisors and/or seek expert help from consultants	

love each other structure must be created to preserve trust and family relationships. Hence, intervening to create formality in the business will create clarity and trust in the business. A symbiotic relationship is created between the business and family regarding trust.

Involving family members in goal-setting and policy-making is important to developing trust and unity.[4] Based on my experience, these policies need to occur on both sides of the family–business equation. The emotional strategies created in families not only strengthen family trust, but also permeate into the business creating a sense of trust. By the same token, creating structure, discipline, and formality in the business not only generates trust, predictability, and profits in the business, but also has a positive impact on family emotional trust. There is a bilateral relationship between the activities done in the family to build trust and its impact on the business. This is the family business trust paradox. Intervening in families to strengthen trust automatically strengthens trust in the business, while enhancing the family's social capital. Table 3.1 lists activities that promote trust in business families.

Trust Building in the Family

Several situations I have dealt with in my work exemplify this bilateral dynamic on the family side. The first depicts building trust and emotional equity in the family through a family retreat. During the retreat, family fun time and business discussions were important. The dad invited all six of his adult children, spouses, and 14 grandchildren to a dude ranch in Arizona. The idea was to strengthen family relations, but also integrate the older cousins, 15 years and older, into the family council discussion.

In this example, the family's commitment to build the emotional equity or strength of their family by having the cousins – who live in different parts of the country – participate in fun activities not only strengthens their family relationship, but also is a mechanism for building trust in the family. In addition, having the younger-generation cousins participate in the family council discussions strengthened their confidence and stature in the family and continued the process of trust and collaborative problem-solving. This ultimately strengthened trust to build a stronger family and family–business relationship.

A second example of the bilateral dynamic combines a family activity with a service project. A family business sponsored a picnic and fireworks for a local charity. Not only did the family strengthen its bonds, but their business relationships improved. Specifically, they have been more generous with each other and are not severed by minor differences. The family collaborated, planned, and executed in a positive way a major service activity for a large group of recipients and as a result of their collaborative efforts they were able to strengthen the trust in their business and family relationships. They are also more receptive to acknowledging each other's perspective on family business issues. As a result they were able to give each other the benefit of doubt and not get so easily stuck by minor differences.

Trust Building in the Business

Two additional examples come from the business side of the equation. The first concerns a father who recruited his son into the business with a promise of being able to run the business. The son had a successful career in a large Midwestern real estate firm, but was eager to take control of the family business. He wanted to show his dad what he could do. Prior to formally entering the business, the father and son had a great father–son relationship. The son worked in the business as a teenager, but upon his return to the family business as an adult, he and his father clashed over the direction of the business and how much risk to take. These business differences played themselves out as father–son issues, resulting in the erosion of trust and the quality of their relationship. The solutions to the father–son family issues stemmed from the business side of the equation.

The first was a strategic planning effort where father and son were able to use a strategic business planning discussion to resolve their business differences and subsequently were able to rebuild the trust and closeness of their father–son relationship. They were able to reunite around a new opportunity for the business. In this same family business, we created an active board of directors with outside advisors who participate in board meetings and objectify the business. Even though the father is on the board of directors, the fact that the son is reporting to a board of directors as opposed to his father has not only strengthened the performance of the business, but has also created more trust and closeness in their father–son relationship.

The second example concerns a large family business that experienced the death of the owner-father. The mother and five adult children owned the business in various percentages. The oldest son was recruited to join the business upon his father's death and has worked in the business for approximately 25 years. The other adult children had careers outside of the family business and were not involved in any capacity. Unfortunately there were no formal family business mechanisms in place such as a family council or an active board of directors with outside advisors. Recently the oldest brother's compensation [salary] was revealed and the revelation shook the foundation of trust between the oldest brother, the president, and his siblings.

The creation of a board development committee, with three family board members, to carefully select and recommend four outside members with expertise necessary to create a governance process was a mutually beneficial activity accepted by the family. The formality of having the board responsible for negotiating a compensation plan that is fair and equitable to all concerned is another factor in the rebuilding of the trust. As in the previous example, the structure, formality, and objectivity of the outside members of the board and the structure of the board are what I believe helped rebuild trust and confidence in the family that all will be treated equitably.

CONCLUSION

A common error in many business families is that they concentrate their efforts on the business side of the equation, while neglecting nurturing trust and emotional equity on the family side. An example of this dynamic is highlighted by a *St. Paul Pioneer Press* article discussing couples in business together.[5] A number of couples who worked together in the restaurant business divorced, but kept their business relationship. While marriage and divorce are complicated matters, this article illustrates how easily couples emphasize their business relationship at the expense of their marriage and the personal side of their relationship. Thus, all of the examples in this paper demonstrate how important it is to set up structure in both the family and the business. Even if trust is implicit in families, it must be maintained and nurtured to survive – just like the houseplant. The best way to accomplish this is to create a family council and charge it with the responsibility to generate a dialogue within the family about the most appropriate structures to promote trust in a business family.

In conclusion, based on upon my experience in working with family businesses, I stress the importance of creating trust on the family emotional side, as well as creating structure and formality in the business. The end result will be a major contribution to trust and social capital, which is the secret to success. Doing both enhances the performance of the business and strengthens family harmony.

NOTES

1. Poza (2010, p. 58).
2. There is some evidence that not only are there factors in the family environment and socialization, but we might also have a predisposition to trust. Dan Gilbert, a Harvard psychologist in a January 2010 PBS Series *This Emotional Life* touches on this topic (see Mcgee and Kinhardt, 2010). It appears that we are wired for the trust response and that the creation of trust is an implicit response to this biochemical process.
3. Forgiveness is critical to the revitalization of trust in a family or family business where there has been a breach of trust. When trust is violated in a family, as regularly happens in many families, there needs to be an internal mechanism that allows the family to begin anew. From my perspective, that mechanism is forgiveness.

   There are two examples that illustrate the point. First is a family business where two sons are active in the business with their father; the older son and father had not spoken in four years and ran all of their communications through their brother. In addition, the five other children, who were not active in the business, vilified their older brother and blamed him for the problems that were occurring in the family. As a result of participating in a family business forgiveness ritual in their family business and forgiving each other, the family was able to have a new beginning and trust was re-established in both the family and family business.

   To further illustrate this point, a second family constituted an uncle and his nephew who were in business together. As a result of a plane crash where the boy's parents were killed, the uncle raised his nephew from childhood. As a consequence of major business differences between the uncle and nephew related to unclear business expectations, trust was broken and parties could barely speak to each other at the time of the consulting engagement. In addition to business interventions that included business planning, the whole family, including the uncle's two sons and wife, participated in a family forgiveness ritual. The family was able to share their hurt feelings, forgive each other, create a new beginning, and rebuild the trust in their family. For a complete discussion see Hubler (2005), which elaborates on these phenomena.
4. Poza (2010).
5. Ngo (2004).

4.   Building ethics in families and business

Kenneth E. Goodpaster

The family is an institution (along with faith communities and schools) to which we look for cultivating ethical values and virtues in our society. I use the term "cultivating" because with morality (as with agriculture) it presupposes already existing "DNA" in the soil – innately given content that is responsive to the "husbandry" of the cultivator.

The family provides the initial experience of *community* for most of us – our introduction to "I" and "thou" and to "we" and "they." The family is typically the birthplace of what the nineteenth-century US philosopher Josiah Royce called "the moral insight" (a gateway to what today we call the "moral point of view"). The moral insight, said Royce, is "the realization of one's neighbor," a liberation from the illusion that one's neighbor is unreal, the "illusion of selfishness."[1] One can understand the moral insight as applying to individual persons, but also to group *cultures*. It is the experience that underlies the Golden Rule.

It is through the family that caring and love are modeled and justice (or fairness) comes to be understood by children. It is through the family that loyalty is learned and respect for authority is developed. And it is through the family that we first come to appreciate virtues like temperance and piety.[2]

It seems reasonable to say, then, that while the ultimate foundations of ethics are innate in human beings, the *cultivation* of ethical values is the special contribution of the family. Families provide the material conditions for procreation, early development, *and* moral formation.

Not all families, of course, are effective cultivators of ethical values. Much depends upon the dynamic relationships among parents and siblings, grandchildren and cousins. But there do seem to be regularities. Swiss psychologist Jean Piaget in his classic *The Moral Judgment of the Child* (1932) offers an account of moral development that progresses in stages from "egocentrism" to "heteronomy" to "autonomy." Autonomy emerges naturally in families that foster individual judgment and choice without authoritarian pressure. Families that encourage open dialogue are more likely to cultivate mature consciences in their offspring – consciences that eventually *extend* respect beyond the limited moral universe of kinship. Dialogue as a process seems inevitably to lead to reciprocity and eventually respect between the communicating parties. Philosopher Immanuel Kant referred to this extension of respect as the "universalization" principle and insisted that it was essential for an ethical community.

The "centrifugal impulse" within the moral point of view has its developmental origins in the family, but then it continues beyond family boundaries to neighborhood, region, nation, and eventually the global community.[3]

When we introduce the idea of a family business, we are joining the *societal* institution of the family to an *economic* institution. In the process we add to the ethical dynamics of family life an economic structure that carries with it practical imperatives associated with products or services for the wider community, revenue generation, employment obligations, supplier relationships, and so on.

Inevitably, the joining of these two institutions will bring both synergy and tension. The synergy stems from the advantages a family business may enjoy in the domain of "social capital." [4] The tension stems from the strains that economic decision-making can bring to enduring family relationships that are more fundamental than are business relationships.

Businesses that embrace what has been called "the family point of view" offer a synergistic model that, when extended or universalized, leads naturally to the broad topic of corporate responsibility.[5] As the "family circle" matures and is enlarged and dialogue becomes more inclusive, the principles of loyalty, caring, fairness, respect, and virtue reach out to an "extended family" of stakeholders: suppliers, customers, employees, and so on.

In this paper, I will explore some of the ethical implications for family businesses of their genesis in the institution of the family.[6] And perhaps we might together discover some moral resources for family businesses to draw upon as they develop what scholars refer to as "family social capital."

RECENT CORPORATE SCANDALS – A COMMON DENOMINATOR

Let's begin by reflecting on the litany of business scandals that ushered in the twenty-first century – scandals rooted not in family businesses but in large, publicly-traded firms. (No essay on business ethics these days avoids mentioning this litany!) We can then explore their relevance to ethical values in family business.

After 9/11/2001, Enron and Arthur Andersen ushered in two scandals, soon followed by many others, including WorldCom, Tyco, and Global Crossing. The Sarbanes-Oxley Act was the public sector's response to these earlier scandals. NASA's *Columbia* Space Shuttle disaster and most recently the mortgage and banking crisis are leading to more public sector involvement. Some business ethics scholars have studied the scandals in a diagnostic way, offering suggestions about how to avoid falling into or repeating the patterns diagnosed.

The *cultural* dimensions of the scandals are particularly striking. This was clearly articulated in the report of the Columbia Accident Investigation Board (CAIB) in August and October of 2003. In the board's view: "NASA's organizational culture and structure had as much to do with this accident as the external tank foam. Organizational culture refers to the values, norms, beliefs and practices that govern how an institution functions."[7] NASA's culture in 2003, as in 1986 when we witnessed the *Challenger* disaster, was driven by an overarching goal, including an "ever more compressed" launch schedule for a critical section of the space station by 19 February, 2003. "The date seemed 'etched in stone,'" the report said, and "NASA employees had a sense of being 'under the gun.'"[8]

More recently, in connection with the mortgage crisis, we have seen the passage of the Troubled Asset Relief Program of 2008 (TARP). Malcolm Salter and Bill George (of the Harvard Business School) had this to say about that crisis:

> Like the Enron board, directors at Lehman, UBS, Wachovia, Washington Mutual, Citigroup, and Fannie Mae *failed to understand how compensation systems drove behavior*, thereby creating the conditions that led to their failures. Directors at these firms failed to detect and deter the inevitable *gambling* that resulted from their compensation plans.[9]

I believe that there is a common pattern among most of these corporate scandals that we have seen not only in this decade but in the last several decades. The characteristics are:

- intense *fixation* on certain goals or objectives;
- *rationalization* of this goal-fixated behavior as essential for one's career or for one's company; and
- eventual *detachment* from the natural reluctance that the human spirit feels when rationalizing – separating "head" and "heart" – both personally and in organizational cultures ("selective perception" was no doubt a major contributor to the mortgage crisis).

Fixation, rationalization, and detachment are symptoms of an occupational hazard in business life – a hazard to which both individuals and groups can succumb. Objectives become idols; obstacles become threats; second thoughts are not allowed – and eventually, second thoughts disappear.

I have called this pattern "teleopathy" – goal sickness – because it leads to personally and socially dysfunctional behavior. Teleopathy is not exclusively a problem in business or corporate life. It also manifests itself in the arenas of politics, healthcare, law, engineering, religion, and even education. But business decision-making is perhaps more at risk because so much of management is driven by "objectives," "goals," "targets," "strategies," and "purposes." And while recent scandals have displayed the hazard of teleopathy in large businesses nationally and internationally, we must note that the scale of the enterprise is not essential to the diagnosis. Let us explore the hazard of teleopathy in relation to family business in what follows – as well as some ways to avoid the hazard.

My conviction is that to avoid the pathology, practitioners must avoid the *causes* that give rise to its symptoms – both in themselves and in their organizational cultures. So let us consider what such avoidance measures might look like.

THE HAZARD OF FIXATION

Recently, a US Air Force pilot made me aware of a well-documented phenomenon in aviation that parallels teleopathy in some striking ways. One of the most dangerous "human factors" related to fatal pilot accidents in the Air Force is "channelized attention." Here is how the US Department of Defense defines it:

> Channelized attention is a factor when the individual is focusing all conscious attention on a limited number of environmental cues to the exclusion of others of a subjectively equal or higher or more immediate priority, leading to an unsafe situation. It may be described as a tight focus of attention that leads to the exclusion of *comprehensive* situational information.[10]

Says one aviation consultant (Jim Murphy, "How to overcome task saturation for flawless execution"):

> Channelized attention is when you focus intensely on just one thing and ignore the rest. Some people call this target fixation. Target fixation happens to fighter pilots when they're on a run in towards a ground target. A target-fixated pilot is focused – too focused – and may forget to fly the jet. With his eyes on the target and his heart pumping, he flies the jet into the ground.

Channelizers are easy to spot. They shun eye contact when they take a bathroom break. They wave people off with a flip of the wrist. "Can't you see I'm busy!" is a common answer when you interrupt a channelizer. And their body language says: "Don't ask." . . . They can get so absorbed in one thing that everything else falls apart.[11]

Soon after I was made aware of the phenomenon of channelized attention in aviation, I learned of similar phenomena in mountain climbing, fire-fighting, emergency medical care, and sports management. I'm coming to believe that much more research is needed into this pattern of individual and group behavior.[12]

How can practitioners avoid fixation without suppressing the virtues with which it can be confused (such as courage, determination, and perseverance)? One suggestion is for them to understand the goals they set for themselves and their organizations as part of a *larger* mission, the common good. Such understanding comes from habits of thoughtful reflection. Professional lives steeped in reflection are less vulnerable to fanaticism and misplaced devotion. In a 2001 article in the *Harvard Business Review*, Jim Loehr and Tony Schwartz observed that:

The inclination for busy executives is to live in a perpetual state of triage, doing whatever seems most immediately pressing, while losing sight of any bigger picture. Rituals that give people the opportunity to pause and look inside include meditation, journal writing, prayer, and service to others. Each of these activities can also serve as a source of recovery – a way to break the linearity of relentless goal-oriented activity.[13]

Businesses can find themselves fixated as well – much as individuals do. Management guru Peter Drucker gave expression to this problem in one of his most widely read articles. Drucker wrote:

In a society of organizations, each [business] is concerned only with its own purpose and mission. It does not claim power over anything else. But it also does not assume responsibility for anything else. Who, then, is concerned with the common good?[14]

Drucker's implied answer to this question was "No one," and this answer was as unsatisfactory to him as it was to his readers. The implication was that organizations, like individual persons, must step back from their single-mindedness to achieve a broader perspective on the needs of society – the common good. *Perspective* is the antidote to fixation.

It seems natural to ask, therefore: can fixation and channelized attention become significant issues in family business? And if so, how can they be avoided?

Perspective in Family Business

Perspective (as an antidote to fixation) can infuse and enrich family business in three ways. The first way is through the creation of "family social capital." The literature on "social capital" – and more specifically "family social capital" – teaches us that: "Intense and enduring information channels lead to closure. Extensive closure in families develops family norms that lead to obligations and expectations, reputation, identity, and moral infrastructure."[15] Information channels, both internal and external to the family, provide expertise, support, contacts, and a sense of belonging to participants in the family enterprise. These channels, and the networking that they require, are powerful tools for avoiding fixation, providing multiple perspectives on problems facing the company and early warning systems against channelized attention.

The perspective afforded by information sharing and networking can also encourage (reinforce) an ethical peer group for the family business, helping it to avoid negative entanglements. In the words of Professor Patricia Hedberg, one of my St. Thomas colleagues, "the very processes and behaviors necessary to build family social capital are the same processes and behaviors that build an ethical culture" (personal correspondence).

The second way in which perspective can infuse and enrich family business is through "stakeholder thinking." The two primary stakeholders of a family business are, of course, the family and the business, each of which has a "bottom line" to which it must attend. In the case of the family, the "bottom line" is the enduring relationships among family members. In the case of the business, the "bottom line" includes the more conventional measures of its financial health. Thus, everyone participating in a family business must adopt at least these two perspectives. But in relation to the business bottom line, there are other perspective-inducing factors worth noting. Since family members who are active in the business frequently play multiple roles, they have experience in identifying (and empathizing) with various stakeholder groups. There is a natural identification in family firms – with roles such as owner/investor, manager, and employee – that predisposes family business members toward the perspective that comes with stakeholder thinking.

One of the methods used by the US Air Force to help mitigate the dangers of channelized attention is to provide support for pilots by insisting that missions always be flown with at least two aircraft in formation. The pilot has a "wingman" to look for fixation and to warn the pilot by providing perspective.[16] I believe that family enterprises have an advantage if they have identified and implemented the role of the "wingman," both between family and business, and within the business, among the roles of investor, manager, and employee. In the end, avoiding fixation and achieving perspective is comparable to respecting multiple voices in a dialogue.

The third way in which perspective can enrich family business is through "temporal awareness." Most family firms have a built-in concern with generational succession, which predisposes family businesses toward a longer-term perspective – and temporal extension is often associated with ethically enlightened decision-making. When the business bears the family name and the family reputation, there is an incentive to make decisions with a horizon that goes beyond immediate profitability and extends further into the future. Let me illustrate this insight and the previous one (stakeholder thinking as well as temporal awareness) with some observations that a family business owner made a year ago at this conference.[17]

Dr. Ron Ward retired as a surgeon and entered the business world as an entrepreneur. Today, as owner of RSW Management, Inc., he successfully creates opportunities for start-up, growth, and re-organization of companies from both financial and management perspectives. Both of his sons are employed by RSW Management, and they seek to carry on the values and vision created by their father, serving globally as well as locally in their community outside of Milwaukee, Wisconsin. In September 2008, at a University of St. Thomas conference on family enterprise, Dr. Ward said this to the participants:

> Family businesses have to have bottom lines other than profit maximization, and they need to value the liberty and autonomy that they enjoy to be patient with their capital. The lament of many businesses is that Wall Street pressure on earnings will drive out their longer-term and less tangible mission-oriented values.

Dr. Ward's perspective in relation to his family enterprise is that it is a business with multiple "bottom lines" including the family, of course, but also financial success, client-focused improvement, and community involvement. His business is guided by both *economic goals* (conventional measures of performance) and *ethical priorities* (measures of performance relating to direct and indirect investment in social benefits).[18] And since his name is clearly attached to the enterprise and his sons will be carrying it on, his temporal horizon is an extended one.

THE HAZARD OF RATIONALIZATION

Rationalization is a mechanism by which fixation is often maintained in the face of criticism or attempts to change an individual's or a group's perspective. And because rationalization is usually instinctive, *avoiding* rationalization takes *practice* – practice at telling the truth when exaggeration or denial appear attractive. Accepting that criticism is an occasion for growth and that hypocrisy is part of the human condition – individual and organizational – allows practitioners to address the gaps between "walk and talk." This kind of *honesty* comes alive in candid conversations with trusted friends and workplace colleagues. It is alive in company cultures that encourage constructive self-criticism rather than blind allegiance.

Businesses rationalize as collectivities just as individuals do – and the remedy is similar. In my own work with companies, I begin by saying "We must make friends with hypocrisy." This causes consternation at first, of course. The executives say to me: "I thought you were the ethics guy!" But soon they come to understand that "becoming friends with hypocrisy" means accepting the *humanity* of business organizations. This means taking steps to align the corporate "talk" with the corporate "walk" – words with actions. So the antidote to rationalization is practicing *frankness* and *honest communication*.[19]

Frankness in Family Business

In the context of family business, frankness and honest communication are first-order concerns. Family norms include mutually acknowledged obligations and expectations, reputation, collective trust, identity, and moral infrastructure. These attributes cannot get a foothold in a family system that discourages frank dialogue among family members. Rationalization is fed by lack of "closure" in a family business.[20] It leads to individual isolation (distrust, fear about others' intentions, absence of collaboration) and group fragmentation (loss of identity, lack of reciprocity).

Dialogue, by its very nature, helps family members to truly "see" one another – to take each other seriously and to treat each other with respect. Dialogue is one of the principal means by which the family serves as a cultivator of conscience and ethical values (the theme with which I began this paper). Forming a moral community *within* the family through dialogue ultimately enables the family to contribute to frankness within the family business and in the larger moral community *outside* the family business.

But true dialogue takes time and patience. It can be resisted in the name of "efficiency." Nevertheless, it represents one of the most important *investments* that a family business can make. Failing to make such an investment because of the pressures of everyday business goals and objectives can result in what might be called a "culture of urgency" that treats family relationships as expendable, superfluous, and contingent.

It is a short step from a culture of urgency to a culture in which family members, employees, and customers are treated simply as tools, as means to economic ends.

Many family businesses (not all) are able to achieve the "family point of view" (FPV). In a recent article in *Family Business Review*, Sorenson et al. defined the idea this way:

> The *family point of view* is the shared perspective – the family's shared moral convictions – that results from family dialogue over time . . . Over time, families articulate the family point of view, "the beliefs that guide the way we do things in our family business." Articulating the family point of view increases the likelihood that the family will call on its moral consciousness when faced with family business decisions. Collaborative dialogue is an interactive process [which] leads to action – and action leads to further dialogue, a process that deepens common understanding and confirms agreed-upon ethical norms.[21]

For present purposes, we need not go into the correlations hypothesized and confirmed in this study. The key point is the relationship that we can reasonably assume between *dialogue* of this kind and the frankness and honest communication mentioned earlier. If frank dialogue is an antidote to rationalization, then perhaps family businesses – at least those that embrace the family point of view – are less likely to succumb to "teleopathy."

THE HAZARD OF DETACHMENT

The third symptom of teleopathy results from repeated manifestations of the first two symptoms. Repeated fixation and rationalization desensitizes individuals and groups from the human consequences of their decision-making. How can business practitioners keep head and heart in healthy communication with one another, avoiding detachment? One way is through effective *service* in their communities, service to the less advantaged. In this way, any tendencies they may have toward *indifference* will be harder to sustain. It is difficult to remain indifferent in the regular presence of human needs. It is *less* difficult to be indifferent if business practitioners distance themselves from those needs.

The social and environmental "bottom lines" of companies are important disciplines for maintaining corporate integrity. They serve as insurance against detachment or indifference, reminding companies of *the larger calling of business* – the calling to contribute to the common good, not just the private goods of owners and investors.

It is essential for businesses to avoid detachment; essential that they join their economic agendas to a social agenda; essential that they join respect to rationality.[22] To avoid detachment, individuals and organizations must maintain practices of service, sharing in the work of what has been referred to as the "social sector." The antidote to detachment is *engagement* with the multiple stakeholders of the business (employees, suppliers, customers, etc.), but especially the stakeholder usually referred to as the *community*.

Engagement in Family Business

In the context of family business, detachment can be avoided in favor of engagement in two important ways. First, both the business and the founding family must be engaged, allowing for the family to perform the "wingman" function mentioned above. In some large family businesses, engagement of the business with the family is lost. (But as was the case with the Ford Motor Company when it declined a "bailout" after the 2008 financial crisis, the family can step forward, become engaged, and embrace its role as wingman.)

Second, detachment can be avoided when family businesses engage in community involvement. Hoffman et al. remind us that "Civic engagement refers to people's connections with the life of their community and includes such things as membership in neighborhood associations, choral societies, or sports clubs."[23]

Family firms are often rooted in their communities, making engagement more likely than detachment or anonymity. Dr. Ron Ward mentioned that both of his sons were employed by RSW Management and that they sought to carry on the company's values and vision, "serving globally as well as locally in their community outside of Milwaukee, Wisconsin." The community involvement aspect of this family business served not only to create goodwill; it also served to mitigate the hazard of detachment. This family enterprise – as a matter of deliberate policy – practices engagement with the community.

In a very different context, although in the same spirit, regular contributions to the social infrastructure of Minneapolis were a deliberate policy of the Dayton-Hudson Company some years ago when it was still a family business, and I believe this involvement with the community was not accidentally related to the company's reputation for an ethical culture.

As we seek to understand more clearly both the business scandals of the last decade and the challenges facing family enterprises, we discover teleopathy (fixation, rationalization, and detachment) and its remedies (perspective, frankness, and engagement).

SUMMARY AND CONCLUSION

We know that there is a natural *synergy* and a natural *tension* within all family firms. Each by its nature is a hybrid combination of moral community ("After all, this is a family!") and economic function ("After all, this is a business!"). Family firms highlight the blending of ethical imperatives and economic imperatives – a blending that is ultimately expected of *every* organization. A family business must be focused and productive, but not to the point that it ignores the reality and the ethical significance of the family that gave it a reason for being. The quest is for a *productive moral community*.

British management guru Charles Handy insists that "The purpose of a business . . . is not to make a profit, full stop. It is to make a profit so that the business can do something more or better. That 'something' becomes the real justification for the business."[24] In the context of family business, the "something more or better" can mean a rich legacy of commitment passing from one generation to another and a contribution to the community in which the business makes its home.

Exclusive concentration on either the interpersonal dynamics of the family or on the economics of the business creates problems. Family businesses are as threatened by neglecting honest dialogue and the relationships that such dialogue makes possible as they are by neglecting the economic needs of the business.

Family firms are ethical to the extent that they draw upon the moral foundation of the family as an institution, developing norms that function as a conscience for the business. They also find ethical strength when those who work in the firm engage the family as a "wingman" to avoid fixation, rationalization, and detachment. Family businesses may not always be *more* ethical than non-family businesses, of course, but they have special resources to support integrity and avoid teleopathy.[25]

The study of family enterprise helps us to discern the importance of balancing purpose and persons; stakeholder roles; short term and long term. It shows the power of frankness and collaborative dialogue. And it helps us to appreciate the value of engagement in the community to avoid detached and uncaring judgment. Perhaps this is why it is not uncommon for leaders of large corporations to invoke family as a metaphor in their pursuit of improved employee relationships or cooperative divisional structures.[26] It suggests that family enterprise can offer a model for business at its best.

NOTES

1. Royce (1885, pp. 155–6).
2. Drawing upon both research and theory, scholars have identified five domains of innate morality (for a summary of research and discussion of domains, see Haidt and Joseph, 2007): harm/care, fairness/reciprocity; in-group/loyalty; authority/respect; and purity/sanctity. They argue that the five domains exist across all cultures. However, different cultures and subgroups may emphasize some domains of morality more than others.
3. The question "Who is my neighbor?" and its boundary-escaping response in the Christian gospels is just one illustration of what we are calling the "centrifugal impulse."
4. Sorenson et al. (2009).
5. Ibid.
6. An earlier version of this paper benefited from collegial comments by Ritch Sorenson and Patricia Hedberg.
7. CAIB (2003, Vol. 1, Ch. 7, p. 177).
8. Ibid., p. 134.
9. Salter and George (2008, p. 5, emphasis added).
10. DOD HFACS (2005, p. 7).
11. http://www.myarticlearchive.com/author/murphy.htm; last accessed 8 June 2011.
12. "Mountaineering tends to draw men and women not easily deflected from their goals . . . This forms the nub of a dilemma that every Everest climber eventually comes up against: in order to succeed you must be exceedingly driven, but if you're too driven you're likely to die. Above 26,000 feet . . . the line between appropriate zeal and reckless summit fever becomes grievously thin. Thus the slopes of Everest are littered with corpses" (from Krakauer, 1997, p. 233).
13. Loehr and Schwartz (2001, p. 128).
14. Peter Drucker (1994, p. 78). Drucker continued: "[We have] to think through how to balance two apparently contradictory requirements. Organizations must competently perform the one social function for the sake of which they exist – the school to teach, the hospital to cure the sick, and the business to produce goods, services, or the capital to provide for the risks of the future. They can do so only if they single-mindedly concentrate on their specialized mission. But there is also society's need for these organizations to take social responsibility – to work on the problems and challenges of the community. Together, these organizations *are* the community."
15. Hoffman et al. (2006, p. 139). The authors add: "Closure occurs when there are sufficient ties between members of the social network to guarantee the observance of norms (Coleman, 1988; Portes, 1998). With the strong relational ties, frequency of interaction, and history of relationship in families, closure will be much more prevalent in family capital than in social capital. Closure places pressure on employees and family members to perform within established social norms. With the existence of closure, the significant possibility of discovery (by others in the social network) exists when norms are violated."
16. The military has long understood that target fixation and channelized attention are phenomena that present mortal danger to fighter pilots. Accordingly, the Air Force has developed strategies that have greatly reduced the number of accidents resulting from target fixation. First, pilots are taught to be *aware* of the phenomenon. Second, a pilot must *limit the time* he or she devotes to a given task. Third, pilots must constantly *cross-check* cockpit instruments and the view outside the airplane's canopy for cues that correlate proper parameters – or identify problem ones. Finally, combat pilots must draw upon and provide *mutual support* to one another, as missions are always flown with at least two aircraft in formation. (Thomas Harrison, "Teleopathy – target fixation and how to combat it," unpublished class journal, personal correspondence).
17. Family Capital, Family Business, and Free Enterprise was a conference sponsored by the University of St. Thomas Center for Family Enterprise, 25–26 September, 2008. In

addition to organizational issues, public policy issues were discussed during this conference, as well as personal family business behavioral issues.

18. The use of stakeholder language signals genuine moral progress for democratic capitalism. It has opened up the consciousness of business leaders to go beyond the single-mindedness to which Peter Drucker often refers, and offers a humanizing or socializing framework for decision-making. In the wake of the collapse of communism at the end of the 1980s, this language offered hope that the globalization of market economies could stand up to moral scrutiny.

19. Here is an example involving Mattel, the toy company. In a recent *Wall Street Journal* article, the following comment appears: "Mattel has consistently employed a formidable team of outside lawyers to deny defects with its toys, in some cases even after millions of them had been recalled and determined to be unsafe and defective by U.S. regulators." This appears to be an organizational form of rationalization. But later in the same article, a change in Mattel's behavior is emphasized: "Mattel takes full responsibility for these recalls and apologizes personally to you, the Chinese people, and all of our customers who received the toys," Mr. Debrowski said. He added, "It's important for everyone to understand that the vast majority of those products that we recalled were the result of a . . . flaw in Mattel's design, not . . . a flaw in Chinese manufacturing." See Blanchard (2007).

20. Hoffman et al. (2006, p. 140): "Without closure there is no opportunity for the organization to develop strong family norms and for identity to begin to take hold."

21. Sorenson et al. (2009, p. 3, emphasis added).

22. To quote Peter Drucker again: "The emergence of a strong, independent, capable social sector – neither public nor private sector – is a central need of the society of organizations. But by itself it is not enough – the organizations of both the public and the private sector must share the work" (Drucker, 1994, p. 80).

23. Hoffman et al. (2006, p. 139).

24. Handy (2002, p. 5).

25. In the words of the late Pope John Paul II: "The purpose of a business firm is not simply to make a profit, but is to be found in its very existence as a community of persons who in various ways are endeavoring to satisfy their basic needs, and who form a particular group at the service of the whole of society." (Encyclical Letter, 1991).

26. University of California historian Roland Marchand has documented this phenomenon in his book *Creating the Corporate Soul: The Rise of Public Relations and Corporate Imagery in American Big Business* (2001). Marchand's book was praised as "an exemplary work of interdisciplinary scholarship."

5. An early warning system for family conflict

Katherine Hayes

INTRODUCTION

Through five generations my family enterprise has benefitted from the creativity, education, and experience of its family members. These many talents and capabilities have enabled us to succeed through several major transitions. However, until recently a growing lack of trust caused family members to withdraw their capabilities as they consumed their energies in avoidance of conflict due to a growing dispute. This lack of trust threatened to destroy the multi-generational enterprise.

While at work one day, I received a personal phone call from a high school classmate, who had previously sent me some threatening letters from jail, asking me to help him get a loan. I was afraid and ended the call quickly. I immediately told the CEO, and she helped me to take appropriate protective action for my immediate family and me. Important to note is that even though our family enterprise is governed by the entire family, I am the only family member employed by the business.

Later, at a family gathering, a cousin heard me say that the classmate asked "about those CPAs [certified public accountants] I work with." From that point a conflict developed and escalated. My cousin expressed concerns about the safety of the family and about employees, including me, to the CEO. I thought that this issue should have been brought to me instead of the CEO. The conflict escalated to the point that my cousin wrote an e-mail saying he wanted to leave our family enterprise. The next day he changed his mind. However, these events triggered a governance meeting. Subsequently the family agreed to hire a facilitator to help the family work through the trust and conflict issues that had become apparent.

I escalated the conflict because I felt my position in the business was threatened. I was afraid, angry, and defensive. I felt that my cousin cared more about the safety of the business than my personal safety. I fixated on what he had done to me and recruited other family members to support my position. My cousin recruited his own allies and soon the whole family was at war. I was so focused on being right and blaming him that I lost sight of what the conflict was doing to family relationships. I became detached from the pain my family was feeling and to my role in perpetuating the conflict.

Thankfully, my family hired a facilitator who helped us resolve the conflict. The facilitator helped me see how both my cousin and I had hurt feelings, the need to be "right," and that the conflict was damaging family relationships. This helped me to stop fixating and see the larger family context. With the facilitator's help, the family identified a common goal – developing a new governance structure for the family.

My cousin and I worked on the new structure together and, during one of the brainstorming sessions for our new structure, I suggested that my cousin and I should have a drink sometime. He took me up on it. With the help of our new experience of working together, we were able to begin to forgive each other. Not everyone let go of the anger at the same time. Nonetheless, once my cousin and I had found resolution, the whole family was able to begin the work toward acceptance of differences and more trusting relationships.

If I knew then what I know now, I might have been able to handle the situation more effectively. Using the concepts of teleopathy and the "four horsemen," I would be able to recognize symptoms of the underlying problem, a kind of sickness. Knowing the symptoms to look for can help to better manage future conflicts.

REFRAMING THE CONFLICT: TELEOPATHY AND THE FOUR HORSEMEN

Behavioral patterns that lead to conflict can be framed by two concepts discussed at the Family Capital, Family Business, and Free Enterprise Conference at the University of St. Thomas. These concepts are Kenneth Goodpaster's "teleopathy"[1] and John Gottman's "four horsemen."[2] First, teleopathy, or "goal sickness," is characterized by a pattern of *fixation*, *rationalization*, and *detachment*. Fixation in this case is a very strong interest in something that prevents you from paying attention to anything else. Rationalization is an attempt to ignore any signals from the environment that are in conflict with the fixation by providing reasonable or self-justifying explanations. And detachment happens when the rationalization has gone on so long that one becomes disconnected from the environment or any challenge to the fixation. Goodpaster sums up the pattern in his paper this way: "Objectives become idols; obstacles become threats; second

thoughts are not allowed – and eventually, second thoughts disappear."[3]
This pattern can be seen in an individual's behavior as well as in groups,
especially family groups where there is the influence of a shared culture.

Second, Gottman has identified a group of behaviors particularly
damaging to relationships, also known as the four horsemen: *criticism,
defensiveness, contempt,* and *stonewalling.*[4] Criticism is the offer of judgment or disapproval that is often felt to be unsolicited. Defensiveness is an
attempt to deflect the perceived criticism. Contempt is a strong feeling of
dislike toward someone considered inferior or unworthy of respect. And
stonewalling is a refusal to cooperate by removing oneself physically or
emotionally from the situation.

Teleopathy can be seen as a sickness that can exist in an individual or
group and negatively influence family relationships. Disease is commonly
defined as a condition or tendency that has harmful effects. We often
diagnose the disease by the symptoms or negative effects. In applying this
to family relationships, the presence of the four horsemen can be seen as
symptoms of the disease of teleopathy. Recognition of these symptomatic
behaviors can help to identify the roots of the conflict and how it can be
resolved in order to promote healthy change within the family enterprise.
My intent is to draw attention to the notion that the presence of the four
horsemen as symptoms may be an indication of the underlying teleopathy;
therefore recognition of these symptomatic behaviors can help to identify
where the conflict has its roots and how that conflict can be resolved to
promote healthy family change.

Goodpaster's teleopathy and Gottman's four horsemen have several
commonalities. To be specific, fixation and criticism go hand in hand, as
do rationalization and defensiveness. To be critical often implies judging
in a detailed way, as if fixated on something to the point of commenting
on it. Rationalization is a form of defensiveness about a belief or behavior
and the feedback from the environment. Even more obvious is the connection between detachment and stonewalling. Both of these involve an emotional exit from the environment. Frequent use of criticism, defensiveness,
detachment, and stonewalling may indicate teleopathy – a goal sickness
or unwillingness to see others' perspectives. Recognizing the behavioral
symptoms is the first step toward positive change. To illustrate, I will
return to my own conflict story and demonstrate the roles of teleopathy
and the four horsemen in that conflict.

Fixation and its Symptom, Criticism

Goodpaster explains the first characterization of teleopathy, fixation, as
being so singularly focused on something that peripheral vision and the

ability to entertain other cues from the environment are lost. During the growing conflict between my cousin and me, I was fixated on my own hurt feelings and fear for my position in the business. In the presence of encouragement from my family to forgive and forget, I felt I needed to dig in my heels and prove I was right and he was wrong. The first of the four horsemen, criticism, is evaluating and judging another person during an interaction. I didn't recognize how fixated on, and therefore critical of, my cousin's actions I was without considering what might really be motivating him.

Rationalization and its Symptoms, Defensiveness and Contempt

Goodpaster explains the second characterization of teleopathy, rationalization, as the temptation to exaggerate or deny details. In my case, I exaggerated my cousin's intentions in order to feel more secure in my "rightness." As if the more "wrong" he was the more "right" I could be. Rationalization also occurs in response to cues from the environment. As more and more family members became impacted by the conflict with my cousin, instead of taking a step back and considering the consequences of my own actions, I became more and more convinced I needed to win for the sake of the business. I interpreted the concern in my family's voices as defense of my position rather than concern for the family and the family enterprise.

The second of the horsemen, defensiveness, is being resistant to acknowledging the other person's position. I was clearly defensive and unwilling to entertain the possibility that my cousin may have had legitimate reason for concern. When my cousin's wife reached out to talk about the situation and that conversation ended with her in tears, I was still unable to see how I might be contributing to the conflict growing in the family as a whole. And I was unable to hear anyone's suggestion of forgiveness. The third of the horsemen, contempt, is communicating a lack of respect or distaste for another person. When the conflict was at its worst, I felt physically uncomfortable being in the same room with my cousin. I couldn't bring myself to greet him, I would avoid eye contact at all cost, and I think my body language reflected my feelings of discomfort.

Detachment and its Symptom, Stonewalling

Lastly, Goodpaster explains the third characteristic, detachment, as an inevitable result when second thoughts are not allowed and eventually disappear. While I don't think I ever became completely detached from the situation, I was emotionally detached from my cousin and resistant to any feedback that did not support my position. And at the height of the conflict, my cousin and his wife threatened to leave the family business. This is an example of the last of the horsemen, stonewalling; physically or emotionally removing oneself from the interaction. I think this was my cousin's last resort. We were in a lose–lose situation and the best option seemed to be to remove himself.

ANTIDOTES TO TELEOPATHY

In his paper, Goodpaster also identifies the antidotes to each of the characteristics of teleopathy. He identifies the antidote to fixation as perspective. With the help of the facilitator and extended family, I was able to gain some perspective. The facilitator met with each family member separately and allowed us to tell our stories. After meeting with the facilitator, who was able to tell me what he heard in my story, I was then able to attend to my feelings and stop focusing on blame. Each family member had this opportunity, and by applying Goodpaster's next antidote, frankness and honesty, we began to make progress toward healing.

Frankness and honesty are the antidotes to rationalization. The therapist offered an honest reflection and frank outside perspective that allowed each family member to better appreciate their role in the conflict. He also met with my cousin and his wife and my husband and me together. This provided us an opportunity to hear each other's stories, using active listening, and better understand our positions in the conflict. Once I had this new perspective on the conflict, and I was able to take a more honest look at my role, I was also able to recognize how often the four horsemen were present in my interactions with my cousin.

Goodpaster's antidote to detachment is engagement. Once I had an idea of my role in the conflict I was able to see there may have been a better way to navigate the conflict. I became motivated to address the conflict and help my family grow as a result. The facilitator helped me to see how I could stop focusing on blame and my need to be right. Then he encouraged me to use the progress we had made working through the conflict as momentum for more positive change. We hired another advisor who helped us direct our attention to our governance structure, which needed to be transitioned. This activity gave all of us an opportunity to work together toward a shared goal. Both my cousin and I were engaged with the process of re-working our structure and this provided us an opportunity to use the new perspective and relate to each other in a positive way.

HOW TO IDENTIFY AND TREAT TELEOPATHY

The behaviors indicative of teleopathy, like the ones outlined in my conflict story, contribute to the conflicts in family business, which can be more emotional and last longer than those in non-family business. Unfortunately, the presence of teleopathy makes it hard to recognize when one is in conflict because the feelings that may have grown out of the conflict have been present for so long. It can become a part of the family culture to hold on to anger, pain, or disappointment even though one may no longer understand the root of these feelings. Nonetheless, there are usually indications that conflict in relationship is present. In the following, I present four steps to identifying and treating teleopathy:

- *Step 1 Recognition of conflict.* Two indications conflict is present are the difficulty in working together and the inability to transition in the business to a new model or generation. If these problems occur, look for the behavioral symptoms *criticism, defensiveness, contempt* and *stonewalling*. The greater the conflict, the more likely the four horsemen are at play. In some cases, criticism, defensiveness, contempt and stonewalling may become the primary mode of communication.
- *Step 2 Identify your role.* If family members can see symptoms of conflict, the next step is for them to identify their role in the conflict. Do you criticize other family members? Are you defensive when other family members raise concerns? Do you find that your contempt for other family members is increasing? Do you engage in stonewalling activities such as avoiding being with some family members or opposing their proposals for no good reason?
- *Step 3 Get perspective.* In these situations of conflict, where the family is having trouble working together or transitioning the business, and criticism, defensiveness, contempt, and stonewalling are ruling, there may be a need for an outside perspective. Perspective is the first antidote to teleopathy. A trusted family advisor can help to identify each family member's role and begin a process toward resolution. With the help of the advisor's perspective, family members are able to step outside of their view to see the bigger picture. Getting some distance is integral to finding the root of the conflict.

  Honesty is the second antidote to teleopathy, and with the help of this new perspective a family member may be able to take an honest look at his or her goals. This can help them regain their peripheral vision, and to see whether or not they have lost sight of the goal for the family and the business.

By being honest with themselves and gaining perspective, family members are able to recognize that just because the family is in business together does not mean they have to like *everything* about each other. It is only important that family members trust each other enough to do business together. Another family member can be trustworthy in business even though he/she doesn't make the same life choices as you do. All of the family members don't need to like the same foods or go to the same church to be successful at running a business together. Someone outside the family may be better able to shed light on what is relevant to being in business together.[5]

- *Step 4 Find common ground.* After gaining perspective, seek common ground. If one can peel back the layers of criticism, defensiveness, and contempt it may be possible to find a place where there is a shared goal. It is helpful to focus on areas where family members agree instead of focusing on the areas where they do not agree. Once a shared goal or concern is found, it will provide a foundation from which to grow healthier relationships. When family members find a place of agreement, it can be easier to put aside all the other grievances not helpful to the more important cause they share. Working together on the shared goal or concern slowly develops trust.[6]

Detachment and stonewalling are the hardest of the behaviors to overcome. If the teleopathy can be recognized and addressed before stonewalling sets in, conflict resolution will be much easier because the parties are still engaged. All of the other phases of the teleopathy and the use of criticism, defensiveness, and contempt involve some level of engagement, while stonewalling and detachment represent a lack of engagement. It is much easier to keep someone at the table than to bring them back to the table once they have left, either mentally or physically. Nonetheless, even in long-enduring conflicts it is possible to bring family members back to the table once a shared goal or concern is identified. It just may take more patience and understanding. For example, it is important to recognize that the family member who has left the table may have a lot invested in their new position or location and that it will take time for them to appreciate the benefits of re-engaging in the family or the business.

The process of recognition is not likely to happen simultaneously for every family member. As friend and family business owner Harry McNeely Jr. once said to me, "Family is like popcorn; all of the kernels don't pop at once." Thankfully, if one person recognizes their role in the conflict and takes steps toward resolution, it can be enough to allow the other family members to gain new perspective and recognize the benefits of a shared goal. Once the family is working together the four horsemen are more likely to be kept under control, and the new momentum can be channeled toward positive change. Eventually, with the worst of the conflict in the past, it may be possible for more family members to recognize their own teleopathy.

When teleopathy is present, the goal-driven individual has likely recruited other family members. If the recruiter decides to stop elevating the conflict these family members may not be willing to give up the fight. They may even feel angry and betrayed by the family member for letting go, especially when that family member brought them to the fight in the first place. Or they may see the family member as a traitor for not buying into their own rationalizations and patterns. Whatever the case, it is important to recognize this for what it is and not let the behavior continue. Modeling a new behavior and attitude while understanding each family member's need to be where they are in the process will be most helpful in the long run. Conflict in families is inevitable, but the conflict does not need to derail the success of the business if it is kept in perspective.

CONCLUSION

Thankfully, in my conflict story my family as a whole was able to recognize the underlying lack of trust fueling the conflict and we hired an outside advisor to help us end the war. It was shortly after this process began that I was introduced to teleopathy and the four horsemen. These concepts provided insights into my family's conflict, including my own role. I feel fortunate to have had the opportunity to understand my own teleopathy with respect to conflict, and now I am also able to see elements of teleopathy in many other contexts. Using the concept of teleopathy to understand conflict, and the tools to address behavioral patterns, has helped me feel optimistic about handling inevitable future conflicts.

If there is attentiveness to teleopathy and its symptoms, conflict might be reframed as a catalyst for change and not as something to be avoided. The framework provided by this analysis of teleopathy can be used to facilitate the evolution of conflict within the family and the business. Keeping an honest perspective, accepting that conflict comes with progress, and recognizing the roots early, allow for an open exchange of information and work toward common goals to strengthen the family enterprise.

NOTES

1. Goodpaster, Chapter 4, this volume.
2. Gottman (1994).
3. See Goodpaster, Chapter 4 this volume, p. 54.
4. Gottman (1994).
5. Kaye (2009).
6. Ibid.

6. Summary of dialogue: observations about trust and ethics in family business

Trina S. Smith

This part of the book provides us with the definition of social capital and how it relates to family business. The authors address questions such as:

- What is social capital?
- What is family social capital?
- Why is family social capital unique and an asset to a family enterprise?
- How is family social capital maintained?

The discussion that ensued among family business members, advisors, and researchers after this session at the 2009 Family Business and Social Capital Conference centered on the unique aspects of trust in family businesses in relation to three main themes:

- avenues to trust;
- hindrances to trust;
- the importance of both the family and business.

In the following, summaries of these discussions, including illustrative quotes, are presented. Following the summaries, derived from these discussions and chapters in this part of the book, are questions to think about in application to family business.

AVENUES TO TRUST

In discussing trust in family business, including ways to generate trust, it is important to recognize that trust in a family business is qualitatively different than trust in a normal business because of the family. Thus, as a participant noted, there seems to be genuine trust in family businesses because the members are looking out for each other's best interests. This allows room for frankness. In other words, as stated by a participant speaking about family members, "If your butt looks too big in those jeans, they will tell you."

This relates to other comments centering on the resiliency of trust in family business. As such, participants discussed that trust is resilient in families because you can stretch bonds further inside a family than you can outside, as there is a strong innate desire within families to trust. Family members do not always have to prove themselves. For example, a participant noted, "even when family members get the sense that, 'I don't trust you,' time can pass, and they can have lunch, and say, 'you know we're brother and sister, we need to get over this.'" Thus, the family bond provides resiliency.

Participants discussed the usefulness of distinguishing between fragile and resilient trust as it is possible for families to move from one to another. For example, one person noted that through extending ourselves to others, it may be possible to trust in ways you had not trusted before. Optimism, such as seeing the good intentions in others, and bravery were also mentioned as ways of facilitating trust. In terms of bravery, a participant stated, "If the emperor has no clothes, it takes a brave family member to confront the emperor." Furthermore, progress and learning, which are possible in a healthy family culture, are other ways of building resilient trust. Yet, families that do not have healthy cultures may not be able to build resilient trust.

Lastly, participants provided examples of rebuilding trust in family businesses, illustrating resiliency. One of the participants told a story about a family business in which one family member was so fixated on making money that he violated clearly stated boundaries. The violation was seen as extreme because the family members trusted each other so much. To overcome this, the family engaged in dialogue with the help of a consultant. While the comments were authentic and painful, with the dialogue the family was able to move on and rebuild trust.

HINDRANCES TO TRUST

Participants noted that the romanticism of families can impede frankness and trust. As a scholar noted during the discussion, when we feel threatened and are fearful, we may get fixated and rationalize on doing whatever we need to do to survive. A by-product is the loss of trust. Even more so, there can be a fixation on the "romance of the family," accompanied by rationalization and detachment at the expense of the business. When this happens, there isn't room to take risks and try new things. Yet, trying something new may lead to more trust and resiliency. Clinging to the past in support of romance of the family limits expansion of trust and change that could allow for increased productivity. This idea was supported by other attendees who noted that because of the romanticized myth of the family, family members often feel that they have to act in a certain way just to sustain this myth, which again prevents frankness and lack of trust.

Relationships beyond those among family members are also important to discussions of trust. Many family businesses are proud that they treat their employees like family and therefore may construct families within the business. A story by a conference participant illustrates this. Someone close to him in the business was hurt by another person. Because he was close to this person and saw them as a mentor, he felt like his father had been hurt.

BUSINESS AND FAMILY

When considering families in business, is important to look at trust within both the family and the business. Two stories from conference participants illustrate this idea. Both relate to how the business affects the family and the family affects the business.

A participant told the story of a small, thriving, and growing family business. The husband and wife both had desks in the same room and their young children frequently came into the room to ask for help. At a consultant's recommendation, they separated the business office from access to the home. Because the wife had primary responsibility for the family, she ended up working very long hours late at night in the business office. Neither the husband nor the wife was happy and wanted things back the way they were. *In making changes to accommodate the business, they had failed to take into account the impact on the family.*

Likewise, a family business participant discussed how fixation and detachment affected both the business and her family:

> In family firms, there are two CEOs. There's the chief executive officer, but there's also the chief emotional officer. The chief emotional officer is the wingman [*sic*] in a family who provides perspective and gives the family business an edge . . . When the chief emotional officer is not present in the company, it's easy to become fixated on business goals, leading to rationalization and detachment. During the good times in my own family business, my mother was our chief emotional officer, and things were great. Then she phased out of the business . . . After I joined our company two years ago, I see that my father,

who is the owner, has become detached . . . We have encouraged him to be more active within the family and to travel less.

PART I   QUESTIONS TO THINK ABOUT

1. Does your family provide opportunities to have open and frank discussions?
2. Why do you trust people in your family and your business? Why do people trust you?
3. When has trust been broken in the family and/or family business? How did you solve it?
4. How do you promote trust among all parties in the family and/or business?
5. How do your business decisions impact the family?

PART II

Co-constructing family-business social capital

In Part II of the book we learn how family social capital is constructed along with the tools to both assess and construct social capital within our own business families. An important theme of the chapters in this section is that in family businesses, the family is often neglected. In looking at family social capital, it is important to address both the business and the family.

In Chapter 7, Danes and Stafford remind us of the importance to the business of having social capital within the family. They provide tools to assess functional family integrity and family-business conflict. They cite research indicating that when families function well together, they have less conflict and are more resilient.

In Chapter 8, Cronin, as an advisor, gives practical ideals regarding trust and family social capital in families and how this relates to the advising relationship. When positive social capital is present, advisors can more easily establish a trusting relationship with the family. More specifically, to produce positive outcomes, advisors can use social capital concepts to promote trust within the family, to establish trust with the family, and to trust that the process will lead to the desired outcome.

In Chapter 9, Bruess presents a scholarly overview of important elements within the family system to construct family social capital and a family identity. She suggests, for example, that families can replace destructive communication patterns with positive rituals and patterns and that contribute to family unity and identity. This is of particular importance for families in business.

In Chapter 10, Sorenson and an anonymous daughter and granddaughter from a family business apply social capital concepts to a family business. They provide an in-depth historical account of how family rituals and communication patterns provide a foundation for a successful family and family business. Drawing upon historical accounts of the family business's founder and his wife, including their courting, parenting children,

and starting the family business, we see how open and honest communication, trust, and family rituals helped establish the social capital in the
family and the business. In Chapter 11, Smith presents summary of the
dialogue.

7. Family social capital as family business resilience capacity

Sharon M. Danes and Kathryn Stafford

Considering the nature of family businesses, which has varying types and degrees of family involvement, one would expect research on owner management to include not only business management but also family/business interface management. However, that has not been the case in much of the family business research literature. As Stafford et al. have noted, when the family is considered in the family business literature, the prevailing assumption is that families cause problems that must be solved and that maintaining the business takes precedence, even if it harms the family.[1]

Because of the emphasis on business functioning, family business research has concentrated on the human and financial capital of family members who are directly involved in the business's operations. Family business research has paid little attention to other forms of family capital and to other family members, all of which affect the family/business connection and family business sustainability.[2] Family business owners must perceive, process, and respond to changing environments and adjust the business's courses of action to ensure sustainability over time, all of which depend on the relationships among those people within the owning family and the business.[3]

Relationships among people and the resulting resources are the essence of social capital. Specifically, family social capital is goodwill among family members and between owning family members and their communities, which can be infused within the owning family and their business to facilitate action.[4] Social capital is embodied in relationships among people as well as formal social institutions. Social capital provides information, access to technological knowledge, markets, and complementary resources. Social capital research focuses on how the quality, content, and structure of social relationships affect the flow of other resources and facilitate family firm sustainability.

Coleman, a leading social capital theorist, claims that family is the key institution through which social capital is transmitted through investments of time and effort, the development of emotional ties, and guidelines about acceptable and unacceptable behaviors.[5] These relational behaviors are based on contextual values, beliefs, and norms that spring from family structure, roles, and rules.[6] The family relies upon social capital to uphold social norms and return favors for the business's benefit.[7] But the family business literature is not clear about the definitions of family capital and social capital. In fact, the terms are often used without definition, leaving readers to supply their own.

Danes et al. defined family capital as the total bundle of owning-family member capital composed of human, social, and financial capital.[8] This definition is more far-reaching than most prior definitions in the family business literature. Such a definition of family capital is rooted in strong family ties.[9,10] This chapter focuses on one dimension of that family capital – family social capital – and draws extensively from the research published by Sharon M. Danes at the University of Minnesota and her colleague Kathryn Stafford at The Ohio State University.

The purpose of this chapter is twofold: (1) to summarize Danes and Stafford's research on family functional integrity, family business tensions, and women's contributions to family social capital that benefit the business; and (2) to present the Family Functional Integrity Tool and Family Business Conflict Identification Tool designed to help family businesses assess their family social capital. Their research is all theoretically grounded in Sustainable Family Business Theory, which they developed. Data are from the National Family Business Panel (NFBP), which is a national, representative sample of US family business owners surveyed in 1997, 2000, and 2007. Drs. Danes and Stafford served as integral collaborators in collecting the first wave of data and were leaders in data collection of the two most recent waves.

Danes et al. defined family social capital as goodwill among family members and between families and their community that can be input to owning families and their businesses to facilitate action.[11] High levels of social capital create greater flexibility, allowing the family business to better address internal or external disruptions that it might face. High social capital stock creates feelings of trust that promote cooperation and team collaboration, whereas low social capital stock does not. High social capital stock attracts other family human and financial capital resources to the business while low social capital stock lessens access to and accumulation of other family resources. High social capital stock creates a reliable supply of resilience that families can draw upon to combat the effects of internal and external disruptions to the family business; low social capital stock, on the other hand, creates vulnerability to disruptions. Resilience capacity is the ability of families to adapt and respond to stressful events and to problem-solve effectively.[12]

Unlike human capital that is embodied in individuals, social capital is manifested in relationships among people and in formal social institutions. With increased family social capital comes improved productivity for family members.[13] Analyses of family social capital focus on how the quality, content, and structure of social relationships affect other capital flows and, at the same time, ease sustainability of both family and business.[14]

Drawing upon this family capital stock can either enhance or reduce its store, resulting in the current period's output, which may be used in the next time period.[15] One must consider the difference between the concepts of the stock of resilience capacity and taking actions that draw upon that capacity. Much of the family firm research incorporating constructs that authors described as family management uses indicators of structures such as presence of family councils rather than flow measures of family management practices that are emphasized in this paper.[16] For example, use of available social capital stock may help develop a sense of trust based on shared norms and values, principles of obligations, and norms of cooperation. Of course, the use of social capital may also lead to the destruction of trust as the result of unshared norms and values.

THEORETICAL GROUNDING: SUSTAINABLE FAMILY BUSINESS THEORY

Sustainable Family Business Theory (SFBT) (Figure 7.1) is a theory that emphasizes long-term family business sustainability rather than business revenue as the primary outcome, and stipulates that short-term business viability is a function of both business and family achievements.[17,18] In other words, in SFBT, family business success depends on support from healthy families.[19] The theory stipulates that individuals in either family or business may affect the other. In contrast to other family business theories, unique SFBT features are its incorporation of change processes as well as processes during times of stability, and the portrayal of the family and family/business interface dynamics.

SFBT does not assume that family is in competition with business. Rather, the theory recognizes that disruptions created by change are normal occurrences where family and business interface. Capital rallies at this interface in order to manage both unexpected disruptions and planned change, and to negotiate family/business roles and decision-making patterns. The degree of family/business overlap adjusts depending upon internal and external demands.

SFBT has several central tenets.[20] Most relevant to this study are that:

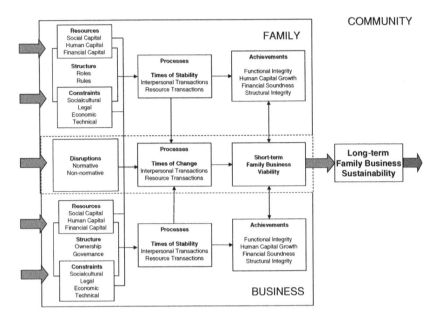

Source: Danes et al. (2008b).

Figure 7.1   Sustainable Family Business Theory

(1) a positive collaboration between family and business is productive for short-term firm achievements and long-term sustainability;[21] (2) family capital transactions in family *and* business may facilitate or inhibit business sustainability;[22] (3) family and business interact by exchanging capital across boundaries;[23] (4) owning families manage family and business jointly to optimize the achievements;[24] (5) after disruptions, processes must be rebuilt to ensure sustainability over time;[25] and (6) conflicts arise when there is a mismatch between demands and the capital that can be used to meet those demands.[26]

Capital is an economic term for resources. Family and business capital in SFBT is classified into social, human, and financial capital. Capital is objects, personal characteristics, conditions, or energies that are valued in their own right or that are valued because they help protect or achieve valued goals.[27] The owning family may either directly or indirectly input community capital to the firm. The theory recognizes the potential for capital to have simultaneous positive or negative effects on firm performance, depending on the circumstances. As an illustration of such phenomena, Field noted that "when people cooperate to pursue their own goals, it is sometimes at the cost of others."[28] Constraints impose limits on available alternative processes and strategies as well as the quantity of available capital. The assumption in SFBT is that the primary business goal is short-term viability followed by long-term sustainability.

In family and business, structure overlaps capital and constraints because it is thought to be both. Family roles and rules clarify who leads and how they lead, manage, or distribute family capital. Family roles and rules also restrict the effects of constraints and clarify how members interact in relation to membership, organization, and bonding.[29] Roles and rules not only cover who is in and out of family, but also include how the family assigns roles to members, how bonded members are, and how businesses define themselves relative to the outside world.[30] Shared meanings are core to family roles and rules, and those meanings include values, norms, and beliefs.[31] Decision authority patterns are also part of family roles and rules.[32] Some roles and rules are outwardly evident to all family members, but some are so deeply ingrained within the family's culture that members act on them unconsciously.

Processes during times of stability take place within both the family and the business, and can be thought of as routines, or standard operating procedures. During times of disruption, routine procedures may or may not be as effective as they usually are during stable times. These processes during change or disruption occur within the family/business overlap. SFBT suggests that at various times, capital transactions (e.g., use or alteration of social, human, and financial capital) and interpersonal transactions (e.g., communication, personal relationships, conflict management) from both the family and the business may affect family business sustainability.

The family/business overlap in SFBT is especially important when one considers intermingling of financial resources between family and business. Understanding resource intermingling is crucial in small business studies because it complicates financial records of both family and business with confusing and potentially catastrophic results. For instance, when family members take cash from the business for personal use, business profits are understated. Or, when a family uses a home equity mortgage to gain money to invest in business assets, those business assets are overstated and liabilities are understated, thus inflating the business's net worth. In instances like these, because the family business may not know if it is profitable, it may be jeopardizing its future and future support for the family. Intermingling can lead to inaccurate, and possibly deceptive, financial statements for the business.[33]

SFBT recognizes that business achievements are evaluated from many angles and that each dimension is important for a complete outcome assessment.[34] Financial success has been the chief concern of most business and economic theories. Using multi-dimensional measures leads to a better understanding of the entire decision set that owners use when strategizing how to invest their time and money.[35] Much of traditional business performance literature is based on the underlying assumption that individuals make economic decisions in a social vacuum.[36] In contrast, SFBT places businesses within the social context of community.[37] As a liaison between community and business, families offer a fertile environment of community values, attitudes, and beliefs that serve as inputs into business culture and add further meaning to the business's direct interaction with the community.

Disruptions in SFBT are classified as normative and non-normative. Normative disruptions are those such as the illness of a family member who works in the business. Previous research has focused on normative disruptions such as peak business seasons.[38] Non-normative disruptions are those that are not foreseeable or are highly unusual. An example would be a natural disaster that forces temporary or permanent business closure.[39]

METHODS

NFBP data are longitudinal over ten years with three years of data collection (1997, 2000, 2007)[40,41] The data were obtained from a national, representative sample of households who own a business. The household sampling frame, area probability sampling, and high response rates mean that the results of studies using the NFBP are representative of business-owning families in the US.

Using an area probability sample of all 50 states, interviewers screened more than 14000 household telephone numbers in 1997 to determine whether someone in the household was either a family business owner involved in the day-to-day operations of that business, or was the manager of a family business that he or she expected to inherit. To assure that respondents could answer the interview questions, the business owner had to have been in business at least a year and had to have spent at least six hours a week or 312 hours annually working in the business. Because the 1997 project focus was on the interaction of the business and the family, the business owner had to live in a household with at least two members. The response rate in 1997 was 71.1 percent. Qualifying families were administered two different 30-minute telephone interviews, one for the business manager and one for the family manager. When the family and business manager were the same individual, a 45-minute combined interview was administered. Data were obtained from 708 family business owners in 1997. In 2000, responses were obtained from 553 households, more than 75 percent of the original 708 households. In 2007, responses were obtained from 290 of the original households. The largest sample business had 250 employees; thus, the businesses in 2007 would be classified as small businesses by the US Small Business Administration.[42]

FAMILY FUNCTIONAL INTEGRITY

In 2009, Danes et al. stated that "strong businesses supported by strong families produce strong family businesses."[43] If that statement is true, then family functional integrity is a critical segment of family social capital. Open communication about goals and a desire to resolve misunderstandings about how to achieve those goals are key components of strong owning families.[44] This type of open communication springs from a stock of resilience capacity that is critical to long-term sustainability of family firms.[45] Danes et al. described this stock of resilience capacity as family social capital; Family APGAR is one way to measure family social capital.[46]

Family APGAR is a self-report scale developed by Smilkstein that characterizes how well the family typically functions in the opinion of the person using the tool.[47] Family APGAR is a well-established measure of family functional integrity that synthesizes features of more than one theory; it is based on theories of stress and change.[48] It consists of five items, and in a pretest with business-owning families, respondents readily understood the statements and answered quickly with sufficient sensitivity to differences in families.[49]

Family APGAR measures satisfaction with five dimensions of family functioning – **a**daptation, **p**artnership, **g**rowth, **a**ffection, and **r**esolve.[50] The measure name represents the first letter of each dimension. Each dimension represents a common theme in the family literature. Table 7.1 includes conceptual definitions and questions used to measure each dimension. Adaptation is the use of intra- and extra-familial capital for problem-solving when family stability is stressed during a crisis. Partnership is sharing of decision-making and nurturing responsibilities by family members. Growth is physical and emotional maturation and self-fulfillment achieved by family members through mutual support and guidance. Affection is the caring and loving relationships that exist among family members. Resolve is the commitment to devote time to other family members for physical and emotional nurturing. Each component has a unique function, yet each is interrelated to the whole.[51]

Each question response was recorded on a five-point Likert scale from

Table 7.1   Conceptual definitions and APGAR questions representing family integrity dimensions

Family Integrity Dimensions	Conceptual Definitions	APGAR Questions
Adaptation	Adaptation is the utilization of intra- and extra-familial resources for problem-solving when family equilibrium is stressed during a crisis	You are satisfied that you can turn to your family for help when something is troubling you
Partnership	Partnership is the sharing of decision-making and nurturing responsibilities by family members	You are satisfied with the way your family talks over things with you and shares problems with you
Growth	Growth is the physical and emotional maturation and self-fulfillment that is achieved by family members through mutual support and guidance	You are satisfied that your family accepts and supports your wishes to take on new activities and directions
Affection	Affection is the caring or loving relationship that exists among family members	You are satisfied with the way your family expresses affection and responds to your emotions, such as anger, sorrow, or love
Resolve	Resolve is the commitment to devote time to other members of the family for physical and emotional nurturing. It also usually involves a decision to share wealth and space	You are satisfied with the way your family and you share time together

Source: Smilkstein (1978).

never (1) to always (5). When summed, the potential range was 5 to 25. Table 7.2 provides Family APGAR average scores for three years of NFBP data. The total APGAR scores increased over time, although they were not statistically different. This increase makes sense because attrition in the sample took place over time. The owning families who were most functionally healthy were most likely to have businesses that survived over time, in part due to their family functionality. The family businesses that remained in the sample over time had an average Family APGAR score slightly above 20. Adaptation was the highest dimension score across the three years. Resolve, referring to satisfaction with time spent together,

Table 7.2   Differences among 1997, 2000, and 2007 NFBP data APGAR means

Family Dimension	Question Asked	1997	2000	2007
Adaptation	You are satisfied that you can turn to your family for help when something is troubling you	4.37 (1)[a]	4.40 (1)[a]	4.37 (1)[a]
Partnership	You are satisfied with the way your family talks over things with you and shares problems with you	3.96 (4)	4.02 (3)	4.06 (4)
Growth	You are satisfied that your family accepts and supports your wishes to take on new activities and directions	4.15 (2)	4.19 (2)	4.06 (4)
Affection	You are satisfied with the way your family expresses affection and responds to your emotions, such as anger, sorrow, and love	4.06* (3)	4.19 (2)	4.21 (2)
Resolve	You are satisfied with the way your family and you share time together	3.96** (4)	3.94 (2)	4.09 (3)
	Total APGAR (sum of items)	20.50	20.73	20.79

Notes:
* $p > 0.10$ = difference between 1997 and 2000 Affection, and 1997 and 2007 Affection.
** $p > 0.05$ = difference between 1997 and 2007 Resolve, and 2000 and 2007 Resolve.
a.   = ranking from high to low level of family integrity dimension.

Source: NFBP.

had the lowest score in the first two waves and then increased slightly in the third year. The growth score (satisfaction with support desired to take new directions) decreased from the second to third year and became the lowest scoring dimension among the Family APGAR dimensions in the third year.

Family APGAR has published norms with which to compare oneself and/or to use to measure "degree of integrity or functionality." Using these norms, 1 percent of the owning families were dysfunctional (scores of < 11), 16 percent were indeterminate (scores between 11 and 17), and 83 percent were clearly functional (scores of > 17) (Figure 7.2).

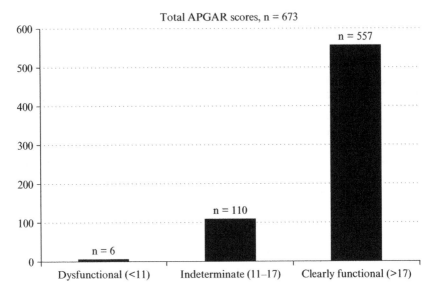

Source: NFBP.

*Figure 7.2   Distribution of Family APGAR scores from National Family
            Business Panel data*

Family APGAR provides firm owners with a valid, reliable, confidential
means of monitoring family functional integrity, and is also fast and easy
to score. Historically, Family APGAR was developed as a quick (emphasis
on quick) screening device to identify which families of hospital patients
were incapable of helping to care for the patient.[52] Reliability measures
from recent studies are good. Family APGAR strengths include its ease
of administration and its focus on perception of satisfaction. The instrument is a self-report, which means it can be self-administered and results
kept confidential. It can be used by families with children or without them.
Family APGAR has also been found to be valid and reliable with families
from ethnic minorities.

In Table 7.3, the Family APGAR questions have been turned into a tool
that can be used with business-owning families. Like all self-report tools,
this one relies on the ability and willingness of the user to admit problems
or dissatisfaction to themselves.[53] If the score on the Family APGAR is
less than 11, the owning family might consider seeking the help of a trained
counselor. Such a consultation is important even if only one person in
the family scores below 11. If the score is between 11 and 17, the owning
family most probably does not need the help of a professional counselor.

In this situation, family members may want to work on shared meanings about family and business goals, making certain family members have written job descriptions in the family business, and establishing clarity and agreement on decision authority patterns. They also might consider taking steps to clarify and maintain both business and family boundaries. If the Family APGAR score is greater than 17, the owning family might continue the processes that it has been using, but the members need to remember to re-evaluate the family integrity periodically and at times of change.

A further advantage of the Family APGAR instrument is that Smilkstein has given permission without charge to use the scale for research, education, and personal information.[54] Caution should be used when relying on the results of this tool because these figures are based on the owning family members' opinions. Different family members might have different opinions. If several family members do the same assessment, a good rule of thumb is to use the lowest score. Caution also should be used when classifying your family's level of functional integrity, especially if you are close to a cut-off point. A good rule of thumb is to seriously consider the lower category and reassess more frequently than otherwise.

Family functional integrity should not be taken for granted as the family and business changes and moves through life cycle stages. A principle of SFBT indicates that after disruptions, processes must be reconstructed to ensure sustainability over time.[55] Most families draw heavily on their social capital and resilience capacity during times of change and, in so doing, must reconstruct many processes in the family and business due to this mix of social, financial, and human capital changes. Family APGAR also might be used when re-evaluating goals. Perhaps your family sets goals with the onset of a new year. If so, use Family APGAR at that time to gauge the functional integrity of family adults. Compare scores and the match between item scores. Then ask how goals have contributed to that score. Would new goals improve scores and better serve the needs of family members? Use Family APGAR also when setting new business goals. Ask the same questions about business goals that you ask about family goals. Has working together or apart to achieve goals helped family functional integrity? Has it jeopardized integrity? What business goals contribute to functional integrity?

FAMILY BUSINESS TENSIONS AT THE INTERFACE OF FAMILY AND BUSINESS

For a family business to remain viable and successful over time, it must change,[56,57] and tensions and stress are normal during these times of

Table 7.3 Family Functional Integrity Tool: Family APGAR for family business-owning families

Item	Never	Hardly Ever	Some of the Time	Almost Always	Always	Your Score
1. You are satisfied that you can turn to your family for help when something is troubling you	1	2	3	4	5	_____
2. You are satisfied with the way your family talks over things with you and shares problems with you	1	2	3	4	5	_____
3. You are satisfied that your family accepts and supports your wishes to take on new activities and directions	1	2	3	4	5	_____
4. You are satisfied with the way your family expresses affection and responds to your emotions, such as anger, sorrow, or love	1	2	3	4	5	_____
5. You are satisfied with the way your family and you share time together	1	2	3	4	5	_____
Your Family APGAR score						_____

Notes:

Directions: For each item please enter in the far-right column the number that indicates how often you are satisfied with that aspect of your family life.

Scoring instructions: Enter your chosen numbers for each item into the last column on the right. Then add those numbers and write that total at the bottom of that column. This total is your Family APGAR score. If the score on the Family APGAR is less than 11, consider seeking the help of a trained counselor. Do this even if only one person in the family scores below 11. If the score is between 11 and 17, you probably do not need the help of a professional counselor. In this situation you might want to consider working on shared meaning about family and business goals, making certain family members have written job descriptions, and establishing clarity on decision authority patterns. If the score is greater than 17, continue to utilize the processes that you have been using, but remember to re-evaluate at times of change.

Disclaimer: Caution should be used when relying on the results of this tool because these figures are based on your opinion. Other members of your family might have a different opinion. If you have other members of your family do the same assessment, a good rule of thumb is to use the lowest score. Caution also should be used when classifying your family's level of functional integrity, especially if you are close to a cut-off point.

Source: Authors.

91

change. However, tension diminishes social capital and resilience capacity that can be used to combat the consequences of both internal and external disruptions. When tension is present, other types of family capital must be used to moderate tension levels so that they are kept in the creative/constructive range rather than the distracting/destructive range.

The SFBT tenet that applies here is that conflicts arise when there is a mismatch between demands and capital that can be used to meet those demands.[58] Family business conflict is not a static phenomenon; it varies based on the stressors that either the family or business is experiencing.[59,60]

Family business literature indicates that conflict is one of the fastest-growing concerns affecting business sustainability.[61] Unresolved conflict is detrimental to business sustainability because conflict is negatively related to the achievement of family and business goals.[62,63,64] Conflict is difficult to manage when boundary, role definition, or commitment issues are present.[65] Thus, these issues also need to be addressed during change, and in so doing, family and business power structures and interactions may be reconstructed.[66,67]

Paradoxically, a certain level of family firm tension acts as a creative mechanism and can increase the health, growth, and success of both the business and family.[68] When properly focused and managed, low and moderate levels of tension (constructive tension) can stimulate changes that keep the family business viable and healthy. On the other hand, higher levels of tension (distracting tension) can have the opposite effect on the business – reduced health and satisfaction, stunted growth, and diminished success.[69,70] However, the balance between constructive tensions that create healthy change and continued viability and distracting, destructive tensions that reduce health and diminish success can be managed.[71]

Each response to a tension question was recorded as a five-point Likert scale from "no tension at all" (1) to a "great deal of tension" (5). When summed, the potential range was 7 to 35. The actual range was 7 to 30 (Figure 7.3). Sixty percent of the NFBP business owners in 1997 reported some tension (scores of 7 to 9), 24 percent reported moderate tension (scores of 10 to 13), 11 percent reported high tension (scores of 14 to 18), and 5 percent reported very high tension (scores of 19 to 30).

The family business tension literature has concentrated on tension content. Only recently has that literature investigated the link between tension content and interactions that occur around those tensions. Tensions and stresses within family businesses fall into five content areas: justice, role, work/family, identity, and succession.[72] Justice tensions refer to problems of compensation [salary], quality of treatment, or allocation of capital across family and business;[73,74,75] the intermingling of financial capital across family and business can lead to cash flow problems and

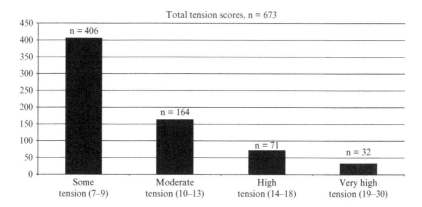

Source: NFBP.

Figure 7.3 *Distribution of total tension scores from National Family Business Panel data*

tensions over money.[76,77] Each spouse has a lens through which he or she evaluates capital demands by the family and business. For instance, time distribution across family and business can result in an increase in justice tensions.[78,79] For example, there may be times when work/family conflict evolves for the business owner because he/she feels they should be spending more time both with family members and managing business operations.

Centered around confusion about role performance, role tensions may be related to types of tasks performed, the level of spousal participation in the firm, or decision-making authority.[80,81,82] Role confusion can arise when family members work together or when the family business employs people who are not part of the family, an insider/outsider situation that can create stress.[83] While business-owning couples may feel left out or excluded from the business decision-making process, resulting in a lessening of couple cohesion, the same can be said about having sole or undue responsibility in decision-making.[84]

In a recent study by Danes and Morgan, work/family balance was the greatest tension producer among issues that surfaced at the intersection of family and business, even though succession tensions have been the primary focus of the family business literature.[85] An example of work/family tension is when business work dominates family needs over an extended period or when business owners have high demands in both family and business simultaneously.[86] In such cases, the business owner feels pulled in both directions at once when they only have time or energy enough to do what needs to be done in just one domain at any one time.

Succession tensions primarily deal with ownership and management transfer issues.[87] Identity tensions involve family members' needs to differentiate themselves and act as independent, autonomous persons amid family expectations. Identity tensions surface through gender conflicts, sibling rivalry, and parent/child relationships. They often remain unresolved over time because they are never openly addressed.[88]

Family business tensions and conflicts are unique in that many business relationships are grounded in the conscious and/or unconscious history of family relationships. For example, sibling rivalry in childhood often continues in adulthood, and when siblings are working in a family business, that rivalry can be an undercurrent of business management. When these tensions aren't clearly acknowledged, they can lead to distracting rather than creative tensions in the family business.

Thus, family business conflicts often have significant features that do not fit established dispute-resolution models.[89] Members of family businesses are often fighting about deeper issues than those that are broadcast; some of these issues include growth, power, management, inheritance, or role definitions.[90] If these deeper issues of symbolic significance are not acknowledged and addressed, the drive to sustain conflict can be just as strong as, if not stronger than, the desire to resolve it. Kaye says this situation is characterized by repetitive conflict and must be addressed with professional assistance.[91]

Business-owning husbands and wives perceived tension through slightly different lenses. Table 7.4 includes the questions asked about the five sources of tension. The table includes responses from wives and husbands of business-owning families. The highest tension in all three years was work/family tension. Both spouses equally thought work/family conflict created the highest tension except in 2000, when husbands reported less tension than did their wives. The second-highest source of tension was capital competition between family and business. The lowest source of tension in 2007 was confusion over decision authority and unequal ownership of the business by family members. Succession conflict was the lowest-ranked until 2007 when the two previously-mentioned tension types reversed in rank order.

Tensions affect the success of family businesses.[92,93] Family business couples are involved in joint activity with collective goals that require them to maintain family stability and creative and constructive conflict patterns, or at least to ensure that conflicts are resolved quickly.[94,95] When family members let their tension build up within the family, the business suffers; in fact, Olson et al. indicated that reducing family tension by only 4 percent could increase annual business revenue by $400.[96]

Table 7.4 Wives' and husbands' tension means of NFBP

Tension Content	1997		2000		2007	
	Wives	Husbands	Wives	Husbands	Wives	Husbands
Work/family conflict						
Unfair workloads among family members due to the business	1.94 (1)[a]	1.74	1.76 (1)[a]	1.57*	1.85 (1)[a]	1.55*
Justice conflict						
Competition for resources between family and business	1.84 (2)	1.54*	1.68 (2)	1.46*	1.67 (2)	1.76
Unfair compensation [salary] for family members	1.51 (5)	1.29*	1.47 (4)	1.26*	1.57 (4)	1.48
Identity conflict						
Failure to resolve business conflicts	1.71 (3)	1.51*	1.55 (3)	1.20*	1.60 (3)	1.54
Role conflict						
Confusion among family members over who does what in the business	1.59 (4)	1.49	1.45 (5)	1.35	1.52 (5)	1.64
Confusion over who has authority to make decisions	1.49 (6)	1.34*	1.32 (6)	1.27	1.38 (7)	1.46
Succession conflict						
Unequal ownership of the business by family members	1.35 (7)	1.17*	1.30 (7)	1.08*	1.42 (6)	1.39

Notes:
* $p < 0.05$ = difference between wives and husbands; asterisks are located at smaller of two means.
a.   = ranking from high to low level of tension.

Source: NFBP.

Table 7.5   Achievement indicators by total tension levels

Achievement Indicators	Total Tension Levels				
	No tension (a) (6)	Some tension (b) (7–9)	Moderate tension (c) (10–13)	High tension (d) (14–18)	Very high tension (e) (19–30)
Husbands' report of total tension					
Family					
Family APGAR	20.6	20.8	20.4	20.6	18.5[abcd]
Business					
Overall success of the business	4.18[e]	4.07[e]	3.90	3.67	3.50[ab]
Success of most important business goal	4.07[de]	3.93	3.64	3.33[a]	3.30[a]
Wives' report of total tension					
Family					
Family APGAR	22.2[bcde]	20.9[ae]	20.4[ae]	19.7[ae]	17.7[abcd]
Business					
Overall success of the business	4.05	4.21[e]	3.95	3.93	3.74[b]
Success of most important business goal	4.05[e]	3.90	3.86	3.67	3.39[a]

Note: The superscripts in the body of the table represent the group(s) where there is a statistical difference in the APGAR score; the letters represent each one of the tension groups.

Source: Danes and Olson (2003).

The functional integrity of the owning family is critical to navigating the conflict environment.[97] When tensions arise, families with higher levels of functional integrity have a greater store to draw upon to manage these tensions and to creatively turn them into change needed to sustain the business over time. When there is sustained tension, the family can buffer the impact on the business. However, if its functional integrity is weak, the family can become further stressed when experiencing effects of tension created by the business.[98] The more stressful events families experience, the less capacity they have to lessen the consequences of the tensions created by the business.[99]

Table 7.5 summarizes the relationship of various levels of total business tension with a number of family and business achievements. This particular study included only six of the seven tension questions in the analysis. The table includes information from both the business manager and the spouse. As tension levels increased, every achievement indicator declined.

For both members of the business-owning couple, the very high tension level (score of 19 to 30 in the tension tool) was statistically different from the other group (Table 7.5).

Although tolerating a certain tension level can stimulate needed change, tensions over goals can become distracting at some threshold point.[100,101,102] When that threshold is reached, setting forth and communicating clear goals becomes difficult. Goals can be a powerful means of guiding a family business, so the consequences may be serious.

In order to remain a viable business, some tension is needed to stimulate change; however, the critical question is, at what point does constructive tension become destructive? Findings show that it was not until families reported "very high tension" levels that statistical differences were found in achievement indicators for family and firm. That may be the point at which the difference between constructive and destructive tension becomes clear. At this point, the family business will definitely be aware that there are problems to be solved. The question then becomes whether at this point the tensions are so high that options that may have been helpful earlier are no longer feasible because of the high tension level. Perhaps a "caution" sign should be drawn at the "high tension" level when it becomes obvious that tensions are nearing the threshold level. At this tension level, people may still be willing to make a major effort to address the sources of the tensions. Studies show that when families communicate more openly about circumstances, the intensity of disagreement over issues is lower.[103,104] On the other hand, lack of opportunity to discuss and make decisions about family business issues can intensify family conflict.[105]

Table 7.6 includes a Family Business Conflict Identification Tool. It helps family business members assess family members' perceptions of tension for each content area and the total tension from all areas. It can serve as a discussion starter or an indicator of changes in tension levels at times of major change. The score only provides a picture of accumulated tension levels present in your family around business issues. What you do with this information is critical to business productivity. Positive responses to identifying tension include clarifying job responsibilities and decision-making roles, negotiating work–family balance, or developing a concrete plan for distributing the family business's capital. Family businesses with a score between 14 and 18 should become concerned about the impact of these tensions on the successful functioning of the business. Scores of 19 or greater suggest that tensions have most likely already hindered the successful functioning of the family business.

Table 7.6   Family Business Conflict Identification Tool

Tension Type	No Tension At All				Great Deal of Tension	Your Score
a. Confusion among family members over who does what in the business	1	2	3	4	5	___
b. Confusion over who has authority to make decisions	1	2	3	4	5	___
c. Unequal ownership of the business by family members	1	2	3	4	5	___
d. Unfair compensation for family members	1	2	3	4	5	___
e. Failure to resolve business conflicts	1	2	3	4	5	___
f. Unfair workloads among family members, due to the business	1	2	3	4	5	___
g. Competition for resources between family and business	1	2	3	4	5	___
					Total Score	___

Notes:
Directions: Within family-based businesses, family and business issues are interconnected. Sometimes tensions arise that can affect the productivity of the business. First, think about how your business may affect the family members who live in your home. Second, choose a number that indicates the level of tension that each issue generates in your home life. Enter that number in the space at the end of each tension question. Use the scale of 1 to 5 that is provided. The 1 represents no tension existing and the 5 represents a great deal of tension existing. To obtain a "total tension score," add the score for each individual tension type and place the total in the space for "total score."

Total tension score: Mean score for business owners within the National Family Business Study was 9.9; for household managers, 11.5.

Interpretation of your total tension score: The score only provides a picture into the accumulated tension level that exists in your family around business issues. What you do with this information is what is critical to the productivity of the business: clarifying job responsibilities and decision-making roles, negotiating work–family balance, or developing a concrete plan for distributing resources of the family business. Concerns about the impact of these tensions on the successful functioning of the family business should arise with a score of between 14 and 18. Scores of 19 or greater suggest that tensions have most probably already deterred the successful functioning of the family business.

Source: Authors.

WOMEN AS CONTRIBUTORS TO SOCIAL CAPITAL IN FAMILY BUSINESSES

Gender research shows a difference in the way the women and men use their social capital. For example, women communicate and problem-solve differently from men. They prioritize life experiences differently from men, and are socialized differently within both family and business.[106] In recent years, increasing numbers of women have chosen business as their career. If business owners were to capture differences in how males and females use their social capital by using the strengths of all involved, they could potentially create a more vibrant business culture. Or business owners could continue to underuse or ignore gender differences, thus losing potential capital to create a competitive advantage for their business. Which approach the family business takes may affect family business achievements that, over time, diminish or enhance the business's sustainability.

The way business-owning males and females experience tensions differs within family businesses. In a decade review of research on couple relationships, Gottman and Notarius asserted that women tend to be the ones who typically raise most of the issues in the majority of marriages.[107] That finding has consistently been found for family business-owning couples as well.[108,109,110,111] The average scores for the five tension types in all three years show that, in most cases, men reported less tension than did women (Table 7.4). Additionally, Stewart and Danes found that women who work in family businesses tend to have a higher need than men to work through tension and conflict in order to work effectively.[112]

Care must be taken in the interpretation of these findings. One interpretation, often found in family business literature, is that women are problems to be managed. Another interpretation recognizes that perhaps women are better barometers of family integrity and leading indicators that change is needed, whereas men are lagging indicators.[113,114] One reason women report higher tensions over business issues is that women often have a greater mismatch between demands and available capital to meet those demands.[115] Furthermore, a certain level of tension is normal when more than one family member is involved in a family business and can help stimulate dialogue about ways to sustain the family business over time.

In a discourse analysis of family business owners, men and women differed in the way they spoke about their business management.[116] Women had a higher emotional discourse-style score (words of personal involvement, concern, preference) for managing the business than men did. Men balanced their emotional language with the practicality of planning tasks and creating efficiencies. Women frequently used "we" in their communication about their businesses, reflecting key female roles identified in the family business literature: building relationships, negotiating, maintaining multiple simultaneous roles, and providing flexible bonds to hold changing family businesses together.[117] These are strengths that women bring to team building.

This same family business discourse study identified a previously ignored role of women in family business.[118] Women in this study placed much greater emphasis on words about "future" and "change" than did men. Women's more frequent use of those phrases shows that women are more likely to act as springboards for innovation within family businesses. In contrast, men used words related to accomplishing tasks in the present.

Women may have a greater effect on family social capital than men. Women's family roles are more likely to lead to greater responsibility than men's roles for investing in or creating social capital within the family. Their emphasis on "we" in business management may also help create social capital. They are leading indicators of tension and conflict, threats to or drains on stocks of family social capital. They are also more likely to express interest in the future and positive change that can further increase family social capital and create competitive advantage for the business. Past assumptions about business management may not work as well now or in the future when more women are part of the business environment. In a study of the impact of disruptions on a family business's gross revenue, the gender of the business owner subdued responses to disruptions (sleeping less, hiring temporary help during busy times, family members donating time to business, and using family income for the business).[119] These moderating effects were so significant that the effects of responses to disruptions on gross revenues were the opposite for females and males.

Just as assumptions that all businesses should be managed in the same manner despite the owner's gender should be questioned, so should assumptions about how businesses are managed in times of change versus times of stability.[120] Much of the family business literature considers only family capital within the business, but both Olson et al. and Danes et al. found that during times of disruptions, family social capital outside the business also impacts business revenue.[121,122] This research supports the SFBT tenets that family and business exchange capital across boundaries, especially during times of disruption and change; this cooperation between family and business is productive for both short-term business success and long-term sustainability.[123]

During family firm consultations, one caveat about gender differences is that information may be biased if some family firm decision-makers are not part of information gathering. In addition, if the consultant does not observe the family business decision team interact as a group followed by the opportunity for individuals to confidentially confirm or refute the information obtained or problem-solving processes used in the observed group interaction, biased information may also be a concern. Biased information results in skewed and/or faulty consultation advice and guidance. It is not easy to gauge intricacies of the use of family social capital within firms, including family and firm roles. By observing group interactions while family members problem-solve and by using individual family members' confirmation or refutation of those group interaction processes, a family firm consultant can unravel power structures and interactions among family members. It is in group interactions that power structures are solidified and maintained.[124]

SUMMARY AND IMPLICATIONS

The purpose of this paper was twofold: (1) it summarized Danes and Stafford's research on family functional integrity, family business tensions at the family/business interface, and women's contributions to business social capital; (2) it described two tools to be used with family businesses based on their research: Family Functional Integrity Tool and Family Business Conflict Identification Tool. Their research is theoretically grounded in Sustainable Family Business Theory (SFBT). Data were from the National Family Business Panel (NFBP), which followed a national, representative sample of US family businesses for ten years.

A basic premise of the SFBT is that short-term family business achievements and long-term sustainability depend on the support of healthy families.[125] However, only recently has family been incorporated into family business research, and then it included only those family members employed by the business. The unique features of the SFBT are its inclusion of change processes in addition to standard operating routines and the recognition of family/business interface dynamics. It is at this crossing point where a give and take between family and business social capital creates a resilience capacity that the business can draw upon to generate short-term achievements and create a solid foundation for long-term sustainability.

Research by Danes and Stafford on family functional integrity shows that strong businesses supported by strong families produce robust family businesses. When families are functionally strong, they have a resilience stock that buffers both family and business against stresses arising from disruptions. But a stock of family resilience is not enough for long-term sustainability. Danes et al. indicated that access to and use of family social capital is more critical to family business success than actual family capital stocks.[126]

Strengths that women bring to family firms are an example. Using the differences in how men and women function can create a more vibrant firm culture, whereas ignoring or under-using them means the business may lose potential capital for creating competitive advantage. For instance, when women report higher tensions over business issues with the family business, should the interpretation be that women are a problem to be managed or that women are a better barometer of family integrity and a leading indicator that change is needed? Family business resilience is diminished when family social capital is not taken advantage of because its competitive advantage is lost.

Tension means the absence of social capital and a diminished stock of resilience capacity to buffer internal and external disruptions. The presence of tension also requires the use of other components of family capital to moderate tension levels so that they are kept in the creative/constructive range rather than the distracting/destructive range. Paradoxically, the business needs a certain amount of creative tension to motivate change to remain viable over time, but it can reach a threshold in the tension level, after which it becomes destructive to the long-term sustainability of the family business.

One of the highest tensions reported by both spouses of family firm couples over time is work/family balance. The tensions occur at the family/firm interface; during times of change and stress, family and firm exchange capital across boundaries, so ignoring the interface in family firm research, education, or consulting is like ignoring an essential body limb. Family firm couples are involved in joint activity with collective goals. This joint activity requires maintaining family stability, creative and constructive conflict patterns, or at the minimum, eliminating extended conflict.[127,128] When families let tension build up, the firm suffers. Although tolerating a certain tension level can stimulate needed change, tensions over goals can become distracting at some threshold point.[129,130] Because goals can be a powerful means of guiding a family firm, when that threshold is reached, it becomes more difficult to provide clear goals and communicate them effectively.

This chapter adapted research measures for family functional integrity and family firm tensions into assessment tools. The Family Functional Integrity Tool assists in assessing the stock of family social capital. It can be used as a discussion starter or as a barometer of how the family is doing during times of change. During change, new processes need to be developed, and the tool can provide guidance about where to begin. Since the tool is based on individual family members' opinions, you should use caution when classifying your family's level of functional integrity, especially if the score is close to a cut-off point.

Tensions in the home due to firm issues can range from creative and constructive to distracting; if sustained over a long period of time, these tensions can become destructive to the functional integrity of the family and firm. The Family Business Conflict Identification Tool assesses the tension level for the seven most frequently identified tensions in the family business literature. The research indicates that there is a threshold at which tension pile-up hinders the successful functioning of the family firm. Even before that, there is a range in which tensions become a distraction to the firm manager. Within this range, it is still possible, with a targeted and united effort, to tackle the root causes of the tensions.

This paper focused on the family social capital research of Danes and Stafford. That research emphasizes family/business interface management with an emphasis on the use of and access to family social capital, the foundation of resilience capacity. It includes two tools, the Family Functional Integrity Tool and the Family Business Conflict Identification Tool, which assess components of family social capital that create resilience capacity and competitive advantage for family businesses.

NOTES

1. Stafford et al. (1999).
2. Danes et al. (2008b).
3. Danes et al. (2005).
4. Danes et al. (2009a).
5. Coleman (1990).
6. Danes et al. (2008b).
7. Zuiker et al. (2003).
8. Danes et al. (2009a).
9. Ibid.
10. Heck et al. (2006).
11. Danes et al. (2009a).
12. Danes et al. (2009b).
13. Danes et al. (2008b).
14. Danes et al. (2009a).
15. Ibid.
16. Gimeno-Sandig (2005).
17. Stafford et al. (1999).
18. Danes et al. (2008b).
19. Ibid.
20. Ibid.
21. Ibid.
22. Danes et al. (2009a).
23. Danes et al. (2007).
24. Danes et al. (2009a).
25. Winter et al. (2004).
26. Danes et al. (2002).
27. Hobfoll (1989).

28. Field (2003, p. 3).
29. Danes et al. (2002).
30. Danes and Olson (2003).
31. Haberman and Danes (2007).
32. Danes and Morgan (2004).
33. Zuiker et al. (2003).
34. Danes et al. (2007).
35. Ibid.
36. Danes et al. (2009a).
37. Danes et al. (2008b).
38. Ibid.
39. Danes et al. (2009b).
40. Winter et al. (2004).
41. Winter et al. (1998).
42. US SBA (2006).
43. Danes et al. (2009a, p. 211)
44. Danes (2006).
45. Danes et al. (2008b).
46. Danes et al. (2009a).
47. Smilkstein (1978).
48. Sawin and Harrigan (1995).
49. Ibid.
50. Smilkstein (1978).
51. Ibid.
52. Sawin and Harrigan (1995).
53. Smilkstein (1978).
54. Ibid.
55. Winter et al. (2004).
56. Danes (2006).
57. Danes and Amarapurkar (2001).
58. Danes et al. (2008b).
59. Danes and Morgan (2004).
60. Stewart and Danes (2001).
61. Danes and Olson (2003).
62. Danes et al. (2007).
63. Danes and Olson (2003).
64. Danes et al. (1999).
65. Danes (2006).
66. Ibid.
67. Haberman and Danes (2007).
68. Danes and Morgan (2004).
69. Danes and Olson (2003).
70. Danes et al. (1999).
71. Danes and Olson (2003).
72. Danes et al. (1999).
73. Danes and Morgan (2004).
74. Danes and Lee (2004).
75. Danes et al. (1999).
76. Olson et al. (2003).
77. Zuiker et al. (2003).
78. Danes and Lee (2004).
79. Danes and Morgan (2004).
80. Ibid.
81. Danes and Olson (2003).
82. Stewart and Danes (2001).

83.   Danes et al. (2002).
84.   Stewart and Danes (2001).
85.   Danes and Morgan (2004).
86.   Ibid.
87.   Haberman and Danes (2007).
88.   Danes and Olson (2003).
89.   Kaye (2002).
90.   Stewart and Danes (2001).
91.   Kaye (2002).
92.   Danes and Olson (2003).
93.   Olson et al. (2003).
94.   Danes et al. (2007).
95.   Danes et al. (2009a).
96.   Olson et al. (2003).
97.   Danes and Olson (2003).
98.   Danes et al. (1999).
99.   Ibid.
100.   Ibid.
101.   Danes and Morgan (2004).
102.   Danes and Olson (2003).
103.   Danes et al. (2000a).
104.   Danes et al. (2000b).
105.   Stewart and Danes (2001).
106.   Haberman and Danes (2007).
107.   Gottman and Notarius (2000).
108.   Danes et al. (1999).
109.   Danes and Lee (2004).
110.   Danes and Morgan (2004).
111.   Stewart and Danes (2001).
112.   Ibid.
113.   Danes and Morgan (2004).
114.   Danes and Olson (2003).
115.   Danes (2006).
116.   Danes et al. (2005).
117.   Ibid.
118.   Ibid.
119.   Danes et al. (2007).
120.   Ibid.
121.   Olson et al. (2003).
122.   Danes et al. (2007).
123.   Danes et al. (2008b).
124.   Haberman and Danes (2007).
125.   Danes et al. (2008b).
126.   Danes et al. (2009a).
127.   Danes et al. (2007).
128.   Danes et al. (2009a).
129.   Danes and Morgan (2004).
130.   Danes and Olson (2003).

8. Building trust in advising family businesses

Margaret A.T. Cronin

> Trust no one unless you have eaten much salt with him.
> Cicero

INTRODUCTION

At my law firm, I advise family businesses and families of wealth in business and estate planning matters. In preparation for this article, I asked one of the owners of a family business that I advise about trust. "George," I wrote, "Do you trust me as your advisor?" "YES," he responded. "If so," I wrote, "why, and how did I build this trust with you?" He replied, "By gaining [the] confidence of my entire family. Also, by [you] being so organized for each meeting. Your attitude, smile and your ability to advise us of necessary changes that need to be made to keep our [documents] up to date."

In reflecting upon these words and my experience with other family business owners, four factors seem to stand out as building blocks in creating trust as an advisor to family businesses: *congruity, value, strategy* and *connection*. Congruity means the compatibility between the advisor's direction and the direction of the family business. Value represents the advisor's technical knowledge and experience in the field upon which the family business can draw. Strategy denotes the advisor's effectiveness in being part of the solution that helps the family get from here to there. Connection means the ability of the advisor to relate to each family member, owner, and manager that is part of the system. I am certain that there are other compelling factors and that each advisor will have his or her own perspective on developing trust. In this article, I offer only my own observations in the hopes that sharing my library of experiences will help build our collective knowledge of what it means to serve family businesses.

An advisor to a family business may feel that he or she is an objective

Figure 8.1   Building trust

third party in the family business engagement. The advisor may see himself or herself as merely a witness to the goings on of the family and the business that they operate. This advisor may roll his or her eyes behind closed conference room doors with the other advisors to the family business – "There they go again with their family dysfunction." He or she was engaged to perform a particular role, such as drafting a document or preparing a tax return, and is not being called upon to interact with the entire system. If the advisor views his or her role with these limitations, the outcome is probably quite predictable: a document or a tax return will be produced. However, if the advisor views his or her role as forging a deeper trust relationship with the stakeholders in the system, what might be possible? Could the trusted advisor then become part of the strategy that helps the system achieve greater outcomes?

I believe that there is a symbiotic relationship between building trust in family businesses and the outcomes that are achievable. If the business-owning families trust the advisor, they are more likely to trust the process, and therefore they are more likely to trust the outcome of the process (see Figure 8.1).

In family business advising, I often refer to the following quote: "People care as much about the justice of the process through which an outcome is produced as they do about the outcome itself."[1] I have found this to be true. In my experience, when a significant action is taken in a family business without a fair process to support the decision, the complaint is more likely to be, "I wish he/she had just consulted me first before hiring this manager," or "If he/she wanted to change strategic direction, he/she should have run it past the other owners," than "The manager is not a good hire for our business," or "I don't like this new strategic direction." The tone of these common complaints is telling us that the process is often not only *equally as important* as the result, but may be *even more important* than the result. I might take the analysis one step further: if the advisor is going to take the lead in establishing a fair process, he or she must have the trust of the family/owner/management groups in order for the process to be deemed "fair" and the outcome to be trusted.

CONGRUITY: LET'S EAT SOME SALT TOGETHER

When I meet with many of my family business clients, the first 15 minutes is often spent talking about each other's businesses, off the clock. We discuss the trends we are seeing in the business community, how the client acquisition process is going, and how new business units are faring in the present economy. I am fascinated by their approach to business and leadership, and I find hearty nuggets of wisdom in each exchange. These conversations help establish that we are business owners together, facing the same struggles and victories that place us in that unique class of entrepreneurs. We wear many hats. We pull all-nighters when needed. We worry about our employees. We leave important meetings to attend our children's or grandchildren's sporting events.

These conversations and the unspoken bond we share as entrepreneurs help to create trust. When I make a legal recommendation to a family business client, the client trusts that I would not lead them astray. I know how busy they are and the family and business demands they face. If I ask them to take the time to focus on a legal issue that impacts their family wealth and business, they trust that it must be an important consideration.

Congruity between the advisor and the client can be established in many other ways than a shared spirit of entrepreneurship. Congruity may surface in a shared understanding of family wealth philosophy, leadership theory, or strategy. For example, Bob is a family business owner whose greatest fear is creating a sense of entitlement in his children. Bob and I have talked about the current research on entitlement and we have exchanged articles with one another on this topic. Bob feels that each child should have some "skin in the game" rather than have the family business gifted to him or her outright. I can assure Bob that he is not alone – that fostering entitlement is one of the primary concerns that other business owners are raising today – and that he has options other than outright gifting of shares to his children. As we walk through the options, Bob can trust that I will be responsive to his goals and will work toward an outcome that accommodates his concerns.

A shared direction does not mean that the advisor and the client need to agree with one another. On the contrary, that would close doors rather than open them. Instead, the notion of congruity refers more to a common awareness than a unity of values – a parity of visioning or a shared plane of understanding. If the client feels that he or she is in a position of congruity with the advisor, the client is more likely to trust that his or her perspective is being taken into account in the process.

VALUE: ARE YOU BRINGING SOMETHING TO THE TABLE THAT THEY DON'T ALREADY KNOW?

In developing trust with family businesses, I am constantly struck by the importance of the advisor bringing value to the relationship through technical expertise. If I am brought into the family business by one owner/family member, I am often tested (consciously or unconsciously) by the other owners/family members on my technical knowledge of taxation, estate planning vehicles, and business structures. During this questioning, I can feel them rationalizing: "She may have been brought in by Joe, but she actually seems to know what she's talking about." This is a great opportunity to build trust. When the advisor can be the bearer of facts, rather than opinions (that may come later), the advisor may have a leg-up in gaining trust in the family business early on. Ultimately, the family may like the advisor, but they are not bringing in the advisor to be buddies. They are opening their family history to the advisor because they know that there are things they need to know and learn in order to progress. As a lawyer, from me they are seeking an analysis of options based on what is important to them, which may, but does not always, include: transfer of wealth, tax-efficiency, promoting the success of the business, asset-protection, self-determination, or multi-generational harmony. Often in client meetings, we use the whiteboard to lay out all of the options for transitioning the family business and list the attributes of each: gift or sale, outright or in trust, immediate transfer or transfer at death; freezes estate for estate tax purposes, helps protect against creditor and divorce claims, provides flexibility and a solid income stream. In doing so, we are able to consider extensively the vehicles that may be used for a transfer of ownership and how each of these may fare against the client's objectives. The client must trust that the advisor has the knowledge base to present the range of options and help evaluate them effectively. By conveying technical expertise in a way that makes sense to the client, the advisor is able to build trust.

STRATEGY: WHERE ARE WE GOING?

I have always believed that the advisor should come prepared with a potential game plan or strategy. This plan may be modified or even completely redesigned as the process continues, but there must be a plan. If the advisor does not have a plan in mind, the whole process may feel aimless and disorganized to the participants. In addition, lack of a strategy limits what the group can accomplish or, worse, caps the exploration of alternative outcomes that may define a "successful" business transition.

For example, one family I advised was convinced that they needed to pass the family business down to the next generation in order to have "success." When they came to me, they had spent years rummaging through family members to find the perfect successor CEO, and had come up short. Together, we created a strategy for evaluating the desires and strengths of the next generation, utilizing other professional advisors who could assist in drawing out the leadership possibilities. It became clear that one son wanted to run the business, but did not have the tools in his toolbox to do so or the consensus of the group. The current owners considered two paths: (1) spreading the ownership among the next generation and giving that son the opportunity to lead, with training and help from supplemental managers; or (2) selling the business. When faced with these choices, the son determined that he would actually rather sell the business, take his share, and start his own business that was uniquely designed around his strengths and interests. The first generation was pleased that their wealth could give this son the chance to fulfill his vision, and the other owners were relieved. Would you call this a success, or a failure? I would call it a success. However, without a strategy in place that might bring forth this outcome, the family might not have had the perspective to evaluate this as a successful solution.

Having a strategy also helps the advisor, who may be occupying the lead role in working with the family business, identify other professional advisors who may be pieces of the puzzle. Making a solid referral to another advisor is a great way to build trust with the family business stakeholders. It tells the family that you are not professing to be the only person who has knowledge and experience that will help them. It also assists in diversifying the perspectives that may lead to a better outcome for the client.

CONNECTION: THE POWER OF THE POSITIVE

> He made an effort to get to know each of the business owners. We all had to make an independent judgment about whether we could work with him. If any one of us had objected, we would not have hired him. He consistently reaches out to each of us to make sure we understand the strategies he is proposing and have a chance to ask questions.
> (A family business owner speaking of his accountant)

In order to build trust, I believe that the family members, owners and managers actually have to enjoy working with the advisor. Do they need to invite the advisor over for dinner on a Friday night or as a guest at family weddings? No, but the advisor must make an effort to have a personal connection with each stakeholder in the system in order to build trust. The result may be a proactive type of trust: "We trust that you are leading us to take action in the right direction"; or, it may be a reactive type of trust: "We trust that you would not guide us in a way that would be harmful to us or our interests." These distinctions can be tricky for the advisor when issues of confidentiality and "who is the client" are raised. However, connections can be formed to create trust with individual stakeholders without breaching confidentiality rules.

Connecting with family business owners may also pave the way for better utilization of the advisor's expertise. I recently had breakfast with a banker, Paul, who regularly advises family businesses. He told me that as a banker, he must overcome the preconceived notion of a banker as stiff, uncooperative, and regulatory-focused. He explained that because owners of a family business are so personally tied to the business – it is their identity and their livelihood – they often view it as a weakness to ask their banker for money. This is even the case if the business is quite healthy and simply needs capital for expansion. In order to gain trust, Paul makes an extra effort to disband the "banker" stereotype and show that he is working earnestly in the best interests of the family and business.

With this personal connection comes the advisor's ability to evaluate the readiness of the family business for certain outcomes of the process. I believe that the advisor must actually feel that a certain outcome is possible if he or she is planning to guide the family business in that direction. If the advisor suggests an annual family retreat, but does not really think that the family is capable of getting organized enough to accomplish that goal, the family will sense this doubt and it will pervade through the process like a wet mop. The advisor has a responsibility to guide the process incrementally toward an outcome that he or she genuinely believes is achievable and beneficial.

Humor should always be a tool in the advisor's tool belt. Many advisors take calculated risks in order to prepare the family, business, or ownership group for personal connection at a meeting. One advisor had an ownership group play a "stepping stone" game in which they had to figure out how to work together to get each member of the group across the room. Another advisor gave each employee in the business a different chocolate bar to illustrate that, while all chocolate is good, there may be nuances about each person's style or preference that must be discovered (this person likes caramel, this person is allergic to peanuts) in order to bring out the strengths of each member of the group. Privately, the advisors were sweating and wondering if the risk would pay off or if the group would just laugh at them. Surprisingly, both results occurred: the risk paid off *and* they got the group laughing. In these two examples, this laughter paved the way to trust with the advisor and among the participants, and each group was able to function positively.

The trust that results from making personal connections with the stakeholders in a family business has another intangible consequence: the advisor may unintentionally inspire the stakeholders to do what I informally refer to as "bring their 'A' game." For example, I once started working with a family business in which the previous advisor was disliked by the family. I got the impression that the previous advisor was a good lawyer who saw himself as a legal expert, but didn't value understanding the needs of the family, business, and ownership groups. The group had not been able to get any traction, there was infighting, and their efforts to work together were collapsing. The family members were ready to give up. Before the group meeting, I talked with each family member and listened to his or her perspective on what was happening within the family and business areas. I also talked with them about their lives and personal goals, and how the family business worked as a propeller toward or a barrier to achieving these goals. There was nothing magical about our conversations, but by the time we met as a group, they seemed ready to work together. We were able to discuss their legal structure and options in a reasonable way. Perhaps this illustrates that if the advisor sets the groundwork for a positive, respectful environment, the family members, managers, and owners may be less likely to try to derail the process. This means that conflict can be dealt with diplomatically rather than explosively.

THE OPPOSITE OF TRUST

I recently participated in a meeting with a family business owner and his son. The topic was how to pass shares of the business down to the next generation. We had spent prior meetings talking about the goals: tax-efficiency, transparency, and deep consideration of all of the available options. I had concocted a detailed gifting and life insurance strategy that seemed to meet all of the goals, and was explaining this strategy when I saw something change in the business owner's eyes. I can recall the exact moment in the meeting when my bucket of trust was depleted and he abruptly terminated the discussion. What happened? How did I lose him? It had been going so well! I realized later that I had heard all of the overt goals, but missed the two most important underlying ones: relevance and simplicity. Many family business advisors theorize that the reason family business owners avoid business succession discussions is a fear of their own mortality. I wonder if it is not a fear of mortality, but a fear of becoming irrelevant. I later understood that my proposed strategy would inadvertently have had the effect of making the business owner irrelevant, which was an unacceptable outcome.

In retrospect, missing the crucial subtext wasn't my only mistake. The other mistake was giving the client the impression that I was attached to one particular outcome. But I thought it was such a brilliant strategy – fitting the pieces together like an intricate and carefully-crafted puzzle. That isn't important. As an advisor, I learned that the best way to create the opposite of trust is to make the client feel that you are vying for a particular result. The goals must be their goals and the result, too, must be of their choosing.

BUILDING TRUST AND FAMILY SOCIAL CAPITAL

An abundance of family social capital can make an advisor's job infinitely smoother. Each of the four trust-building factors described in this article – congruity, value, strategy and connection – seem to flow like water when family social capital is present. If the advisor can identify social capital in the form of shared family values, the advisor can explore how these values might translate in each of the family, business, and ownership domains. If the family brings meaning to the transition of the business by seeking to carry on the founder's legacy, the advisor is able to leverage this family social capital in gathering consensus among multiple generations. If the family demonstrates trust with each other, they are more likely to view an advisor with trustful eyes, as a helper or facilitator rather than an outsider. Ultimately, the existence of family social capital can expand the scope of possible outcomes in the advisory relationship.

Conversely, lack of family social capital for an advisor can be like scraping metal. There is no cushion that family members can draw on when the hard questions arise. When the going gets tough, the family members are more likely to take their marbles and go home. There is no incentive to collaborate or compromise. Identifying the lack of family social capital can either shrink the menu of available outcomes or drive the decision to engage an advisor whose specific role is to help the family begin to build enough social capital that greater outcomes are possible.

The question becomes whether the advisory process itself can promote or diminish family social capital. For example, if it is part of the process for the advisor to gather input from each of the family, business, and ownership groups before a significant decision is made, doesn't family social capital become a self-perpetuating asset? On the other side of the coin, if the advisor works with one group to the exclusion of the others, doesn't the lack of family social capital become a self-fulfilling prophecy? I would suggest that in designing the process, the advisor can influence the presence or absence of family social capital. In the example above in which the family initially experienced infighting and a resistance to working together, a key component of the advisor's role was building up enough trust to unlock the family's social capital. In this example, the process was able to facilitate this result.

CONCLUSION

If only it was easy, and trust was a script we could write out and perform with each family business client! It isn't, and as advisors we are both capped and propelled by our ability to read the situation and respond as we deem appropriate. In my practice, I have observed that congruity, value, strategy, and connection are four factors that help build trust between the advisor and the stakeholders in the family business. Perhaps family businesses are the most remarkable in their uniqueness rather than their sameness. However, in each family business, trust among the advisors, family members, owners, and managers becomes a root that anchors the process, and the participants, together. The presence of family social capital becomes a fuel that helps the system achieve greater outcomes.

NOTE

1.   Chan and Mauborgne (2005, pp. 174–5).

9. Family rituals and communication: the construction of family identity and social capital

Carol J. Bruess

INTRODUCTION TO FAMILY RITUAL: CREATING FAMILY CULTURE AND IDENTITY

The idea of ritual often conjures images of religious or anthropological practices; in early studies, ritual did frequently imply magic, myth, or taboo. However, family ritual as central in constructing family social capital refers to all acts of communication – from the routine family dinner to the celebratory family holiday traditions – which pay homage to something that is sacred, such as a person, relationship, object, or event.[1,2] As "symbolically significant" interactions, rituals become important places where family "business" is indeed accomplished, including the work of keeping in touch, updating each other on daily events, sharing fleeting (or ongoing) emotions, creating and perpetuating family identity, expressing positive or negative regard, touching base, planning, organizing, coordinating schedules, and transmitting family values between generations, among multiple other functions. Family rituals, from the mundane to the celebratory, reflect the dynamic lives of twenty-first-century families. Rituals are particularly important for family members who also share a business. In many ways, family identity is expressed in family communicative and ritual activity. Family identity – those beliefs, values, norms, rules, and expectations shared among members – is also sustained by family rituals.[3,4]

Most relationship scholars in the field of communication agree that maintaining a relationship, the work it takes to keep a relationship going, is the most important work of all.[5] The communicative strategies people use for sustaining long-term relationships – especially those most intimate and complex relationships of family – hinge on daily communication and the joint development of a family relational culture.[6,7,8,9] Families are mini-cultures in which we develop our own language, rules, worldviews, identities, customs, and rituals. Created in and through communication, a family's relationship culture – similar to Sorenson et al.'s notion of a "family point of view" – is a co-constructed and shared perspective.[10] Based on a family's common moral convictions as well as from a jointly-constructed identity and repetitive, symbolically significant experiences (commonly known as family rituals), a shared and strong family culture is a basis for shared dialogue that has meaningful applications in family business.[11]

From the communication discipline comes a perspective on family and symbolic interaction that places meaning construction at the center of study; communication is viewed not merely as a tool used *by* family members to build business, create dialogue, and/or negotiate conflict. Rather, family is formed *in* and *through* the daily, routine, and mundane communication of members. Through a communicative lens, families *are* symbolic systems in which interactions – large and small, celebratory and routine – compose our understanding of self, other, and the world. For members who also share a family business, such compositions have an even greater stake. As one of the single most illustrative and important types of symbolic family interaction, family rituals allow members to examine and reflect on family communication dynamics. Family rituals, for instance, serve as powerful sites of the routine conversation and communication that create our individual and collective relationship identities.[12] In total, family rituals have a host of positive functions and provide many opportunities for building and sustaining family social capital. Let's take a closer look first at some of the meaning-making activities in which rituals are developed, and then explore the way rituals might be used to consciously shape family and family member identity.

MANIFESTATIONS OF FAMILY RITUAL: FAMILY RULES, PATTERNS, IMAGES, AND STORIES

The study of family communication has grown rapidly in the past decade; from multiple disciplinary perspectives, our understanding of both macro- and micro-communicative variables is stronger than ever. From a meaning-making perspective, the building of family capital is similar to the construction of a strong family culture. The complexity of a family system increases the range of possible interpretations within that system. In such a system, family rules, communication patterns, images, stories, and rituals serve as ongoing central communicative acts through which family identity is created and sustained. As communicative enactments, rituals build identity development; they are created in and through

– manifestations of – a family's rules, image of self and members, and stories. In so many ways, "ritual is a genre of communication events."[13] Rituals specifically, and communication more generally, are "perform-ances" of family identity. Let's take a look at how this process works.

Family Rules as Ritual

One of the primary ways that families develop their sense of identity is through shared rules. As shared understandings of what communication means and what is expected behavior in certain situations, rules are central to family functioning and even more so for families sharing a business. All families develop rules for interaction in the family, although family rules are often unstated. Think of some of the rules guiding what you are *not* allowed to talk about in your family. Common taboo topics in families include discussion of family finances or sexual activity. Where and when did you learn such rules? Most of us learn these rules over time through observation of other family members or because we actually broke the rule. Not all rules are implicit and learned only through experience or observation; some rules in the family are explicit rules: "Do not talk back to your mother!"

All families, regardless of the number of explicit or implicit rules, are rule-governed systems; members interact with each other in an organized, repetitive fashion. Over time, such repetition creates the communication patterns that steer family life. Often, we find it difficult to recognize the patterns of our own families because we take them for granted and view them as normal. As you uncover rules, you start to see communication patterns more clearly.

Communication rules in families who share a business are vital because they provide necessary boundary management in the family, aid in the development of relationships among members, and contribute to a sense of family satisfaction. Typically, communication rules come in three forms: What can be talked about? How can it be talked about? To whom can it be talked about? As Galvin et al. explain, three communication rules provide a framework for unearthing the communication rules in any family system.[14] For instance, can you talk about money, death, sex, poli-tics, religion, and drug use in your family? Do you have rules about those topics that can be discussed face-to-face and those that are okay to discuss via e-mail or text message? Can you use vulgar language, only technical terms, or slang when talking about any of these topics? Are you allowed to talk to only certain people in your family about specific topics? As you think about the communication rules in your family and family busi-ness, consider when and how the rules are enforced and in what context.

Examine how the creation of and response to these rules are actually communicative acts, or forms of ritual.

Communication Patterns and Behaviors as Ritual

Greater social capital – in the form of happiness, success, and trust – is a topic of much interest to researchers and therapists who study a variety of relationships. As someone who reads voraciously and studies the communication patterns – think "ritual" – of many types of intimate relationships, I believe knowledge about the communication characteristics of happy, long-lasting couples is particularly useful to our discussion of family social capital. Why? Because decades of research all point to one very similar conclusion: the primary predictor of family and marital satisfaction is the communication between members of those relationships. If you want a happy family, you have to consider – on a micro-level – communication patterns. And while research on family communication patterns is abundant, the scientific findings on marital satisfaction and communication from one of the largest research teams in the world (Gottman et al.) [15,16,17,18,19,20,21] are groundbreaking, extensive, and reliable.

Gottman, a social psychologist and head of the Gottman Institute at the University of Washington, has identified the communication behaviors most destructive in relationships.[22,23,24,25,26,27,28] Conducted with thousands of couples over four decades, Gottman's research represents a science of marital communication unmatched by any other. In fact, Gottman and his research team have been able to predict, with over 90 percent accuracy, which marriages are headed for divorce. Evidence from his studies suggests that if certain negative communication patterns are not reversed, eventually they will – in a majority of cases – lead to the end of a relationship. The key is in how members of relationships handle their conflicts and incompatibilities.

What can his findings tell us about improving family social capital? I believe quite a bit. His findings are practical and applicable not only to the dyad, but to all human interaction, particularly that of close families. For instance, after analyzing tens of thousands of marital interactions in their data base, Gottman and his research team have found that a simple ratio of positive to negative behaviors is one of the key differences between those relationships that survive (enjoy happiness) and those that do not. Happy couples were those that maintained a five to one ratio of positive to negative moments in their relationship. It didn't matter if couples fought a lot or very little, or had great passion or very little; what did matter was the overall *balance* (5 to 1) of positive to negative interactions. This seems like a meaningful concept as we consider social capital.

The second striking conclusion of Gottman's research, and which also has easy application to family communication choices, is that all forms of negativity are not equal. Gottman and his team found that certain negative communication behaviors are more toxic than others and should, as he says, be "outlawed" from our relationships. These five particularly corrosive behaviors work like a cancer in our interactions, destroying the relationships and the goodwill between its members. They are: (1) criticism: evaluating and judging the other person in an interaction; (2) defensiveness: responding in an oppositional manner that does not acknowledge the other person's ideas or opinions; (3) contempt: the act of despising or communicating a lack of respect for another person (Gottman suggests that a simple non-verbal behavior such as the "roll of the eyes" can communicate contempt in a relationship); (4) stonewalling: removing oneself physically or emotionally from an interaction, like putting up a stonewall (eighty-five percent of stonewallers in Gottman's research were male); and (5) belligerence: acting in a hostile or combative manner, as if looking for a fight.

Gottman cautions us to recognize the often subtle differences between these five behaviors and other forms of negativity, such as anger and disagreement. Anger, for instance, is perfectly fine in a relationship as long as it is not expressed with insult or criticism. He also says that all people engage in these behaviors from time to time, but we should be aware of their destructive nature when they begin to monopolize interactions between members of a relationship. In so many ways, learning which behaviors foster goodwill and happiness is learning to enhance our family's social capital.

Family Image as Ritual

Families also develop a shared identity, and greater social capital, by creating a shared image. Metaphorically, a family image is an understood or created likeness; it reflects what the family is like, what is expected in the family, how important family is, patterns of communication among members, and between members and the outside world. Family images and metaphors construct the reality of family members. Frequently, a family image or metaphor is shared among members, although sometimes each member's image is different from the rest. In family business, family members must have an opportunity to share their images with one another, reflecting thoughtfully on how each member's metaphor might instruct others about how the family and business function and interact.

What image do you have of your family? Do you see your family as a football team, a concert band, characters in a comedy skit, waves in an ocean, or the components of a salad? Is your image reflected in the mission statement or daily practices of your business? Below are excerpts of two family images written by students in an undergraduate family communication course, and while the students were not necessarily members of a family business, their viewpoints are instructive. As you read, think about what these writers convey about the identities and cultures of their families and their communication patterns. Then consider the practical idea of asking members of your own family "team" or "orchestra" or "band" to share their images, listening attentively to what you can each learn about the strengths and weaknesses of your family's identity heard in and through members' verbal renderings of "family."

Family as a team

> I feel my family is like the USA Olympic Team because we all have our individual strengths that we are encouraged to use, yet we all work together as a team for one common goal: to strengthen our family ties. Like in the Olympics, we each strive to be the best that we can regarding school, work, and our personal lives (like our own athletic events). But if someone needs help, comfort, support, or just a hug, we all come together as one team. When it's all said and done, there will be no medals conferred, but something much stronger that will last a lifetime.

My family: a fruit salad

> To me, my family is like a fruit salad. My father is like a banana; he is tough on the outside but soft on the inside. He is a stern enforcer with a temper while other times he is a quiet observer. On the interior, he is a deeply emotional man who feels things intensely and who has a great respect and love for his family. My mother is like a strawberry. She is bright, beautiful, and colorful, with a wonderful appreciation for life. She is a favorite among her friends and is the one that everyone gravitates toward. My sister is also hard on the outside but very deep in the inside. I would compare her to a watermelon. She is tough and strong, a natural athlete. She is quiet and sometimes seems shy. On the inside she is full of seeds of information and intelligence. She has a beautiful exterior but her true beauty lies within. I think that I am like an orange. I wear my emotions on my sleeve and contain a lot of "juice." I am colorful and bright but can sometimes be a bit sour when I am moody. I have many sections inside of myself. All together we mix to form a beautiful, colorful mixture of different tastes and textures, but complement each other and work well together.

The image a family has of itself is an important reflection of that family's relationship culture and shared sense of identity. Often, alliances are formed in the family along the lines of shared images. The daughter who sees her father as "tough as nails" might align with her mother, who also views dad as "strict as a warden." The father, who sees his family as a place to be "run like a business" where order is a priority and rules are meant to be followed, might align himself with the son who expresses respect for the rules and guidelines of the family, and enjoys how the family "runs like a well-oiled machine."

Family Stories as Ritual

A cornerstone of family communication research is found in the literature on family stories and storytelling. As a means for creating family identity and sharing meaning, stories reveal and build family capital. As ritual activities in families, they shape our families in ways often unnoticed until a primary storyteller is gone or until decades after the event inspiring the story has passed. Stone was among the first to examine family stories and their function for members.[29] Stories define rules, teach members about the idea of family, identify family values, provide a sense of history, tell us what is expected of us as family members, and construct identity. They also provide a chance to remember, to socialize new members, and to connect members over generations. Because a story is not "right" or "wrong," its lessons are often embedded within the plot or characters, allowing members to interpret and apply them to current or future decisions.

Family stories are also memorable in ways that other forms of communication are not, such as sharing information through instructions, mandates, or reports. In many family businesses, for instance, the story – or saga – of the founding members is memorable and serves as a powerful force to guide members toward mindful and moral decision-making. Family stories are important in that members develop a sense not only of family, but of self that comes from what the family believes and values.

CHANGING YOUR FAMILY RITUALS TOWARD (RE)CONSTRUCTING YOUR FAMILY IDENTITY

Without ritual interaction, our families would lack many intricate, delicate, multi-vocal, multi-layered, sometimes painful but always powerful interactions, negotiations, and creations of identity. Rituals are pivotal yet often mundane acts of family identity, unveiling themselves through cues both big and small, each a kind of "moral commentary about what is valued, or an expressive hope for what could be."[30] Knowingly or not, families use rituals to create and recreate family identity, consciously and unconsciously relying on them through both the spectacular and the banal events of every family's life. But can we intentionally change our rituals to enhance, alter, and/or recreate our family's identity? Yes, yes, and yes. However, such work – because it is relational work – is often emotional and not immediately or clearly successful; it can also cause upheaval as the family system tries to adjust and respond to change. Let's explore why and how you might consider both the practical and theoretical work of family identity and ritual (re)creations.

Fiese et al. point to family rituals as conveying messages about the culture of a group.[31] In their classic study of family rituals, Bossard and Boll tell of the many ways families use family rituals to resolve the "emotional business" of members.[32] Bruess and Pearson point out the way rituals develop, maintain, and enhance the daily lives of married couples and adult friends.[33,34] Rituals have so many positive functions in families that books have (literally) been written on the topic (e.g., most recently Fiese).[35] Here, let's review those findings that are most useful toward our goal of creating, sustaining, and transforming family identity in the context of family business. Specifically, how do we replace negative rituals with positive ones; change rituals that prioritize business over family; restructure family communication to change the identity and roles of family members; challenge and change family images, rules, and norms; and change communication patterns related to alcohol addiction?

Replacing Negative Rituals with Positive Rituals

Clearly, rituals play an essential role in the positive development of individuals and families.[36,37] Especially in the early years of marriage, for example, repetitive symbolic actions establish and affirm commitment between partners[38] and rituals help maintain most types of relationships over time.[39,40,41,42] In fact, a lack of patterned interactions might hint at relational dissatisfaction.[43] Although ritual is recognized in research as an overwhelmingly positive act, rituals can also come to feel like obligations, reflect outdated tradition, feel empty or uncomfortable, and/or represent negative patterns of interaction not welcome by all members. Let's look at the story of one business owner, a case from an actual family business, revealing how the father in the firm changed a negative pattern of interaction into a positive ritual with his son, with whom he hoped to share the business some day (note: all names and identifying information have been changed to protect the identity of those illustrated):

> John is a family business owner who hoped his son Calvin would join him in the business. However, John had a tendency to consistently criticize and "nitpick" his son's performance, especially on the job. No matter how hard he tried, Cal's performance was never good enough. John believed his criti-

cism was an effective way to improve his son's performance. John's pattern of interaction with his son was deeply engrained; to him, his criticism seemed "normal," and he had no idea of its impact. Over time, Cal's attitude toward his father hardened, and he did not want to continue the relationship. Not until Cal threatened to leave did John become aware of what he was doing. John got feedback from his wife and then asked a trusted manager to supervise his son, providing a more objective assessment of his son's performance. In addition to changing his pattern of criticism, John replaced his old ways with a new and more positive ritual: catching his son doing something right and letting him know about it.

Because rituals – especially those reflecting our patterns of interaction – are often tightly woven into the fabric of our daily lives, we often don't recognize when and how they are perceived by others. A negative ritual can often open the door – once recognized – for a more positive and productive communicative act. As John did, begin by seeking and being open to feedback about your habits and patterns. Then make small but meaningful changes. You'll likely be pleasantly surprised by the significant results.

Changing Rituals that Prioritize Business Over Family

In families specifically, rituals help create intergenerational bonds and preserve a sense of meaningfulness.[44] They convey family values, attitudes, and beliefs,[45] are related to family strength,[46] provide members with a sense of belonging,[47] bond and promote closeness,[48] help families maintain and perpetuate a paradigm or shared belief system,[49] create and maintain family cohesion,[50] and afford means for maintaining family contact.[51] In their review of over 50 years of family ritual research, Fiese et al.[52] conclude that in the enactment of rituals "[t]here is an affective commitment that leaves the individual feeling that the activity has felt rightness and provides a sense of belonging." As in the lesson above – replacing a negative ritual with a positive one – when rituals no longer "celebrate common family identity" in a way that all family members wish,[53] they should be examined, changed, or abandoned. Here's an instructive example:

> Joanne, the family matriarch, began to notice that holiday gatherings were filled with discussions about the business. She became increasingly concerned that the business was taking precedent and being viewed as "more important" than the family. More and more, she worried that establishing congenial family relationships was no longer a priority. Finally, she decided to take a stand and create a new rule: No discussion about business at family holiday gatherings! The focus of holiday gatherings would be on fun and enjoying the relationships among members, not discussing business successes, challenges, and opportunities. Period.

Joanne's actions reflect a key tenet of rituals: they are created by and are reflections of rules. Changing a rule can change a ritual and/or provide means for a new one to take its place. If the rituals in your family tend to prioritize business over relationships, take a stand. Make a change. Create a new rule (or two). Rules, theoretically, are guides for our actions; make sure your new rules (rituals) are clear and compelling enough to follow.

Restructuring Family Communication Toward Changing Family Identity and Roles

Classic ritual researchers Bossard and Boll[54] made the poignant suggestion that ritual represents the essence of a family's culture. As we've been seeing time and again in this chapter, most researchers believe rituals are not only communicative enactments themselves, but create and sustain the identities, communication patterns, and roles in families. When such patterns and/or roles become troublesome and/or no longer serve positive functions for some or many members, change is not only desirable, but necessary if the family business is to succeed. How does a family change long-held and deeply-engrained patterns and approaches? Often, it takes the assistance of a professional consultant or therapist. And commitment. And time. And a willingness to change. But a combination of some or all of the above can bring about dramatic improvements in family relationships and, as a result, the family business. Take a look at the story of how one family took the step to make such a shift:

> Frank and Brenda owned a large family farm and hoped their children would want to continue working in the family business, raising their own children on the farm. However, Frank and Brenda's children became discontented as adults when the communication patterns they experienced as kids did not appropriately change as they matured. The parents shared information only between themselves, made most decisions, and managed the farm without meaningful input from their adult children. Finally, many of the children were upset enough to either leave the business altogether or state a desire to leave. Frank and Brenda realized they needed some external input and sought help from a family business consultant. The consultant helped the family restructure their ways of interacting and their decision-making patterns. She had the family meet and for the first time engage in open discussion as equals about farm-related issues. As expected, at first the children aired their frustrations. Frank and Brenda felt emotionally torn apart by such open communication; the norms, rules, and roles they had known for so long were radically changing right before their eyes. Over time, they all settled into a new pattern of regular meetings in which the adult children had a role, and everyone participated in discussions. The family also added new rituals of recreation for all members to enjoy together. Children who had left the business came back. All members began to feel like active participants. In the end, the family's identity – as a result of

changes in communication patterns, norms, and roles – was dramatically and positively transformed.

Challenging and Changing Family Images, Rules and Norms

Rituals hold symbolic significance, paying homage to relationship histories, norms, images, and rules of interaction. In other words, rituals shape our families and give us something to hold on to. In honoring something of historical value, rituals can also reveal a "backstage" of family life.[55] According to scholars who take a dialectical approach (e.g., Baxter),[56] we must be attentive to the interplay of different, often contradictory, voices in every ritual. From a dialectical theoretical perspective, we should consider how social reality – the rules, norms, images, and expectations of our family members – are produced and reproduced in ritual.[57] The following story of one woman in a family business illustrates this idea:

> Mia had become increasingly insulted that she was excluded from meetings regarding the family business while her brothers were included. The established image in the family was that a woman's role was in the family, not business. But she was determined. She had the education, skills, and aptitude for management. She appealed to her father for opportunity. Not until he attended family business seminars and learned that other family business owners had daughters who made positive contributions to the business did he relent. When he let his daughter participate, managers were impressed by her performance and participation. This change resulted in women being invited to other meetings that had traditionally been reserved for men in the family business.

Rituals are "expressive of social relations,"[58] depicting not only the norms of family life and thus the images families create of themselves, but cultural norms for members as well. Although we each – as family business members and individuals in families – are situated within a larger cultural system, we can work to change those roles and images in our own family systems by challenging the assumptions by which they are created and sustained.

Using Ritual and Communication to Protect Family from Alcoholism

As we have seen, rituals are quite powerful in the positive impact they can have on family strength, individual and family identity development, and the health and well-being of family and members.[59] One important finding – supported by the work of many other researchers interested in substance abuse and family systems – points to the role of rituals in reducing the generational recurrence of alcoholism.[60,61] For families who have experienced or are currently experiencing alcoholism, it is probably not a surprise that any illness, especially alcoholism, affects families – and their special occasions – in powerful ways.[62] Bennett and colleagues found that in families where rituals were sustained and kept intact (e.g., the family dinnertime ritual and other similar patterned daily interactions), children were less likely to continue the alcoholic tendencies in their own adult lives. Rituals act as buffers, giving members a sense of predictability and stability. They organize family life. They also provide opportunities for support from other family members to confront – instead of enabling – the alcoholic's ability to control or dominate interactions and behaviors.

According to Black,[63] families of alcoholics often develop a 'Don't Talk' rule. They develop a rule – often implicitly – to ignore and not discuss the drinking or any of the behaviors that result. The Don't Talk rule is one rather powerful way members rationalize the alcoholic's communication and interactions. Below is an illustration of how alcoholism can, over time and with lasting impact, negatively affect family relationships and thus the family business. As you will see in this case, even though the communication and erratic behaviors of the alcoholic member are not discussed, they have created negative perceptions that affect the decisions of family members.

Carl was a successful owner and vice-president of a bank and prominent in his community. Carl's rituals dramatically influenced family communication patterns. They also restricted his children's interest in following his footsteps as a third-generation bank owner and leader. Carl felt much pressure in his job and was frustrated by some of his co-workers. Driving home from work, he reached for a bottle of whiskey to drown his worries. When he got home, he said very little to his family. Instead, he stared at the floor. When frustration and anger built, he occasionally exploded at family members, at the smallest provocation. After dinner, he often drove off to spend time with drinking buddies. Within a year of his retirement, he casually mentioned to a son, Robert, the option of becoming an owner and working in the bank. This was the first time Carl had mentioned such an opportunity, and Robert was quite surprised. Robert had already established a successful career in another community. But the primary issue that determined his response was his father's erratic communication. In part, Robert had moved to distance himself from his father. His answer was no.

CONCLUSION

What do we learn here? First, families are constructions of our own making, requiring a mindful, knowledge-driven approach to their maintenance and success. Second, family rituals are commonly underestimated and overlooked; as decades of research supports, family rituals are some of the most powerful sites of rich and meaningful family interaction, and are primary contributors to family identity. Third, building a strong family culture is essential, and we are wise to be deliberate about the process, giving attention to language development, rule structures, our daily patterns of negativity and positivity, and to the stories that sustain our legacies and satisfy our needs to create identity as part of a family group. For all family members – especially those working together in business – conscious attention to making and maintaining a strong family is difficult and ceaseless, yet fruitful and highly satisfying work. From a communicative perspective, making smart choices toward effective and constructive – not mindless and destructive – communication is essential to success and satisfaction. I hope you learned a bit more about the former and will apply these lessons in your own family and business. Working toward an improved communication climate in our families will, no doubt, provide a high return on our investment. As Bossard and Boll (1950) long ago suggested: Just as those religions with the most elaborate and pervasive rituals best retain the allegiance of their members, so families that do things together prove to be the most stable ones.[64]

NOTES

1. Bruess and Pearson (2002).
2. Goffman (1967).
3. Fiese (2006).
4. Fiese et al. (2002).
5. Stafford and Canary (1991).
6. Baxter (1987).
7. Baxter and Clark (1996).
8. Orbe and Bruess (2005).
9. Wood (1982).
10. Sorenson et al. (2009).
11. Ibid.
12. Bruess and Hoefs (2006).
13. Baxter and Braithwaite (2006, p. 260).
14. Galvin et al. (2004).
15. Driver and Gottman (2004).
16. Gottman and DeClaire (2001).
17. Gottman and Driver (2005).
18. Gottman and Gottman (2007).
19. Gottman et al. (2006).
20. Gottman and Silver (1999).
21. Shapiro and Gottman (2005).
22. Driver and Gottman (2004).
23. Gottman and DeClaire (2001).
24. Gottman and Driver (2005).
25. Gottman and Gottman (2007).
26. Gottman et al. (2006).
27. Gottman and Silver (1999).

28.   Shapiro and Gottman (2005).
29.   Stone (2000).
30.   Baxter and Braithwaite (2006, p. 261).
31.   Fiese et al. (2002).
32.   Bossard and Boll (1950).
33.   Bruess and Pearson (1997).
34.   Bruess and Pearson (2002).
35.   Fiese (2006).
36.   Baxter and Braithwaite (2006).
37.   Fiese et al. (2002).
38.   Weigel (2003).
39.   Bruess and Pearson (1997).
40.   Bruess and Pearson (2002).
41.   Fiese et al. (2002).
42.   Homer et al. (2007).
43.   Aylor and Dainton (2004).
44.   Schvaneveldt and Lee (1983).
45.   Bossard and Boll (1950).
46.   Meredith et al. (1989).
47.   Wolin et al. (1980).
48.   Meredith (1985).
49.   Reiss (1982).
50.   Wolin and Bennett (1984).
51.   Meredith (1985).
52.   Fiese et al. (2002, p. 382).
53.   Baxter et al. (2009).
54.   Bossard and Boll (1950).
55.   Jorgenson and Bochner (2004).
56.   Baxter (2004).
57.   Baxter and Braithwaite (2006).
58.   Ibid., p. 261.
59.   Compan et al. (2002).
60.   Wolin et al. (1980).
61.   Wolin and Bennett (1984).
62.   Bennett et al. (1987).
63.   Black (2000).
64.   Bossard and Boll (1950a; foreword).

10. Creating family and business social capital: a co-investigation with a daughter and granddaughter

Ritch L. Sorenson in collaboration with an anonymous daughter* and granddaughter**

What gives family businesses an advantage, or a disadvantage, over non-family businesses? While all businesses have financial and human capital, family businesses are unique because they have family social capital.[1] Family social capital is defined as the social relationships in a family that help define social relationships within the business and attract resources from other family members. In this paper, we examine how family social capital is developed and influences the business.

Historically, community developers focused on solving multiple individual social issues to develop community progress. Yet, about 20 years ago, they found that by identifying individuals with control of assets and capabilities in the community, and by developing working relationships among them, they promoted projects for the common good and enhanced community progress.[2] Simultaneously, literature emerged demonstrating how social relationships, also known as social capital, enable community action.[3]

The primary components of social capital are communication, common identity, and collective trust.[4] The foundational component of social capital is *communication*. Communication creates relationships, which are referred to as ties in the social capital literature. Two types of relationships that can be formed are *bridging*, defined as distant ties, and *bonding*, defined as close emotional ties. Varying degrees of common identity and collective trust are developed over time as individuals communicate, which can lead to confidence about working together.

In this paper, we present an in-depth test case analysis assessing whether, and in what form, components of social capital exist in the courting relationship of a young couple that would later own a business. Furthermore, we also examine if and how the components of family social capital influence social capital in the business, particularly the business identity.

This study uses three sources of information obtained from a business family. The first source is approximately 380 letters written between a couple during their courting years. Family and business names have been changed to protect the family's privacy.[5] The couple will be referred to as George and Sandra Johnson. To further protect the privacy of her grandparents, the granddaughter reviewed letters to determine whether and in what form there was evidence of the development of social capital.

The granddaughter and I worked as co-investigators not only because I was not privy to all the private family documents, but also because she was interested in the topic of social capital in her family. I mentored the granddaughter in helping her understand the concepts associated with family social capital. Thus, her review of letters was instrumental in identifying evidence of the social capital element.

The second source is a family history written about the family and the family business, which I was allowed to read. The history was compiled and written by a historian who had access to family and business records, and who conducted interviews with family members, business associates, and others who were familiar with the family. This historical source was examined for evidence of the development of social capital in the family and in the business. The third source is reflections of George and Sandra's oldest daughter about her parents after the business was started.

FAMILY SOCIAL CAPITAL

Family social capital begins with a bonding relationship.[6] For example, when a couple marries and has children, bonds form. Relational bonds are characterized by a strong, emotional commitment. Family social capital is the extent to which family social relationships enable and encourage family members to contribute their resources and capabilities for the general good of the family. When family relationships are positive, they are considered to be capital because they are a resource or asset that can be employed for a variety of purposes, including in business and the larger community.[7]

However, family relationships can also be a social liability. This happens when family relationships interfere with the ability of the family to combine their efforts and work together.[8] In some cases, much of a family's emotional energy, time, and financial resources are used to defeat or somehow punish relatives. For example, family member resources may be consumed in lawsuits against one another. Thus, family relationships can exist along a continuum from high liability to high capital. When family sentiments and activities are primarily negative, relationships are a liability. When family feeling and activities are primarily positive, relationships provide capital. This paper will focus on the elements of family social capital that promote high levels of trust, strong relational bonds, and positive relationships.

BRIEF FAMILY AND BUSINESS HISTORY

George and Sandra's relationship began in the latter part of the 1940s while George was in college, and Sandra, who had completed a college degree, worked full-time. They were from the same city and had similar backgrounds including being members of the Catholic Church. While courting, they lived in separate communities. The distance between communities was about a day's drive by automobile. Because long-distance calls were expensive, they wrote letters to stay in touch.

After George graduated, he and Sandra started their own business because they did not like the unethical practices of George's early employers. For the first couple of years, Sandra ran the business office out of their home while George established his first manufacturing facility. As the business grew, the office was moved to the manufacturing facility, but George and Sandra continued to have some business meetings and many business social events in their home. After the fledgling business was established, consistent with gender roles of the times, Sandra became a stay-at-home mom and was not involved in the day-to-day business activities. While George continued to develop the business, Sandra transitioned to full-time care of their seven children.

FAMILY MEMBER CAPABILITIES AND ASSETS

Similar to the community movement, families who have social capital build relationships that can access the capabilities and assets of family members to promote the success of a family firm.[9] Both George and Sandra brought many assets and capabilities to their relationship. They completed college and had a strong work ethic. George was very practical in planning for future financial stability. He often talked about his future vision of developing a successful manufacturing facility. Sandra was a caretaker, honing her skills for future maintenance of husband and children.

Given their positive relationship and desire to help one another succeed, George and Sandra were capable of doing much more together than they would have as individuals. For example, Sandra used her networking skills and understanding of people to introduce George to manufacturing and engineering contacts of which she had become aware through relationships established in college. Sandra was a networker and was gifted at building relationships. When they were courting, Sandra wrote to George, "Glenn [Jensen] is an architect and now is out of the business of building and selling homes – he's a smart man. Has a degree in civil eng. from the U. – you should meet him."

George studied engineering and business while in college. That combined with experience in small entrepreneurial ventures while he was in high school led to aspirations to start his own manufacturing facility. George found a willing listener in Sandra when he described the potential for a manufacturing business. Sandra encouraged George to set goals and to achieve success in college. Both George and Sandra were willing to explore starting a new business, one that was consistent with their moral beliefs and values. Both were willing to do what it took to make the firm succeed. For example, in the early years when George was developing manufacturing concepts and processes, they ran their fledgling business out of their home, and Sandra managed office operations. George often worked through the night, reviewing plans and preparing bids for manufacturing services.

George and Sandra clearly brought many capabilities and assets to their marriage. But just as important, they established a strong and productive relationship in the years before marriage that enabled them to work together and complement one another's strengths for both family and business. Below, primarily from letters and the family history, we see glimpses of how George and Sandra's relationship was formed to enable their combined success.

ELEMENTS OF FAMILY SOCIAL CAPITAL

Basic elements of family social capital include communication, common identity, and collective trust. We discuss each one of these elements and illustrate how they were developed in the lives of George and Sandra. As will become evident, the nature of George and Sandra's communication established a strong bond.

Communication

Communication is the basic building block of social capital. Without establishing communication channels, social capital cannot be established. However, as will be described below, the nature of the communication also makes a difference in establishing relationships.

Communication in the family

As the granddaughter examined the letters, much of what she found in her grandparents' communication was what one would expect in relation to social capital: communication frequency, information sharing, and transparency. In addition, the granddaughter discovered that consistently expressing positive feelings and affection, recalling memories, and acting as a supportive sounding board contributed to strong relational bonds.

Communication frequency Communication between George and Sandra was very frequent during their entire relationship, including their courting. They exchanged as many as five letters a week. Sometimes a day would go by without a letter and then one would arrive the next day. They also exchanged occasional phone calls. They encouraged communication by describing how grateful they were for letters and how they missed it when letters did not come. They also visited in person as often as time and money would permit.

Later, when they were married, they established a ritual of discussing the events of the day around evening dinner. When the children were old enough, they joined in on the conversation. Typically, each family member described the day's events. These conversations enabled family members to stay informed about and involved in one another's lives. Importantly, these also allowed George to keep abreast of home life and for Sandra to keep up with the business.

Information sharing The granddaughter notes that a pattern emerged as George and Sandra became more comfortable in their communication. The majority of letters began by voicing affection, expressing longing for the other, and recalling shared experiences. They also shared everyday occurrences; he talked about driving his car and what he ate for dinner, while she described going to mass and perfecting her latest recipe. They spared no details; college classes, work, and the activities of their family and friends were all discussed.

This information sharing helped them see and understand the other's world and to participate in one another's lives. In time, when one brought up an issue, the other quickly understood and could converse about it in an informed and meaningful way. The pattern of sharing information continued later in their marriage each night around the dinner table and in other conversations. When the children were older, George and Sandra conversed over gin and tonic while the kids put dinner on the table. Information exchange provided the foundation for involvement in both the family and the business.

Transparency   George and Sandra openly expressed thoughts and feelings on a range of subjects. Sandra expressed her longing to be with George and her aspirations to have and care for a family. She also revealed detail about everyday activities and how she felt about them. George was not shy in revealing his apprehensions and insecurities about the future, and his occasional struggle with grades. He also expressed his aspirations, once saying, "Another thing I'm learning is to look at the present more than at the future . . . at being an engineer at all before [starting a company] . . . at doing something small right away rather than dreaming about something big in the future." George openly expressed his misgivings about teaching an engineering course to older students while he was still enrolled as an engineering student himself.

Their transparency continued into their marriage. When either had concerns or thoughts about either the family or the business, they were expressed. Many conversations occurred over the years. Her oldest daughter indicates that Sandra was a willing and helpful listener. These kinds of open interactions strengthened trust between George and Sandra.

Communicating positive regard   George and Sandra expressed frequent blissful feelings about one another in most letters. The granddaughter notes that letters were almost always positive and expressed "pure and steadfast affection." George usually addressed his letters to "My Darling Sandie" or "My Wonderful Darling." He would continue with saying, "All alone again and missing you so already. I know I'll never be satisfied Honey, until we're together always." In a similar fashion, Sandra expressed, "Darling, I love u so – it is always the first and last thing I would be telling you if you were here, so I should tell you so everyday." Such expressions established a powerful emotional bond.

The positive and affectionate nature of George and Sandra's communication helped establish a strong emotional bond. Research indicates that the most robust marriages are those in which the frequency of positive to negative comments is four or five to one.[10] During their courting, one would expect affectionate communication. However, George used the affectionate name of "Sandie" and other loving expressions, such as "Sweetheart," throughout their marriage. Similarly, Sandra used the title, "Georgie Boy" and "Honey."

Recalling memories   They not only expressed affection, but George and Sandra relived memories of their time together, which reignited warm feelings. For example, George wrote in a letter, "Honey, remember last weekend?!! It sure makes a difference when we have a lot of time to do nothing but enjoy each other. And, my Darling, how I enjoyed you." He also expressed, "Remembering last weekend . . . about this time we had just arrived home . . . and how much we enjoyed it. Honey, I love you and it keeps getting deeper and deeper."

Throughout their marriage, George and Sandra kept their memories alive. As noted earlier, they hired a historian to write a history of the family and the business for their children and grandchildren. At family gatherings, they enjoyed reliving memories. One of the prominent features of a recent anniversary celebration was sharing memories by the family members. Forgotten memories and stories were recalled. For example, George reminisced that they courted for two-and-a-half years so they could pay off college debt before they got married.

Supportive sounding board According to the granddaughter, the progression of communication made it apparent that George and Sandra developed not only a way to keep in touch, but a way to act as a supportive sounding board for each other. For example George, after learning of Sandra's anxiety about an upcoming talk, reassures her, "Tonight was the night of your talk. Hope you don't get as anxious as I always do when I give a speech. But I know you won't have any trouble with it." Sandra, after reading of George's successes early one week, offers both validation and support. "I hope the rest of the week will be just as successful for you – in school, and in happiness – that is, in not missing me too much, in financial success, and in your general welfare!"

One of their children noted that throughout their married lives George relied on Sandra as a sounding board regarding business personnel matters, and that Sandra's insights and judgments were extremely acute. She had a gift for evaluating people. George took Sandra to dinner with prospective employees. On the way home, he sought Sandra's opinion about hiring the person. George also valued Sandra's perspective and guidance in executing promotions.

Communication in the business
George developed some communication processes within the business that paralleled communication at home. At home, the family met every evening to talk around the dinner table. During the formative years at work, George gathered all the employees together, no matter their position, to have brown bag lunches together. Brown bags gave way to a communal kitchen in which employees took turns preparing meals for one another. The family history indicates that one employee indicated that communication during lunch was more important than the meal; it made them all feel very close. That and other early practices established cultural norms and values that enabled lawyers, engineers, managers, and other

employees to talk with one another, even when the company became very large.

In addition, George found direct ways to express his positive regard for employees. At Christmas, he personally handed out hams to them. In the early years of the business, George and Sandra hosted an annual Christmas party at their house. In the summer, Sandra was in charge of a company picnic for all employees and their families. After the completion of major manufacturing projects, parties were held with employees to celebrate. These events enabled George and Sandra to communicate with all their employees and to get to know their spouses and children. Thus, the business culture became one in which employees could communicate in a personal and informal way, as well as across functions.

Common Identity

When individuals develop a "we," a common identity is formed based on common beliefs. The common moral beliefs, values, and norms of the family become a comparative frame of reference. This common identity helps "we" know how to relate to "them" – other individuals and groups. Over time, the nature of *shared* moral beliefs, values, and norms becomes clarified. When encountering new circumstances, individuals consult with one another to decide how "we" should interpret the situation and respond, so the response is consistent with their common identity. A common identity promotes cooperation and ease of information exchange because "our" common point of view can be taken for granted.

Common identity in the family
Consistent with social capital literature, common moral beliefs, values, norms, and expectations emerged over time evidenced by George and Sandra's communication.

Moral beliefs and values   According to the granddaughter, George and Sandra's most important moral beliefs and values centered on their faith and family. Building a foundation on religious beliefs was relatively easy. Both Sandra and George were Catholics and they both cherished Catholic values. They wrote about faith being a part of their lives, their relationship, and their future lives together. "I guess the good Lord knows best," George wrote. "In fact, I believe he kinda designed us for each other – and we're a perfect match (as perfect as it's possible for humans to be matched)." Both Sandra and George fully believed their marriage would last forever and were anxious to begin their wedded life together.

Reflecting a prominent Catholic value, George and Sandra planned for a large family. George heard a speaker talk about Catholic parenthood. In telling Sandra about the speech, he stated, "His main point was the pressure brought on young couples not to have children because of financial reasons. And he was definitely in favor of large families. And I agree with him." George and Sandra agreed to have a large family, regardless of financial circumstances.

As noted earlier, George became earnest about starting a business when he did not like the unethical practices of two different employers with whom he worked after graduating from engineering school. Sandra was receptive when George proposed they start their own manufacturing facility founded on principles of honesty and integrity, ethics and morality, and rewards for hard work. Integrity was their core value. They never did something that did not pass the integrity test. Sandra was a consistent sounding board, helping him instill their values and principles in the business.

Catholic values were a prominent part of their family life. Priests were often guests in their home. They attended mass regularly and visited sacred Catholic sites in the United States and Europe. The Catholic value of contributing to the common good influenced their approach to business. They contributed a percentage of their earnings to charitable causes and encouraged their employees and family members to engage in community outreach.

Norms and expectations   Many times, the way George and Sandra broached new norms while they were courting was by asking questions that suggested a norm. Frequently, Sandra figured out George's schedule and suggested frequency of visits while he was away at college. After he became a teaching assistant at school, she asked, "Dear, will that new job of yours require weekend work??" In this way she seeks to establish a relationship norm for availability. She revisits the subject almost every week in her letters, without demanding or added pressure, and always with a simple question – confirming her desire to be with him yet being patient and understanding. For example, she wrote, "Please don't [drive by yourself], Sweetheart – 'cuz I love you too much. But please do come," and, "Honey, I'm praying and hoping so hard that your ride will come thru next weekend – will it be Fri?"

Sandra also expressed in an appealing way the desire to be closer together distance-wise. She wrote, "Right now I don't know of anyone who has a fiancé as far away as you are. Oh, how I wish spring would come and you would come with it! This waiting is awful – I envy everyone else so! And at times I get just sinfully jealous." She also promotes norms for her role as caretaker. When George was not feeling well, Sandra stated,

"Darling, I worry so about your colds – I don't know a thing about them and what can I do to take care of you? I'll try, though, my Darling, as hard as I know how."

In developing relationship norms, George and Sandra talked with friends and acquaintances about issues. Those conversations were followed by discussions between themselves that enabled them to form "their" view, the norms that would govern their relationship. George wrote, "Tonight I rode home with two married guys and I asked them what they thought of being married and going to school at the same time . . . and they both said it was fine . . . and to not worry about it cause they were both worse off than I am when they got married." This comment invited Sandra to voice her view.

As their relational bond deepened, new norms were formed. In their case, the most prevalent of these norms were associated with gender roles and family rituals. For Sandra, a home economics major, norms for herself as a future wife and mother included perfecting recipes and learning how to care for babies. She frequently talked about her goals of developing these skills. "Honey, we'll have lots of chicken, won't we? And I'll practice on the dressing – there's room for improvement in everything I do."

They also developed norms for decision-making. For example, when it came to wedding gifts for friends and family, Sandra was responsible for suggesting a gift and coordinating the logistics. George always gave her selection approval and covered the cost. George wrote, "What are you doing about their gift? Honey, I guess I won't be much help in helping you to decide. But whatever you say is all right with me."

Family holiday and special occasion rituals were also discussed in letters. George wrote about Christmas Eve rituals in his family, which he intended to make his own. "We always have oyster stew for supper and then open up the presents afterwards. But you'll have to learn to like oyster stew!!! After all, you're going to be a part of the family!!!" And Sandra communicated her disappointment when George is unable to make it to her birthday. "Birthdays always meant a lot in our family." The granddaughter expressed that when each had voiced an expected norm, the other was quick to respond in a thoughtful and compromising manner, and with an apology, if necessary. In this manner norms and expectations were gradually established.

The granddaughter expressed that there were definitely expectations for frequent letters right from the start. If either waited too long to write, he or she heard about it. George once teased Sandra by stating, "What happened? Did you break your arm? Here I am, waiting for a letter so I can answer but looks like I'll have to wait a while."

As the relationship grew, expectations became centered on family.

Sandra described many times what she thought of as the perfect family, insinuating the type of family they would have someday. In speaking of a friend, she once said, "He is the best family man and so patient with the children – oh, what an ideal husband . . . just like I think you'll be, if you have the chance." George echoed her enthusiasm for raising a family and fulfilling the norms of their life together. "Darling, it's going to be so wonderful . . . living together, planning together, working together (you do the dishes, I'll mow the lawn) ha-ha – and having a whole bunch of kids – blondes, brown haired, red haired, large, small, all sizes and shapes." According to the granddaughter, they did accomplish this.

George also expected to have a *family* business. They started their first business as a family business. When they were very young, George took the kids with him, one at a time, to the office on Saturdays, when no one else was there. The kids played while he worked. All the children were expected to work as a regular summer employee. They were treated as regular employees in the business and never reported to George. If they were going to work professionally in the business, they were expected to gain experience similar to other employees.

The granddaughter summarizes their relationship by saying that the norms in George and Sandra's relationship were formed somewhat easily and naturally, likely due to their similar backgrounds. Each came from a large family, in neighboring towns, and with shared religious beliefs. They shared an equal eagerness for the future: to be together and start a large family of their own. They discussed roles for the "everyday patterns" of their future, including typical Sunday mornings and weekday dinners. They both discussed and anticipated the way they raised their children and how many they would have (12 was projected by Sandra). They could not wait for "forever" to begin. Common backgrounds, experiences, and consensus on beliefs and values created a platform for the family business; accepted norms and expectations were developed out of this common belief system, which started with two individuals and the sharing of their vision for family life. This shared vision helped build a strong family bond.

Common identity in the business
From the beginning, George hoped to establish a business that was consistent with the moral beliefs, values, and norms that he and Sandra shared. He wanted to treat clients and employees with decency, honor, and respect. George wanted a company that kept its word and behaved according to high moral standards. He discussed his feelings repeatedly with Sandra. Finally, George told Sandra, "I want to start my own business – will you help me?" And so with her unstinting support, they

started a business that would be consistent with their shared moral beliefs and principles.

Honesty and integrity became the bedrock for the business. George repeatedly stated that ethics do belong in business. Employees were expected to be ethical and honest in their dealings with one another and with clients. Their business's Code of Conduct states, "There is no substitute for personal integrity and good judgment." As the business grew, the importance of ethics was further emphasized by publishing a Code of Conduct that emphasized the importance of honesty, integrity, and quality. Each employee in the company, no matter their position, was required to subscribe to the Code of Conduct.

In addition, from the beginning, the company contributed to community programs. George led the company in joining with other companies in pledging 5 percent of pre-tax profits to charitable causes. Later, the amount was increased to 10 percent. Their company led the way in establishing an addiction recovery program that over time affected thousands of lives. Foundations established by the company were instrumental in supporting many charitable causes. The company encouraged employees to contribute to the community by giving them time off and resources to support projects.

Clearly the family identity influenced the business culture. In addition, the business culture also influenced the family. In thinking back about family life, one of the children noted:

> The family and the business have always been entwined. The family values are in the business, and the business values are a part of the family. That has affected our work ethic and the way we treated other people and expected to be treated and how we were expected to do things honestly and fairly.

Collective Trust

Collective trust is the assurance that family or organizational members can rely on one another to be true to their common identity, to sustain common beliefs and values, and to follow norms and expectations. As new events and challenges come, frequent and transparent communication enables the individuals to develop a response that is consistent with its collective identity. Common identity gives relationships stability, and provides consistency for both the family and the firm.

Collective trust in the family
As is the case for all couples, confidence has to be developed about a very fundamental issue – will the other person be true to his or her commitment

to the relationship? Early on that issue was broached in an abstract way by Sandra:

> I'll never forget when you kissed me good-bye and I made a promise which I should have made long ago – it's a promise you never did make to me – I'm the one who is beginning to become worried – [Georgie] Boy, please always let me trust you – I'll never forget what you once said – if it's going to happen, it's going to happen in or out of a coed school – you're so darn sensible!

The granddaughter believes this statement concerned marriage and the trust necessary for a committed long-distance relationship.

As illustrated in this paper, George and Sandra devoted much time and attention to developing a common identity. The common identity gave them a good working relationship. That is, they became each other's most important confidant and advisor. It was important to them to build a family and a business that was consistent with their identity. To maintain high levels of trust, they communicated frequently and openly, and consulted one another when there was a possibility of variance with values, norms, or expectations. After discussion, they would seldom disagree on their position.

They started a family business because the individuals with whom George worked were inconsistent with his and Sandra's moral beliefs and their identity. They wanted a business built around their core value of integrity. To be true to their common identity, George made many decisions in consultation with Sandra, including hiring, over the life of the business. Throughout their lives, internal strength came from their commitment to the identity that was initiated while courting. Over time, a married couple that retains its commitment to one another and sustains frequent communication can develop a sense of oneness, a deep common identity.

Late in their lives, Sandra had a debilitating stroke that prevented communication and kept her in a nursing institution. George visited her often, just to spend time with her. But, without the give and take with "Sandie," his closest confidant and sounding board, George was very lonely. He felt like half of him was missing – his identity incomplete. While the children and grandchildren were close by, he did not have the same kind of deep bonding relationship and common identity with them that he had enjoyed with Sandra. He had trusted Sandra more deeply than anyone. George obtained comfort by reflecting on what "Sandie would say." Their identities were so intertwined that George knew what Sandra would say if she could say it.

Collective trust in the business

George's approach to the family business was to delegate responsibility and authority to employees and let them do their jobs. His feeling was that people feel better when they feel a sense of ownership about what they are doing. Thus, his firm was highly decentralized, with decision-making authority given to the lowest level possible. George's approach was, first, to carefully select talented employees who were a good fit for the organizational culture. To help assess the fit, Sandra helped make selection decisions early in the history of the business. Later, the search and selection process was institutionalized. And second, George clarified how employees were expected to do things, defined the quality of work that was expected, and clarified how they were expected to work with clients and with one another. With these things in place, he felt that he could trust them to do their jobs.

The approach that emerged was one that had a sense of teamwork combined with integrity. When something went wrong, concerned individuals took a quick look at the problem, found a solution, and then they moved forward. When a decision needed to be made, relevant experts in legal matters, engineering, and manufacturing worked together to make decisions and implement them. The underlying theme in this approach was to trust one another to do their jobs. With this sense of collective trust and confidence, individuals could be creative and find support for creative solutions.

SUMMARY

The purpose of this paper was to determine from the evidence, including a written family history, family letters, and insights from family members, whether components of social capital were present in the family, and if the nature of the social capital in the family influenced social capital in the business. We discovered evidence indicating that elements of family social capital were present in the lives of George and Sandra, and that the nature of their social capital in some ways influenced the nature of social relationships in the business.

Communication was a priority for George and Sandra both when courting and later in marriage. They shared much information so that each partner fully understood the context and activities of others. The nature of their communication was largely positive and supportive, inviting input and support from one another. Thus, their relationship was a source of capital, not liability. Moreover, there was evidence that the nature of family communication provided a guide for communication at work. The work lunches with employees were similar to family dinners.

Much attention was given by George and Sandra to defining common identity, consisting of moral beliefs (what is right), values (what is important), and norms (how we do things). Their moral beliefs were a primary motivator for starting their own business. When developing the business George consistently relied on Sandra, his sounding board and confidant, to think through issues related to ethical beliefs, values, and norms so they could be in accord with their common identity. Evidence of family identity influencing the business was the Code of Conduct for employees.

There was evidence of collective trust demonstrated through confidence and sharing intimate thoughts and feelings throughout their marriage. Sandra was a sounding board and chief confidant for George on business issues, and George provided the same for Sandra regarding the family. Similarly, confidence and trust was communicated in the business by allowing employees to do their jobs, obtaining their expertise in making decisions, and pushing decision-making to the lowest level possible.

Thus, communication, common identity, and collective trust were all present during George and Sandra's courting years and throughout their married lives. And, there is evidence that the family social capital influenced the business culture.

DISCUSSION

According to Schein,[11] the primary influence in establishing an organizational culture is the assumptions, here called beliefs, of the founder. Schein suggests that culture begins with the founder's beliefs and then is developed as he/she interacts with the group of individuals that join the founder in figuring out how to handle problems and challenges. The founder, guided by his/her beliefs, works through problems with the group he/she has assembled who are guided by their beliefs. Together, they figure out what they will do and how they will do it. Over time the beliefs, values, and norms that make up the organizational culture are established. This culture guides who is hired and how things are done in the organization.

Family beliefs influence beliefs of the founder of a family business to varying degrees. At one extreme, the family may have almost no influence: initial investors are not family members, the founder does not identify with family beliefs, and the founder has relatively little communication with family members, particularly about the business. At the other extreme the family's beliefs may have heavy influence: all investors are family members, multiple family members work in the business, and the business is discussed frequently and openly by family members. In this case, the family beliefs likely have heavy influence on the founder's beliefs, and in turn, on the organizational culture.

In this case example, although Sandra worked in the business for only a brief time, she had considerable opportunity to influence George's beliefs as he developed the organizational culture. She had a role in selecting the founding group of employees. She understood the business context well enough to engage in meaningful discussion about it, which George and Sandra did every day. And, George valued her perspective. Furthermore, Sandra was heavily involved in organizing or attending business social events.

Thus, while not all family businesses are the same, this paper illustrates how the social system in one marriage can influence the social system in the business.[12] In the case of George and Sandra, the core identity formed in marriage influenced the culture in their business. Their business became well known and respected for its ethical business practices and its contributions to the larger community. George and Sandra's commitment to a common set of values and norms provided a basis for expectations in the business.

Perhaps the most telling influence of family involvement is that like family relationships, their businesses are established with the intent to endure.[13] George and Sandra's business is an example of this ideal. Their relationship and Sandra's influence help to explain why family businesses often last longer than other businesses. One board member indicated that Sandra constantly reminded them that the business, like her relationship with George, was in it for the long haul and that its reputation was to be carefully maintained.

Some philosophers suggest that the family is society in embryo. It is the soil from which the larger society emerges.[14] Moral practice is established in the home and then widened to include other human relationships in general. This paper illustrates how the marriage of George and Sandra provided a small, strong social system denoting common identity. That identity became the anchor around which they built a family, established a business, and influenced the larger community.

NOTES

*   "The daughter" is a second-generation member of a family business founded by her father. She has been a director for her father's business, a trust company, and the family office. She is also the founder and president of her own company, which has been in business for over 20 years.

**   "The granddaughter" worked for several years in a public relations firm after completing her undergraduate degree. She recently received her Master's Degree in Integrated

Marketing Communications. She also serves on a foundation board and on a family governance committee.

1. Danes et al. (2009a); Sorenson and Bierman (2009).
2. Jacobs (1965).
3. Coleman (1988).
4. Nahapiet and Ghoshal (1998); Hoffman et al. (2006).
5. As the language in the letters is very intimate and personal, the granddaughter, who shared these materials, asked that the identities of her family be kept confidential.
6. Putnam (2000).
7. Sorenson and Bierman (2009).
8. Ibid.
9. Sorenson et al. (2009).
10. Gottman and Driver (2005).
11. Schein (1983).
12. Sorenson et al. (2010).
13. Miller and Le Breton-Miller (2005).
14. "The Family" (Hexagram 37) *I Ching* (Chinese Book of Changes).

11. Summary of dialogue: using communication and family practices to develop social capital

Trina S. Smith

As the chapters in this section have shown, communication and relationships are key elements of family social capital. In this session of the conference, the participants' discussion raised the following questions:

- How do our connections within and to the family affect relationships?
- How does communication serve to both perpetuate family conflicts and solve them?

The discussion centered on the following themes:

- breakdown of the family unit;
- criticism;
- strategies for solutions;
- advisors and outside perspectives are key.

THE BREAKDOWN OF THE FAMILY UNIT

A family seems like a stable place, but life happens, which causes uncertainty or change. As one participant noted, you may have a family situation where everything is going along fine, including rituals and shared communication. Then a major change happens in the family, such as medical issues, disruption occurs, and this leads to destructive tension. So, in their words, "How do you upright the ship?"

Likewise, two different, yet similar, issues about the family unit and relationships were noted in the discussion. According to one participant:

> In our family, we have some harmony. But we're a small family, and we have pressure to be included, to be in the same boat. If somebody steps outside the boat, the rest of the people in the boat say, "Wait a minute, you can't do that."

We resent the people who have the courage to take the step outside the boat, which creates tension for us.

In a similar, but different perspective, another participant stated:

In my family, there is a tension between who's in and who's out . . . We have a huge family, and so there are a few people who are in, and a lot of people who are out. Among those who are out, there's resentment and sometimes undermining that goes on, not necessarily because they want that position, but just because they're there and I'm not.

CRITICISM

Participants clearly noted criticism as an issue in communication. All agreed that it is the most common negative communication behavior. One participant noted the reasons why we criticize others:

Because we like the way we do things, we criticize others for not doing it that way . . . [W]hen criticizing we tend to fixate on one little aspect of another's behavior. Because you are fixated on it, you go so far as to criticize.

STRATEGIES FOR SOLUTIONS

Conversations ranged from the specific to the more general in regard to solving communication issues within families. One participant summarized why developing communication skills and trust is important to a family business:

One of the gifts and one of the challenges of a family business is that the business itself adds another developmental dimension to the family. The business calls on the family to develop as it develops . . . Furthermore, relational skills and patterns that are developed in the family can and often do carry over to the business. Skills learned in the business can carry over to the family. So, being a family in business provides additional opportunities to develop relationship skills.

Likewise, family dynamics can impede communication, but at the same time provide a reason to work on these skills. As one participant noted, "[T]he business can give a family a reason to work on and improve relationships." Another family business story supports this idea:

One family business owner I know moved here to work with five adult siblings in the family business. She had a psychology background, so she immediately started working to improve family relationships. She said her efforts went nowhere; her siblings weren't interested. But they started working together on the business and found that they weren't working very well together. This then gave them a reason and permission to work on sibling relationships. *Some people may build good relationships to accomplish a purpose.*

From a different, but related perspective, participants noted that in some families there is forced harmony. Speaking of her in-laws, a participant first described forced harmony as the refusal to have conflicts and pretending everything is "hunky-dory," which ultimately leads to negative consequences. She told the story of her husband's family and compared it to constructive conflict:

> In my husband's business, every holiday we get together with his whole family who works there. One of the things they do is go around the table and say their favorite memory of the person. It seems like superficial harmony because they're really not that close. Then you have other families that are a little bit combative, competitive, and teasing – a good conflict. It creates competition and pushes one another and creates innovation. *Each family is complex. Harmony can be good and it also can be bad. Constructive conflict and discussion can be good.*

And sometimes the solution is not always staying together as a participant's story illustrates:

> I come from a family business. I served the mediating role in our family because I wanted this family business to stay intact for my lifetime and hopefully another lifetime. I had good relationships with all my siblings and I remember when I called them shortly after a rift and in their own way they both told me to "butt out sis." The feelings were just too tender. So I left it for a while and then I went back in, and we worked on things. They did end up splitting the business. But, they still talk. That was the best thing that could have ever happened . . . [S]plitting up is not the worst thing in the world.

Family business researchers at the conference highlighted what the research says about families when people come from different backgrounds (i.e., race, ethnicity, social class, religion, and so forth). Research recognizes that the dynamics, implicit rules, and structures that you bring from your culture are deeply embedded in your socialization. Thus, when two people come together and try to create a family system and they are from very different cultural backgrounds, they face much greater difficulty. Some evidence states that divorce rates and rates of unhappiness are more than double that of couples who come together with similar backgrounds.

Some specific strategies were also noted by participants from a variety of perspectives. For example, one participant noted:

In dealing with conflict look at what kind of outcome you want and consider three dimensions: inclusion, control, and outcome. *To understand conflict, you have to understand the root causes.* Is the cause an issue of control, inclusion, or outcome? Within the inclusion dimension, there is shared meaning, connectedness, and structure. In addition, it is important to remember that the gulf widens between people when there is less communication. There are natural communications with the immediate nuclear family, which makes that group more powerful and makes everybody else feel left out. *A family council enables communication with the rest of the family and makes them an insider. It creates shared meaning and connectedness.*

In a similar light, another person talked about Gottman and the soft start-up:

The soft start-up is when you have a complaint. The soft start-up isn't a hostile start-up . . . It doesn't start with contempt or criticism. It starts with something softer, something about my observations, something about what I need, something about my motive for saying what I'm about to say. There are lots of ways for a soft start-up. *We need to have a general set of guidelines. For example, understand what criticism is and do something besides criticize. Develop language to deal with it and know that although it creates real tension and conflict, it's not solvable for them in the long haul* . . . Lastly, it is important to quickly repair when we slip up; we all criticize; we're all contemptuous.

ADVISORS AND OUTSIDE PERSPECTIVES ARE KEY

It is clear from the family business members, advisors, and researchers that advisors are key to building positive communication and helping both the family and business. They have an outside perspective, not tangled in the emotions of the family. A family member participant summarized this nicely:

A family is a complex system. Small changes reverberate through the family. I don't believe as a family we can always fix ourselves and make us right again from the inside out. Because we have a history and are so invested emotionally and communicatively, we can't see the forest or the trees because we are a tree. When things aren't going well, it helps to seek third-party assistance to get a perspective on your family system and take the steps to be balanced again instead of off kilter. Help could come from a close family member, but I think the trained professionals are very helpful.

Furthermore, a participant discussed why an outside perspective may be needed when habitual patterns of behavior, such as rituals in the family and standard operating procedures in the business, are used when change occurs. Using these may not always be the best course:

In general, we tend to rely on standard operating procedures. However, when we have disruptions and change, we need different kinds of processes to deal with and reconstruct shared meanings, connectedness, and structure. For that, we sometimes need a third party. However, we tend to rely on rituals or standard operating procedures and that's not usually very successful.

An advisor to family businesses shared her story about the different tools that may be needed to solve conflict in the family versus the business:

> In my law practice, there seems to be a continuum of tension. Sometimes families call me because there are two family business owners that want to sue each other . . . So I'm trying to find a legal conflict resolution model that can help them have an amicable split without suing each other and making even worse rifts among the family . . . But it is important to remember that some patterns and practices used in our professions can transfer to the family effectively, some can't. Legal litigators may have communication characteristics that make them very successful. Using those skills in the family may be quite destructive. So if it's good in one system, it may or may not be good in the other.

Lastly, in this section, we present a story of a family business member who speaks of how seeking education and perspective from the outside improved their family, the interaction of the family and the family business, and promoted understanding among generations:

> After attending family programs at St. Thomas, we talked about the business and the emotions of the people outside of the family versus inside of the family, which brought sanity to our family on so many levels. My mother, the chief emotional officer, made a rule of no more talk about the business on holidays. It's not a board meeting between those in the family. It brought sanity to understand generational differences and that everyone had a good point of view, just different. There's nothing better than having a third party who has been there, done that, being able to come in and say look, here's what the research shows and have the authority, pedigree, and credibility to be able to speak to these issues.

PART II　QUESTIONS TO CONSIDER

1. Have you taken family business programs or courses to enable a successful family and family business? If not, what holds you back?
2. How do you deal with change in your family and family business? Do you rely on habitual rituals and/or standard operating procedures or are you willing to address new ways of solving issues?

3. How do you communicate with family and employees? What role has criticism played?
4. Are you able to name and discuss tension in your family and/or family business? How can tension be a good thing?
5. Do you utilize outside perspectives? Do you work with advisors?

PART III

Complementing social capital in family and business

Building upon the themes already addressed in the first two sections, Part III begins with Chapter 12, in which Rothausen and Sorenson first provide us with the concept of "family-enterprise-first" firms in which a business is developed prioritizing the family. Hence, both the business and the family systems benefit from each other. Based on this premise, they address the scholarly management literature on work–family to give us tools to examine not only how the business culture can be family-friendly, but how the family can also be sympathetic to the business. This in turn allows productive work and families.

In Chapter 13, McEnaney, from a family business perspective, illustrates how her family's business fits the family-enterprise-first framework, giving us examples related to governance, family member inclusion, and work–family balance. In Chapter 14, Pritchard, from a family business standpoint, gives a personal example to show the interweaving of family and business in another example of a family-enterprise-first business family. Focusing on the permeating roles of family members in a family enterprise, she discusses the role of "chief emotional officer" in her family as well as discussing how creating a family logo further infused a family identity.

In Chapter 15, Eddleston, from a scholarly view, addresses the consequences internally and externally of defining one's family business as a family firm. Cultivating a family-firm identity has a competitive advantage as social capital may be developed both internally and externally. In Chapter 16, based on a family business perspective relating to Eddleston's work, Shepard, utilizing the example of her family's business, shows how the identity of a family firm may differ in each generation. Furthermore, she also gives us ideas based on her family's story about how to cultivate a family identity by doing such things as establishing a family council, writing a family history, and teaching children about the business. In chapter 17, Smith concludes with a summary of the dialogue.

12.   Leveraging family member capacity for the business and the family

Teresa J. Rothausen and Ritch L. Sorenson

"Social capital" is a term used to describe relationships within a system or community – *social* because relationships are the basis for community action, and *capital* because the relationships themselves become an asset. This concept was developed about 20 years ago, when innovative leaders established it as a new approach to building communities. Rather than focusing on social problems in isolation, which together became an unending list of insurmountable social ills, they found ways to build relationships among individuals and institutions to capitalize on capacities and assets to build community. To achieve this, community builders helped individuals within institutions to see value – for themselves and for the larger community – in combining their capacities and assets in new ways. For example, a former prison inmate worked with a university professor to obtain a grant to teach entrepreneurship in a prison, which enabled prison inmates to develop work when they left prison. With this model, working norms and relationships of trust are used repeatedly for causes that benefit each institution, but that each institution could not do on its own. Thus, a variety of seemingly unconnected individuals and institutions might assemble capacities and assets to benefit each other and the community in multiple ways.

We apply the concept of social capital to families in business by exploring the nature of the relationships among individuals and two institutions – the business and the family. Family social capital exists when the nature of the relationships within a family, and between the family and the family business, enables individuals to give human capacities/assets and financial resources to the family and to the family business. We examine how such relationships permit families to leverage human assets and capacities to benefit both the family and the business. Specifically, we focus on two characteristics of these systems: values and norms. Values and norms may either promote or hinder using these relationships to benefit the family and the business. Just as community builders introduced new norms that capitalized on the capabilities and assets of individuals from different institutions, families in business can capitalize on the human and social assets within the family to benefit both the family and the business. When a family totally separates business from family life, potential assets may be overlooked to the detriment of the family, the business, or both.

Research suggests that a subset of family firms already govern their family businesses in ways that use some of these capacities and assets to benefit both the family and the business. A recent study of 732 family businesses in Spain found two primary kinds of businesses.[1] "Family-enterprise-first" businesses – hereafter termed enterprise-first – govern the relationship between the family and the business, which together is called the enterprise. To a large extent, these businesses already develop the capacities and assets of both family and business to benefit the overall family business enterprise. Governance systems are developed to identify and develop family human assets to benefit the business, and to design the business to meet family objectives. Thus, the entire family enterprise system and individuals within each system benefit. This study also found a second group of businesses focusing governance only on the business system, similar to non-family corporations – these businesses will be referred to as business-first. Unlike enterprise-first family businesses, these family businesses keep family and business issues separate.

Both enterprise-first and business-first firms in the Spanish study had comparable business performance, but the enterprise-first firms had significantly better family outcomes, such as family unity, loyalty, support, and interest in the business. Below, we first extract what we can learn from the study of enterprise-first firms that might help us understand how the family and business systems can benefit one another. Second, based on the work–family research literature in management, we suggest ways both types of family firms might benefit more fully from potential assets and capabilities in both the family and business systems.

FAMILIES THAT LEVERAGE FAMILY AND BUSINESS TO BENEFIT BOTH

A review of the Spanish study suggests that enterprise-first businesses have considerable integration between the family and the firm. The governance of the family enterprise can provide stewardship for both family and business. When enterprise-first businesses form strategy, both the family and business provide input. The board of an enterprise-first firm includes representatives of both family and business systems. In representing family interests, family shareholders typically rely on family councils and other collaboration mechanisms to develop common vision, values, and purpose for the family. Transparency is the goal within the entire enterprise. The family is transparent in its desires for the business, and the business is transparent in its goals and how well it is achieving the goals, especially financial goals. The family develops policies for family involvement in the business, the formal mechanism for enabling individual family members to use their assets and capabilities in the business.

Financial budgets help finance the family and enterprise relationship. Such budgets can allow for development of family members through experience and training to prepare to work in the business. Budgets can also support family member education about business to better understand the business system. Family meetings promote family member relationships that help the members develop a common family point of view about themselves and their involvement in the business. A family point of view is a set of values, attitudes, and norms about the business.[2] A family council is often the mechanism used for making decisions about the family and the business. In these councils, family members learn to work together. When needed, councils bring in counselors or mediators to help them resolve conflicts and improve decision-making. In the process, family members improve communication and relational skills, resulting in improved family relationships.

Focusing on governance of both the business and the family requires family members to develop a family point of view about the business and their involvement in the business. Use of resources from the business to develop family members enables the business to benefit from the assets and capabilities that are fostered within the family. Family members who understand and participate in governance of the enterprise can work with the business to prepare other family members to be potential leaders and employees, board members, active shareholders, representatives in the community, and participants in family foundations and philanthropy. These family members may also equip children with the appropriate norms and knowledge to participate in various meaningful ways in the family enterprise.

One advantage of governance mechanisms that enable family input to the business and business input to the family is that businesses that are closely aligned with the family have long-term development and planning horizons. Because family relationships are enduring, businesses benefit from family involvement in establishing vision, strategy, and goals that are also enduring. The knowledge and experience accrued in the family over time provides tremendous resources and advantages to the business. Family members can provide long-term leadership and stability in the business. In consultation with other family members, they can design and promote long-term education and development programs for upcoming family members and employees. As the business moves forward, it can rely on this stock of family human and social resources that have been developed over many years.

For the family and the business systems to thrive over the long term however, they need to retain important elements of their family cultural values and norms and, at the same time, they need to adapt. The family and the business can adapt gradually over time through educating individual members, adopting professional practices, and being involved in professional organizations. Enterprise-first firms have learned to develop and take advantage of some of these assets and capabilities in both the business and the family to the benefit of both systems – the overall enterprise. However, as part of adapting and learning, enterprise-first firms may also benefit from findings in the work–family management research literature. Family-first firms, on the other hand, operate much like large corporations. Although family members benefit from the financial success of these firms, the two systems are kept separate. Thus, family-first firms might gain even more from understanding the work–family research literature. Below, we summarize the work–family literature and then apply concepts from that literature to family businesses.

OVERVIEW OF WORK–FAMILY RESEARCH

Similar to the early focus by community builders on problems and needs, the origin of work–family research in the 1980s focused on a problem: "work–family conflict."[3] Conflict was the focus due to norms that developed during the Industrial revolution. In pre-industrial times, work and family were interwoven with other primary life facets (found in research to include citizenship/community, religion/spirituality, leisure/friendships, learning/education, and ethnic identity) into a fabric of life.[4] With the Industrial Revolution, norms changed so that work was segregated in both time and space from other aspects of life. In the US, paid work and home/family were largely viewed as "separate spheres."[5] These spheres were also gendered, with women at home and men at work. In the last four decades, however, changes in technology, law, workforce demographics, family roles, and the economy suggest a movement toward a new interweaving of work, family, and other facets of life.[6] Societal realities have shifted, but norms and values in families and in businesses have been slow to adapt to these shifts.

To fix the "work–family conflict problem" that emerged when women joined the workforce in droves in the 1970s and 1980s, remedies such as flextime, telecommuting, compressed workweek, and job sharing were implemented.[7] These fixes alleviated some of the work–family conflict and in some cases increased satisfaction. However, one author reviewing work–family research concluded that although these fixes do enable more involvement in both family and work spheres, because underlying family norms and business norms have not changed, rewards and opportunities at work remain greater for individuals who focus only on work.[8] Thus, apparently, these "fixes" did not change the underlying norms related to separation of work and family.

For example, one norm associated with the Industrial Revolution was that the capacities and assets of men were best leveraged primarily at work and those of women primarily at home. The notion that the capacities and assets from both genders could benefit both spheres was overlooked. However, evidence is slowly changing these normative expectations. In the US over the last four decades, women have become essential in the work sphere. Similarly, men have demonstrated added value and important contributions in the home and family. As with the community asset movement, recent work–family research focuses on norms that promote access to the capacities and assets of individuals both as workers and as family members, including research on family facilitation, work–family enhancement, and work–family enrichment.[9,10,11,12]

These approaches suggest that when values and norms of both the family and the business promote capacity and asset sharing, the institutions and the individuals in families and in businesses can benefit. This research has shown that, although being involved in both work and family may cause some conflict, when freely chosen and under certain conditions, it can also lead to higher levels of life satisfaction, self-esteem, skill and competency, relationship or social capital, and performance in both spheres.

LEVERAGING THE FAMILY FOR THE BUSINESS AND THE BUSINESS FOR THE FAMILY: INSPIRATIONS FROM RESEARCH IN MANAGEMENT OF WORK–FAMILY

The difference between family businesses and businesses in general, we argue, is that family businesses have more power to change the norms and values that promote access to capacities and assets to benefit both the family and the business system. In contrast to other businesses, family firms have overlapping sets of stakeholders in the family and the business.[13] Adult family members are shareholders, and children may be future owners as well as a labor pool from which to draw for management and technical expertise. For example, family businesses can take advantage of opportunities to raise children with capacities and assets that benefit the business if children exhibit interest in the business or develop abilities in line with the business. Family businesses can also design the business to benefit the family. For example, the business might offer benefits in line with what the family values, such as tuition reimbursement or quality child care.

Research on work–family suggests that it is the quality of the roles and the support built into the family and the business systems that determine whether conflict or enrichment result for individuals and their organizations when organizational members take on both work/business and family/home roles.[14,15] Since family businesses share stakeholders between the business and the family, members of family-owned businesses have more opportunity to take advantage of potential collaboration in daily choices and in important executive decisions by intentionally designing work and family roles and building support in each system for the other system. That is, family business leaders can influence family and business norms and values to encourage the leveraging of assets and capacities for the well-being of both family and business. Enterprise-first businesses already do this, and will likely be interested in additional ideas to further that goal. Business-first firms may want to consider the potential benefits of this approach practiced by enterprise-first family businesses and suggested by findings in the work–family research literature. Even if business-first firms decide to keep family and business systems separate, these companies may benefit if these ideas are adopted for employees.

Step 1: Values and a Family-supportive Work Culture

A recent development in research on work–family is studying the impact of family-supportive work culture, also called work–family-supportive culture.[16] Simplified, culture is defined as shared values and norms. Thus, when a business organization has a family-supportive culture, its values reflect respect for, and acknowledgment of, the importance of members' families. Having such a culture in a business organization has been shown to positively impact workers' organizational attachment, job satisfaction, organizational commitment, and intentions to stay with the employer.[17] Evidence of a family-supportive work culture may be co-workers who know and take an interest in workers' family members, who are willing to "chip in" when family duties call, and who show appreciation to workers' family members for contributions to the business.

Strongly masculine and "single sphere-oriented" work cultures may make it more difficult for individuals to engage meaningfully in both family and work roles. Many businesses, including family businesses, have cultures of masculine norms deeply embedded from their formation in the separate spheres era. For example, long hours rather than an efficiently produced work product may be the accepted sign of true commitment; an aggressive and hyper-competitive internal culture may discourage cooperative effort even when it is more effective; "up or out" career tracks may be at odds with the life cycle timing of having young children; and the expectation of responding to work calls at any hour of the day or night may be a condition for promotion.[18,19]

Such work values may unintentionally create hurdles to the full involvement in the business for family members and for employees with more balanced values; unfortunately, these barriers often mean that the business doesn't take full advantage of its human and social capital. These norms may appear gender neutral (everyone should work long hours and compete with others in the organization, not just men), but they are masculine separate spheres norms because they value masculine qualities (independence) over feminine qualities (cooperation), and they assume that a supportive family member or spouse is at home to take care of family concerns for the worker.[20] Wives, mothers, and daughters are the family members whose contributions are most likely to be blocked by such norms although increasingly in younger generations, husbands, fathers, and sons who want to be truly involved in their own children's and family's lives may also be affected.

Some steps to check for a family-supportive work culture include:

- Perform work culture and work climate assessments. Do you know what your business's organizational culture is? Do you know whether workers have the same perception of the shared values of the business?
- Explore the family-supportive elements of your business. Are families acknowledged and included? Are family-supportive policies in place?
- Assess your requirements for career tracks. Is it possible to move up in your business, even if more slowly, while being significantly involved in raising children or caring for elderly family members?
- Examine the gender balance in various departments and job types in your family business. If you find concentrations of men in some areas or at some levels, and women in others, conduct focus groups to find out why. Unexamined gendered values may underlie this finding.

- Do business leaders honestly value family and the work involved in caring for family members? If so, exactly how is that demonstrated in the organization?

Step 2: Values and a Business-supportive Family Culture

Just as a work–family-supportive culture has been shown to decrease work–family conflict and create the conditions for workers to contribute more fully and be more invested in both family and work, it stands to reason that a work–family-supportive culture in the family can decrease work–family conflict and create conditions for family members who are also highly involved and invested in work to contribute more fully to the family. Family culture can be thought of as shared values and norms among family members. If a family culture is work supportive, or if the family has a strong work–family culture, individual family members' parents, partners, and children value their work, which in turn facilitates not only work, but partnership or marital satisfaction, family satisfaction, and commitment to family. Evidence of a work-supportive family culture is a spouse who demonstrates interest in and support for one's work role, who knows co-workers and contributes to the building of relationships with co-workers, and who is willing to take on more of the duties at home when more time must be spent at work. A family-business-specific example is a family that takes pride in the family business and whose members identify with it.

Just as strongly gendered notions of roles at work can create unintended barriers to the full engagement of women and men who value their family roles, the opposite is also true: strongly gendered roles in the family may create unintended barriers to the full engagement in the family of men and women who value their work roles. In fact, men who want to be fully involved in both family and work may face a "double jeopardy" of potential conflict because of harsher social sanctions against men who embrace norms of emotional and physical care of dependents. That is, the social disapproval of men who want to physically and emotionally care for dependents may be greater than those for women who want to work outside the home. Some authors have suggested the tendency of some mothers, for example, to unintentionally discourage their husbands from caring for children because these men may have different ways of child care than the women are used to or that seem right to them.

Some steps to take for a work-supportive family culture include:

- Ask family members to characterize the family's shared values, both positive and negative. Check for agreement. If everyone agrees on the family's shared values, you have a strong family culture. In that case, explore whether the culture values feminine and masculine roles, and fosters access to both for both men and women. If, however, family members disagree on values, you have a weak culture. Fortunately, you can take this opportunity to create a stronger culture around the shared values members see as more positive or productive.

- Ask family members involved in the family business whether they feel more supported in their work by their families or more stressed about their work because of the reaction of family members to their work roles.
- Ask family leaders to honestly assess the extent to which they value providing (1) opportunities for all individuals to care for dependent family members and spend time building and maintaining family relationships; and (2) enriched work opportunities in the business for all family members.
- Ask family members strongly involved in work if they feel that their contributions toward the physical and emotional care of dependents is valued.

Step 3: Norms and Role Design

Research on work–family has shown that, when given good roles – characterized by flexibility, support, and autonomy that are recognized and rewarded – more roles generally leads to better outcomes for individuals.[21,22] For example, one recent study showed that job complexity and control over work time were positively related to satisfaction and that when work hours increased, workers with low control experienced decreases in satisfaction, whereas workers with high control did not.[23] Thus, control over time is one characteristic of role quality. The same could be true at home, although we are not aware of any research in that area. However, it's easy to imagine that complexity in family roles and some control over the time spent would increase one's satisfaction in the family role despite high demands. At home, this control over time may be afforded by family members who are willing to share family tasks and are "cross-trained" in all of the arenas of housework and dependent care, rather than holding rigidly to traditional roles.

Work, jobs, and performance standards were created in the separate spheres era. Thus, in many business organizations, the assumption of primary or exclusive involvement in the work sphere is embedded in job design, performance norms, and career tracks. When family members are highly involved and invested in both work in the business and in the family at home, the business must find new ways of designing jobs with more flexibility, control, and back-up support. In addition, family members can choose family roles and work roles in part based on the extent to which the role facilitates involvement in the other sphere; in addition, work groups and families can cross-train on everyone's tasks, thus maximizing flexibility as demands in the two domains ebb and flow.[24]

One interesting and very important finding from the work–family research literature is that data dispute the widely held assumption that long work hours always worsen, and reduced hours always ameliorate work–family. There is strong evidence that the nature of a role, as well as the flexibility and control built in, is much more important than the total number of hours the role demands.[25] Thus, families and family businesses that design both organizational and family roles to allow family members choice, control, autonomy, and support will likely find that higher accrued levels of human and social capital benefit the family and the business.

Some steps to check for family- and work-supportive role design include:

- Assess the job design in your business for overall workload, flexibility, control, and autonomy along with interesting complexity.
- For roles with less flexibility and control, ask whether the lack of flexibility or control is really dictated by the nature of the work or if it is more because of accepted or unquestioned custom or tradition.
- Some roles will require less control over time – for example, answering customer service calls. However, even here, some accommodations can be built in for flexibility. For example, a business could cross-train multiple people in answering calls, and create jobs in which a smaller part of each person's job involves taking a shorter shift at this less flexible work.
- Offer family-supportive policies and programs to aid in workload management. Two primary types of support are time-related and benefit-related policies and programs. Time-related policies include leaves, flextime, telecommuting, compressed workweek (e.g., four ten-hour days instead of five eight-hour days), part-time work, and job sharing (also see the point below). Benefit-related programs include on-site child care, subsidized child or elder care, or other care resources.
- Think about how many other people can perform each person's role and cross-train in your business, increasing flexibility for everyone. Consider allowing the team to choose and negotiate who works what shifts, rather than having a centralized and depersonalized scheduling function.

- Do an assessment of the families in your family system. For each individual's family-related work and care, how many other people are qualified to do that person's task? The more that people can fill in for each other on housework, child care, socializing schedules, transportation, and other family work, the more flexibility family members will have in their family roles to accommodate work demands.
- Look at the number of hours devoted to nurturing the family as well as the number of hours worked in the family business. Ask how each role is valued and managed, and whether this seems fair to all family members.

Step 4: Norms and Rewards

As noted above, one aspect of good roles is recognition and reward. In US culture, despite rhetoric to the contrary, productivity in work organizations is more financially rewarded than caring- and family-related work. One only has to look at the pay levels of teachers versus mechanics, nurses versus medical technicians, to see this. In fact, research shows a gendered work premium for work involving more masculine (assertiveness, linear thinking, independence, rationality, competitiveness) than feminine (empathy, listening, cooperation, care, sensitivity) qualities. When we recognize the value of and reward traditionally feminine work, both men and women with skills and interests in these areas will be more likely to bring these to bear for the good of the family business.

Some steps to take for a work- and family-supportive reward systems include:

- Examine the criteria for rewards such as higher pay and promotions in your business. Honestly look at the qualities of the highest-paid and highest-level employees. What qualities got them there? If they were single-mindedly devoted and on-call at all hours, you may have unintentionally built barriers to the fuller participation of a broader range of family members. We often think, "of course, those who spend long hours should be rewarded" without asking how efficient those long hours actually are. But some organizations have found that shorter hours actually lead to more productivity per wage dollar. If you start rewarding outputs instead of time spent at work, you have a better chance of enabling family members with differing levels of involvement in non-work aspects of life to contribute more fully and get things done in more efficient or collaborative ways.

- Consider how those who use family-supportive policies and programs are viewed. For example, if a family member has the opportunity to work a flexible schedule but key decision-makers then view him or her as a less serious contender for succession, ultimately workers will be discouraged from using the very programs and policies put in place to help them invest in both their families and the family business.
- Examine the criteria for both women and men to be judged "good family members" in your family. How gendered are these criteria? Are women judged negatively when they choose to work hard in the family business? Are men who choose part-time work when their children are young judged harshly? We often assume that specialization of labor results in more efficiency, when in fact involvement in more arenas of life may result in better performance in each arena. For example, skills learned in supervision can be applied well to parenting, and communication skills learned within the family can be leveraged in the business.

Step 5: Relationships

The quality of relationships in family businesses has an exponential rather than a merely additive effect, because the same relationships are often significant in both domains. Your son may be your direct report, and your aunt may be your boss. If those relationships are strong, respectful, and healthy, they create social capital both in the family and for the business. Relationships are also the conduit for both role demands and rewards. Managers, co-workers, life partners, spouses, children, and elders in one's family all contribute to the level of demands made and rewards given. Thus, the quality of those relationships can determine the difficulty or ease with which an individual engages in family and work roles.

Social support is one reason relationships are so important. Research has shown that social support buffers individuals from stress resulting from adverse conditions, life events, work roles, and it seems likely from family roles as well. Social support relates to better work–family social system outcomes by buffering an individual from stress and conflict, and by facilitating positive outcomes.[26,27,28] Families and businesses that invest in relationships, and in modeling the norms and values of supporting one another in both domains, will likely benefit both the family and the family business.

Some steps to take to check for work- and family-supportive relationships include:

- Treat time and resources devoted to building family relationships as investments that will pay dividends both in family life and in the life of the family business, rather than as non-productive time. Building family relationships can take the form of anything from generous vacation time to retreats and workshops with the focus of teaching relationship skills like listening, acknowledging, and showing appreciation for the contributions of individuals, as well as how to give constructive feedback and criticism that builds rather than destroys relationships.
- Include "supportiveness" and "network building" on annual performance evaluations. Do 360-degree feedback to learn if your managers have critical team-building and relationship management skills.
- Participate in family business seminars and classes that acknowledge and address the importance of family relationships to the health of both the family system and the business, and that teach skills to improve relationships.

CONCLUSION

Although we believe that work–family research has applications to family business since "business is work" and "family is family," we also acknowledge that attitudes are likely quite different when a family owns the business. The applications provided above from management research on work–family may have different nuances when applied to family businesses. Nonetheless, family business is part of the larger society in which the old assumptions of separate spheres and gender roles have been challenged. We believe that not addressing this shift, or overlooking the potential competitive advantage to be gained by active management responsiveness to these changing realities, would be a mistake for any business, and particularly family businesses, given the potential for increased benefits in both spheres of concern: the family and the family business.

Work–family research suggests that the business will see conflict as well as enrichment when family members and the business's employees are heavily involved in both family and business tasks, roles, duties, and rewards. Whether family or business predominates depends largely on the norms and values promoted by family business leaders in both the home/family and in the business, and the relationships among the individuals involved. The days of separate spheres are over, assuming they ever really existed. Use this realization to design, or re-design, your family business to give you the strong competitive edge represented by family social capital.

That the norms and values of family business leaders define the nature of the relationship between the business and family systems was illustrated by one of the authors' recent experiences when teaching a seminar for families in business. During a breakfast conversation with the wife of one of the family business owners attending the seminar, she explained that she planned to shop while her husband attended the seminar. The author suggested that if she attended the seminar, she would better understand the family business and as a result might learn how she could contribute her talents to the business or how to develop her young sons to participate in the business. However, when she suggested the idea to the owner, he reacted negatively. The owner apparently wanted to maintain the business-first model and its separate systems.

As suggested by this example, family norms and values in business-first firms likely would need to change even more than those in enterprise-first firms if business-first firms are to benefit from these insights from work–family research by taking full advantage of potential family capacities and assets. Norms and values are deeply embedded, and families are likely to resist change.

As a result of conversations with others in his network, one owner, George, who one of the authors met at a family business event, decided to change his approach to business. He had originally had a business-first firm with his brother. Sisters, who were minority shareholders in the business, sued the company because they weren't given a voice and did not receive what they thought were fair dividends. The brothers ended up dividing the assets that remained after the resulting legal settlement. George, having talked about his experiences with other owners, envisioned an enterprise-first business, and started his own company. He took his adult children to seminars about family business, provided them with opportunities to learn about the business, and then gave his daughters and sons choices about becoming involved. Education and opportunity to learn about the business led the siblings to take on the challenge, and they committed their capabilities and personal assets to the business. Their firm is now a thriving enterprise-first business.

In conclusion, when more family members are aware of and involved in both the business and the family, and have a voice in both spheres, they will likely design an overall family enterprise system that allows family members to answer the needs of both systems and, at the same time, make both work life and family life more fulfilling.

NOTES

1.   Basco and Rodriquez (2009).
2.   Sorenson et al. (2009).
3.   MacDermid (2005).
4.   Barnett and Hyde (2001).
5.   Fletcher and Bailyn (2005).
6.   MacDermid (2005).
7.   Den Dulk (2005).
8.   Sutton and Noe (2005).
9.   Carlson et al. (2006).
10. Gordon et al. (2007).
11. Grandey et al. (2007).
12. Hanson et al. (2006).
13. Rothausen (2009).
14. Barnett and Hyde (2001).
15. Kirchmeyer (1992).
16. Gordon et al. (2007).
17. Thompson et al. (1999).
18. Rothausen (1994).
19. Thompson et al. (1999).
20. Ibid.
21. Barnett and Hyde (2001).
22. Kirchmeyer (1992).
23. Reynolds and Aletraris (2006).
24. Rothausen (2009).
25. Barnett (1998).
26. Adams et al. (1996).
27. Cohen and Wills (1985).
28. Ganster et al. (1986).

13. Our family enterprise

Terri McEnaney

In Chapter 12, Rothausen and Sorenson suggest that family businesses can consider both business and family goals in their approach to business. Our family business does place importance on both the family and the business. Thus, our family business can be classified as a family enterprise business – one that seeks to use the business in a variety of ways to meet both business and family goals. Much of our approach is developed around the family point of view, to develop the family and meet its needs. I illustrate with an overview of our family business.

FAMILY OWNERSHIP

Bailey Nurseries was founded in 1905 by J.V. Bailey when he began selling fruits and ornamental trees at the St. Paul farmers market. Currently the company sells over 2000 varieties of ornamental shrubs, trees, and evergreens as well as annuals and perennials focused on the northern two-thirds of the US and Canada.

Today, the third generation of owners remains active as advisors and participates in the overall strategic discussions while the seven fourth-generation members hold varied positions in the company. Family members must be active in the business to have ownership in the business. These family members help manage the business–family relationship to achieve business *and* family goals.

The plan is now in place for transferring ownership to the fourth generation (and of stock from the third generation is in process transferring). A Limited Liability Corporation (LLC) was formed in the 1990s. Our policies insure company ownership is retained in the family. We have a buy–sell agreement. If a family member were to leave the business today, they must sell their stock to the company or to another family member.

FAMILY DEVELOPMENT

From our family point of view, we believe in family member development, which is consistent with a family enterprise first business. For example, we recently held a family ownership retreat guided by a consultant who helped us identify issues, clarify the issues, and resolve conflicts. A survey was completed by each family member that clarified personal values and goals, business values and goals, and leadership and communication. The consultant compiled the results and presented key findings and recommendations to the Bailey family. We discussed the findings and planned actions to improve our relationships and how we operate as an ownership team.

As just one example, our family has a firm belief that we need a strong balance of business and family. And, the results of the consultant survey showed that there was some confusion and frustration related to family involvement in decision-making as it related to an individual family member's level in the company. We have planned a follow-up session to clarify our policy.

We also discussed the role of spouses of blood relatives in the family business. Currently there are no spouses working in the business and their involvement is limited to a few company functions during the year. We decided to include our spouses in more company functions and will likely include them in a future retreat.

COMMON VISION FOR COMPANY

We are fortunate that our family and our employees share a common vision for the company. Our vision is to be recognized internationally as providing the best in horticultural products and services. We recently revisited this vision and confirmed our commitment, which is an advantage of a family enterprise firm. We refer to the vision statement when setting strategic direction and list it in our employee newsletter every month.

Thus, organizing from our family point of view is reflected in our mission and vision and is expressed in our values. As we need to change and adapt, we draw upon the perspective of the family to develop and protect the overall enterprise.

PROTECT BOTH FAMILY AND BUSINESS

Since so many family members rely on income from the business, we strive to both grow the business and protect its future. To grow the company, we strive for 5–10 percent sales growth and an 8–10 percent profit. We do not have dividends but pay out a discretionary bonus to owners based on company performance. We strongly believe in reinvesting in the company to maintain consistent growth and regularly spend $3–5 million annually on capital investments. We also have a conservative philosophy toward the use of debt. For example, we recently made a land purchase and upon evaluation of our cash flow position decided not to take out a loan. This approach has not held us back from strategic expansion, but we are not opposed to using debt for further expansion in the future if necessary.

We also have an active operating ownership approach. This means to have ownership you must be employed by the company. By working in the business, understanding and being a part of the direction setting and implementation of strategies, we can better understand financial risk and reward. It has served us well to have multiple generations share experiences, good and bad, in order to make decisions that are right for the business and the family. Since we value both family and business, we incorporate caring for family as part of our approach to business.

CARING FOR THE FAMILY

Family is very important to our business. We believe that time given to caring for children in this generation will yield its fruit in future generations in the business, a key characteristic of the family enterprise type of family business. Furthermore, the current generation has a traditional family philosophy of having a parent stay at home to be the main caregiver. There is a great deal of respect for our spouses and the important role they play in our work and home lives. Family business can take a tremendous amount of time commitment. To have a supportive home life makes everything come into balance and makes it all worthwhile and rewarding.

Our families have been blessed to have the support and flexibility when needed to address important family needs. When needed, other family members step up and make sure necessities at work are covered. This same attitude pervades the workplace. This value of care work is embedded in our entire business culture, including for non-family employees. When family issues arise, others around the affected employee step up, help and provide support. We are proud to share this family feeling with our employees.

Family enterprise businesses not only place importance on the value of caring for families, but also have a family culture supportive of the business. As Rothausen and Sorenson show in their chapter, a respectful work–family culture decreases conflict and allows employees to be vested in both work and family. A work–family-supportive culture allows those heavily involved in the business also to contribute to the family. A supportive family culture also promotes strong and healthy relationships in the family.

INCLUSION AND COMMUNICATION

Family relationships are an asset that we leverage to benefit both family and the business. The Bailey family works hard to maintain common values, loyalty, unity, and support. For example, our ownership group (both third and fourth generation) meets regularly to discuss current activities and future direction. During meetings we may discuss a recent management team decision, an upcoming board of directors meeting, or whether to buy season tickets for the Twins professional baseball games. The leader of the meeting is rotated, sets an agenda ahead of time, and facilitates the discussion. Another family member takes and distributes minutes.

These meetings can last half an hour or two hours depending on the topics and depth of discussion. It is an excellent way to keep all owners, especially those not participating on the management team, engaged, providing input, and participating in decisions.

MANAGE THE FAMILY BUSINESS RELATIONSHIP

Our hope is that members of future generations will find our family business exciting and challenging, and will participate actively in its management in order to perpetuate its success. So, we have developed policies to manage family and business relationships. For example, one of our policies is that you must have three years of work experience outside the family business prior to joining the company.

We have established a Family Member Involvement Policy that includes six parts: (1) vision; (2) family involvement philosophy; (c) family involvement roles; (4) employment; (5) accountability and relationships; and (6) family meetings. Highlights of this policy follow:

1. Vision:
    Future generations of the Bailey family will find the business exciting and challenging and will participate actively in its management in order to perpetuate its success. We hope that the Family Member

Involvement Policy will encourage members of future generations to join the business and continue its tradition of success and profitability.

2. Family Member Involvement Policy Goals:

   (a) to guarantee professionalism and productivity;
   (b) to insure family control as a source of wealth creation and competitive advantage;
   (c) to preserve unity within the family;
   (d) to assure that family members, despite whatever disagreements or conflicts they may have, support consensus decisions with employees, customers, and competitors.

3. Family Member Involvement Roles:

   (a) Shareholders' ownership of voting stock will be vested only in family members active in the business.
   (b) Stock redemption agreements will provide for terms of divestment of voting stock from persons no longer active in the business to other active family members or to the corporation.
   (c) Management level of employment for family members and non-family members:
       • There is no special treatment for family members in management.
       • The Board of Directors or hiring manager has the sole responsibility for hiring family members.

4. Employment:
   Qualified family members are encouraged to seek employment in the company:
   (a) Full-time employment eligibility for management includes a Bachelor's degree or equivalent, preferring two years' full-time experience with at least one promotion.
   (b) Family members' participation in high-level management:
       • New family member employees must rotate among job responsibilities in the nursery for at least a year.
       • Employment is not a birthright. Placement and advancement are based on dedication, effort, and demonstrated ability. Compensation [salary] will be based on responsibility and performance. Year-end bonuses may be paid for ownership and will be distributed to family members based on overall company performance and subject to tenure with the company.

- In-laws and spouses of family members are eligible for employment the same as non-family.
- No mandatory retirement.

5. Accountability and relationships:
   Family members are accountable to the same review procedures as non-family:
   (a) Family members, like non-family employees, will receive regular reviews and performance evaluations.
   (b) We prefer that an employed family member does not have a direct reporting relationship with another immediate family member.
   (c) The appropriate supervisor will make final decisions on promoting, demoting, or firing a family member in accordance with company accountability and reporting procedures.

6. Family meetings:
   Held annually to involve all family members with ownership in the business:
   (a) Purposes:
       - To keep all informed about the company, to provide a forum for discussion, and to provide opportunity to express satisfaction or dissatisfaction with anything involving the company and/or family.
       - To provide an opportunity for discussion of family/business issues where family members can be open and honest with each other without negative implications.
   (b) Decisions at family meetings are limited to ownership issues and family issues, but can provide input for family members of the management team who make the day-to-day decisions.
   (c) Annual meetings of the immediate family include an annual report, tour, and an opportunity for questions, answers, and discussions.

FAMILY BUSINESS GOVERNANCE

A management team was formed in the mid-1990s including three family members and two non-family members. This group makes the day-to-day operational decisions of the organization. Other family members not on the management team receive agendas and minutes and are welcome to sit in on these weekly meetings. Our Board of Directors is made up of outside executives who bring a varied range of experience. Third-generation family members serve on the board. Two of the external board members, from multi-generational businesses, have been instrumental in assisting us to set up family business policies.

We expect that the board, in addition to addressing business issues, will help us find ways to develop family members to work in the business. We look to the board for advice about policies and planning related to family positions, employment, and development. Any family member may attend board meetings. However, no one in the fourth generation currently sits on the board.

Our board has been instrumental in guiding our organization through difficulties and challenges. We are fortunate to have people with diverse backgrounds, keen listening skills, and a knack for asking the tough questions. Our aim is to focus on strategic direction and implementation. We use the board's expertise and outside perspective to make us a successful company that will last for generations to come.

Our approach to governance demonstrates the importance of our family point of view about the business and family member involvement in the business. As Rothausen and Sorenson show in their work, this type of governance strategy allows for the business to benefit from the relationships that are already established in the family. Furthermore, because of the involvement of many generations in the family business, family members who understand the business are able to teach and prepare future family business members how to be involved with the business. This is beneficial as it promotes long-term development and planning. In addition, by keeping family members in the business, family enterprises have the ability to not only draw upon the assets of future family members, but also to have a greater ability to be able to revise norms and values that promote both the family and business.

SUMMARY

In summary, our organization might best be described as a family-enterprise-first company. When relevant, we separate family and business, but we also interweave work, family, and other facets of life. We have similar interests, enjoy being together, and we design the business to maintain strong family relationships.

There are many challenges ahead for our family and our business – future successions, continued leadership development for ownership, continued involvement of non-family managers, dynamic changes in our industry and our economy, and our ability to adapt and implement change.

We recognize the importance of our spouses and their involvement, and will look for ways to engage others to better understand the significance and pride that goes along with being part of a multi-generational business. It is what affords us a comfortable life but also includes the challenge of making tough decisions that affect hundreds of employees and their families. It is an awesome responsibility and we are grateful to have the opportunity to contribute hopefully to a legacy that will set the stage for a fifth generation of Bailey Nurseries operations.

14. Putting family in family business: the role of the chief emotional officer

Angela Pritchard

INTRODUCTION

CEO. What does that acronym mean to you? For me, like many, those letters, placed side by side, stand for chief executive officer. However, beyond those letters lie other words, such as leader, mentor, strength, and ambition; words that personify what that title represents. Now what if I told you that CEO, as an acronym, stood for something else, yet maintained those same characteristics?

The position of chief emotional officer is one that is essential within family businesses. For clarity, I'll utilize CEmO as the designed acronym for this role. You could use this acronym and search hundreds of company directories, yet I would be shocked if you happened upon a single find. However, if you looked at the dynamic of family businesses, the CEmO would be hard to miss. This is the person who works alongside the CEO to effectively manage the business and the family, and, as a result, is usually assumed by the CEO's spouse. This relates to Poza and Messer's notion that spouses play an instrumental role in the life of the family business.[1]

In the beginning, my family's business was no exception to Poza and Messer's rule. My father was the CEO, and my mother easily assumed the role of the CEmO. As a result, I grew up in a household where family and business not only co-existed, but also served as defining functions of one another. However, as I got older and the company expanded, I began to see how the role of the CEmO, although rewarding, did not come without its challenges. With those challenges came a shift, but not so much in regard to the roles and responsibilities of the CEmO, but with who would be assuming them.

Pritchard Auto Company was founded in 1913 by my great-great grandfather Walter Pritchard. In 1929, Walter's son John took over the company and added a second dealership. By the 1950s, my grandfather William Pritchard had entered the business full time, and in 1983 my father Joseph Pritchard, at the young age of 19, joined the team. In 1994 my father began diversifying the company and by 2007 it evolved into Pritchard Family Auto Stores, a fourth-generation family-owned and -operated company consisting of seven dealerships, representing all domestic franchises. After graduating from college in 2007, I took on a full-time position at Pritchard Family Auto Stores. Signing on as the Business Manager of our fleet division, I did not foresee the shift that would occur, leading me into one of the most challenging, yet necessary roles within our company. It was the position that my mother had held and unknowingly groomed me for: CEmO.

CHIEF EMOTIONAL OFFICER IN THE BUSINESS

It is clear from our legacy that Pritchard Auto Company has been owned and operated by a series of talented, hard-working, dedicated business-men, and my father is no exception. However, he was the first one to test the true strength of the company by rattling its foundation. Up until 1994 Pritchard Auto Company was a Ford, Lincoln, Mercury dealer. Given the circumstances of the auto industry at that time, my father wanted to diver-sify the company by adding a third location with different franchises, so that year, Chrysler of Forest City opened, offering Chrysler, Jeep, Dodge, and Sprinter products. The decision to expand and diversify created tension because Pritchard Auto Company now had a competitive brand within its market. Even though both franchises were part of the Pritchard group, they were competing for business against one another.

With the opening of the third location, my mother had the opportunity to work for the family business. For years she had been a supporter of my father and his role within the company. As his partner, she had come to know his concerns about the business and undoubtedly offered her sugges-tions on how to address and resolve those issues over the years. So what a wonderful asset she would be to utilize within the company.

Although her title read fleet administrator, my mother's most valuable contribution to the company was within the realm of human resources. Even before working full time for the family business, she was an integral part of the hiring process. After sifting through applications, my father would turn to my mother for her opinion on his top hiring choices. She has an uncanny ability to read people and determine whether they could be an asset to the company, and as much as my father does not always wish to admit it, she has a proven record of being spot on pretty much every time. For example, there have been a few occasions where my father has been set on hiring an individual, whether that was for relationship or experience purposes, but my mother did not support the decision. She would voice her opinion on why that person was not the best fit, but my father insisted on hiring them. Soon enough he began to see what she was able to sense from the beginning and before we knew it, they had either left or been asked to leave the company. As a result of those situations, she became a sounding board. She was the person my father could trust for an open, honest opinion.

Not only was she a sounding board for my father, she assumed that role amongst the employees. Rather than sitting in an office and keeping her distance, she would make an effort to get to the different locations each week and talk to the employees. Whether it was catching up on what was new in their lives or discussing a problem they were having at the office, my mother felt it was important for them to know we were a family-first business and they were an extended part of our family. Her role as CEmO reflected what Poza and Messer described as "the unique yet usual role as steward of the family legacy, facilitator of communications, and touchstone of emotional intelligence in family relations."[2]

CHIEF EMOTIONAL OFFICER IN THE FAMILY

Keeping the lines of communication open was essential, which was something my parents reinforced not only in the workplace, but in their home. Beginning their relationship as high school sweethearts, my mother and father were able to develop a system over the years that structured their communication patterns. As a result they had an unspoken ability to identify what could be talked about, how it could be talked about, and when it could be talked about. That pattern was tested as children entered the picture and the business began to grow. Their communication patterns had to be modified and honed.

When my father expanded the business, he relied more upon my mother to not only care for the family if he had to put in long hours or be away, but also to be there to support him, to listen to his ideas, his frustration, or his uncertainty. Should he acquire another dealership? Should he apply for another franchise? Did he need to look for a partner or could he fund an expansion on his own? The added pressure forced her to juggle family and business in an entirely new way. Although she had worked full time with another company prior to her employment with Pritchard Auto Company, being a part of the family business brought on new challenges. She was no longer the bystander who was able to listen to her husband's business concerns, offer her advice, and wake up to go work for a different employer the next day. Business and family started to take on similar characteristics. It could have been difficult for us children to separate the two, but with the help of our CEmO there were structures, rituals in place to help us utilize our unique situation to build a stronger family and business dynamic.

One of the most important rituals our CEmO sustained in order to protect the importance of family was dinnertime. Regardless of the situation, dinner was a priority at the Pritchard house. It was a time when business was shut off and we could simply be a family. My mother would coordinate our schedules so that even when we had volleyball or football practice, or if my dad was working late, we would have at least one hour to sit down and be a family. She would not simply have something delivered. Our CEmO would spend her mornings before leaving for the office, or the evenings after coming home to cook and bake a beautiful meal. The dinner was always a reflection of our family's current dynamic: pasta for the older girls because they had a track meet the next evening, but with asparagus because that was my dad's favorite; some carrots for our littlest sister; and a side salad in case my brother was cutting weight for wrestling. Each dish was chosen for a specific reason and made with love. We all made dinner a priority to show our respect for the work that was put into the meal. It was a ritual, a symbolic act, which we unquestionably maintained because of the value it added to our lives. And it was a ritual that was consistently sustained by our CEmO.

During dinner we also had other rituals that facilitated and over time honed our communication techniques. After sitting down together, praying, and dishing up our food, we would go around the table and ask one another about the best part of our day. Even on the nights when we already had an idea what the best part of someone's day may have been we always made sure the question was asked and the answer communicated. That one small ritual was like a green light, giving our family the go-ahead to communicate with one another about our lives. It would lead into discussions about school, sports, friends, and anything else we felt like sharing. As the years have progressed, our average dinnertimes have evolved into two- to three-hour-long conversations of telling stories, reflecting on life, sharing goals, and making memories. Thus, although we are a family business, during dinnertime we are simply a family.

TENSIONS AND GROWTH

My mother continued working for the family business and maintained her position as the CEmO in the family and the company for 12 years. During that time she stood by my father as he became the majority shareholder. Between his drive and the support system she provided, Pritchard Auto Company added four new locations within three years (2004–07) and came to represent all domestic franchises. In order to open and maintain four additional locations, the focus had to shift from family to business. With the number of employees doubling and distance between the stores spreading, it became more difficult to demonstrate and advocate the family aspect within the business. The foundation of Pritchard Auto Company had been built with a family mentality; employees were more than just one more person working for our company and customers were not simply another person walking through the door. However, the family mentality was slipping as bottom lines became more pressing.

Rather than allowing the business-first mentality to progress, our CEO and CEmO brainstormed and developed a way to tie all of the businesses together. They gave the foundation of the dealerships an identity, a name that reflected what truly made the company what it was. Pritchard Family Auto Stores became the organization that each individual dealership was linked to. Not only did that name put the family part back in the business, our CEmO designed a logo to reinforce the family aspect and pay tribute to the foundation on which the business was built. The logo, from a distance, is a circle with a stenciled P in the middle. However, if you look closer, within the circle is a little bit of the new company and a little bit of the old, reading Pritchard Family Auto Stores, Est. 1913. It is a symbol that reflected our pride as a family, as a business, and as a family business. It gave us a new platform to build from while keeping those values intact.

The expansion allowed our company to grow locally and nationally; however, the growth did not come without its hardships within the home. My father was now responsible for seven dealerships located in seven different towns across Northern Iowa. Starting as a family-first business, my father made it clear from day one that he would rather lock up the doors and walk away from the company than have it ruin our family relationships. Yet, it was clear that the family-first business was becoming more of a business-first entity.

In order to provide for the family, our CEO had to focus on making the businesses successful, yet that meant sacrificing time with the family to be in the businesses. So although it appeared that business was being put first, it was the result of our CEO putting family needs first. The intentions (family-first) of our CEO were clear when this cycle began, but as time went on, it became more and more difficult to determine whether business or family was being put first. Our CEmO saw that the safe haven where we could simply be a family was diminishing. With the household only consisting of my mother, father, and youngest sister (as the rest of us had gone to college or moved away), family dinners were fewer and farther between, and it appeared as though business had personified itself and filled the empty seats my brother, sister, and I no longer sat at.

It became clear to our CEmO that something needed to be done. Although she enjoyed being a part of the family business, she felt it would be best to distance herself from the business and focus on the needs of the family. She left her position with the company and thus retired her position as the CEmO in order to rebuild the family system. So on the nights when my father was exhausted and needed someone to talk to, my mother could simply be his wife and listen. In many ways she became what Poza and Messer describe as the "chief trust officer." By taking a step back, she was allowing herself to be "the glue that keeps the family together through the predictable challenges families, especially families that work together, face."[3]

A NEW CHIEF EMOTIONAL OFFICER

As one family member exited the business, another entered. In December of 2007, I graduated from college and was offered a full-time job by my father to work for Pritchard Family Auto Stores. As someone who had worked in various facets of the company since my freshman year in high school, I was looking forward to being an official part of the Pritchard legacy. For the first six months, I worked as my father's assistant. This allowed me the opportunity to learn about the industry and see at what capacity I could be most beneficial to the company. During those six months, I lived with my family. With my mother focusing on her own business venture, opening and managing a fitness facility, I would work with my father during the day and came home at night to re-establish an important part of our family's foundation – dinnertime. Since I had the time, I would prepare a meal for the family. Some nights my mother would be home to help, while other nights she was tied up at work. However, we started to make an effort to sit down and share family dinners together and take the time after long days at work to simply be a family again.

Along with preparing family dinners, I began taking on more and more of the CEmO roles my mother used to play. For example, I started serving as a sounding board in regard to certain business decisions our CEO made. Sometimes this meant looking at employee applications or discussing potential hires, while other times it was simply a matter of talking about accounts that we were looking to take on and whether we could handle the additional business. I also found myself making a point to interact personally with other employees and customers, especially those I worked directly with, in order to reinforce the concept of what it means to be a family-first business.

Additionally, my father and I have done our best to address and resolve issues while we are in the office, rather than bring the stresses of work home with us. However, we have found ourselves discussing business outside of working hours. For instance, at dinner while we are discussing our day, one of us will remember there is an upcoming meeting or task that needs to be completed and remind the other of it. At times it is simply an casual comment, while other times it can lead into a full conversation. Yet, we are able to take a step back and realize that there is a time for business and a time for family.

I feel the reason we are able to do that is because we are father and daughter, as opposed to husband and wife. The additional degree of separation is what allows us to maintain a healthy working relationship while still maintaining our personal relationship. As a result, my mother and father can be partners once again. They no longer have to balance family and business, day in and day out. My mother can offer her advice on how my father should handle a situation, without having to worry about whether or not he takes the advice, as she is no longer directly affected by the business decisions he makes. For example, if he wants to hire an individual she does not feel is suitable for a job, she can offer her advice and from that point he no longer needs to stress about the situation. If things work out, great, and if not, then it is simply a matter of finding the next qualified individual. The result of business situations no longer consumes or affects their personal relationship. They can simply be husband and wife. All the while, I get to assume the role of CEmO at Pritchard Family Auto Stores.

Through my exploration of the idea of the chief emotional officer in family businesses, I have been able to identify the presence and importance of that position within my family's business. Historically this role has been assumed by the spouse of the CEO and in the beginning, our company was no exception. My mother served as the CEmO of the business and our family in order to create an environment where both could coexist. However, I have learned that we were able to modify the concept of the CEmO in order to fit the particular needs of our business. For us, that meant adding a generational degree of separation into the mix. Regardless of who assumed that position, the need for someone to fill it remained. I am confident that the reason our company has been able to achieve success is in large part due to the presence of not only a chief executive officer, but a chief emotional officer. Our family-first model and family time have been preserved by our modification of the chief emotional officer role.

NOTES

1. Poza and Messer (2001, p. 26).
2. Ibid., p. 25.
3. Ibid., p. 29.

15. The family as an internal and external resource of the firm: the importance of building a family-firm identity

Kimberly Eddleston

To further the family business field, advances need to be made to explain why and how family firms are different from non-family firms, as well as how family firms vary.[1] The key questions to address in understanding the uniqueness of family firms and why some family firms are more successful than others are: "What comprises a family firm?" and "How can the family contribute to firm success?" A current conceptualization of family firms tries to address these questions by considering the family's involvement and essence.[2] The involvement approach posits that only firms with family participation in ownership, governance, and management are identified as family firms. The basic assumption here is that relatively objective assessments of family involvement can distinguish family firms from non-family firms. However, a flaw with this approach is that it assumes that simply because a family owns firm stock, the family will have influence on the firm's decisions. As such, Chrisman and colleagues added the essence approach to their conceptualization of family firms.[3] The essence approach suggests that family involvement is merely a necessary condition to define a family firm. To truly understand a family's involvement in a firm, one should carefully examine the family's influence on the firm's vision, behaviors, perpetuation, and growth.[4] While the essence approach provides a more fine-grained view of family involvement, it may not quite capture when the family is a significant resource for the family firm, a resource that distinguishes the most successful family firms.

The entrepreneurship literature has recognized the assistance a family can provide in the launch and growth of a business. For example, research has revealed the importance of help from a spouse in establishing a new venture.[5,6] A spouse may provide administrative assistance within the

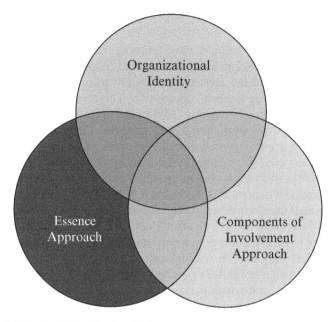

Figure 15.1   Defining the family firm

business, for instance, or support to the entrepreneur by assuming responsibility for the majority of household tasks. Family is a key source of intermittent unpaid labor, which is necessary during the start-up and expansion phases of a business.[7,8] Further, some entrepreneurs, particularly women, start businesses to accommodate family demands.[9] Therefore, given recent advances in the entrepreneurship literature acknowledging a family's influence on any business – family and non-family firms alike – a more comprehensive approach that delineates the unique resource a family bestows a family firm is necessary.

Family business literature needs a complementary viewpoint to the components of involvement and essence approaches. This approach should distinguish when the family is a substantive force, guiding the decisions of the family firm leader, versus merely a symbolic element that is not integrated into firm decision-making. Drawing from organizational identity theory, I argue that since people behave in ways that are congruent to their identity,[10] firm leaders that label their firms a "family firm" will behave and make decisions differently than those who call their firms a "non-family firm." Below, I discuss organizational identity theory and then offer a three-circle model for defining the family firm, as seen above in Figure 15.1.

ORGANIZATIONAL IDENTITY THEORY

Organizational identity includes those features of an organization that are thought to be the most central, distinctive, and enduring.[11] Organizational identity reflects members' consensual view of "who we are as an organization" and "what we do as a collective."[12] The core features of organizational identity have a sense of continuity since they are tied to the organization's history and shared with members through the value and beliefs arising from repeated interaction with others.[13,14] The social constructionist view of organizational identity highlights organizational members' collective beliefs and values that create a shared interpretation of organizational experiences.[15] Research in this tradition examines how organizational members develop shared understandings of their organizations and how these affect organizational behavior, strategic decisions, and change.[16] In this way, organizational identity helps members make sense of what they do,[17] providing the context within which members interpret and assign insightful meaning to their behavior.[18]

While the social constructionist view emphasizes the sense-making function of organizational identity, the institutional view emphasizes the sense-giving function, focusing on the deliberate attempt by organizational leaders to shape others' interpretation, thus influencing "how members of an organization should behave and how other organizations should relate to them."[19] The institutional perspective sees organizational identity as a reflection of clearly stated values and formal claims of what an organization is and represents.[20] In turn, organizational identity is expected to create a strong sense of responsibility for the organizations.

In particular, family businesses may be skillful at fostering organizational identification since their unique identities are composed of elements from both family and business systems, which overlap to various degrees.[21] Through discussions, often around the family meal, the family can create a common set of beliefs about their family firm's identity.[22] Families can shape a strong family-firm identity by establishing a corporate brand that reflects the family's importance to the firm and/or an organizational culture that supports the family's role in the firm. By doing so, the family forges an organizational identity that reveals its values and strategies through communication, behavior, and symbolism.[23] The organization's identity reflects the unique features of the family firm and the organization's persona, depicting the firm's heritage and setting a course for the firm's future. Thus, a family-firm identity conveys "who we are as a family business."[24,25]

Yet, firms vary in the degree to which they integrate the family into their organizational identity.[26] Family firm leaders often struggle to decide whether the business exists for the family, or the family exists for the business.[27] While some leaders choose to separate their family from the business, others choose to integrate their family and business roles to create a family-firm identity. Behavioral expectations drawn from the family role center on nurturing, care giving, commitment, and loyalty to family members, and reflect a collectivistic orientation.[28] In contrast, behavioral expectations derived from the business role center on devotion to the business, pursuit of business success, and legitimacy in the marketplace.[29] Leaders who define their business as a "family business" therefore aim to integrate their family and business roles, viewing the family as a key component of the business. When the family is central to the firm's identity, the family's values provide a foundation for decision-making[30] and contribute to a culture of identification and shared identity.[31]

When family members believe their firm, its history, or their family is impressive, they strengthen organizational identification. The successes, accomplishments, and triumphs of one family member can become a shared identity for the entire family.[32] When family businesses integrate the family into the firm's identity they may provide the business with an important source of competitive advantage that others cannot imitate.[33] Kinship, a shared family name, common history, and familiarity can promote a strong, shared identity in family firms, all of which encourage organizational members to uphold organizational values and pursue organizational goals.[34] For those family firms with a strong identity, the family and the business are seen as one. Family firm leaders build a consistent view of their organization and shape organizational members' beliefs about who they are and what they do as an organization. In this way, family-firm identity can serve both sense-making and sense-giving functions, thus helping to explain as well as predict family firm behavior. In other words, the degree to which a firm sees itself as a family firm may have a profound impact on its values, goals, and behaviors.

The Family as an Internal Resource

The strong ties among family members can create a common set of values and goals that guide family members' behavior. When family firm membership contributes to family members' self-worth and esteem, family members strongly identify with the organization. Being a member of a family may prompt people to identify with the organization, strengthening their goal commitment and motivation as a result. As such, "fulfilling family obligations can be a source of pride, serve as an important non-monetary incentive and provide a common rallying ground for members of the family firm."[35] Strong family-firm identity can even cause family

members to monitor one another's behavior, enhancing firm performance.

As a matter of fact, research indicates that the most successful family
firms are those with loyal, interdependent, committed and altruistic family
members.[36,37] When family members are deeply committed to the business
and members believe that they have a common family responsibility to see
the business prosper, they are highly motivated to fulfill organizational
goals and maximize firm performance. When a family feels a sense of unity
with the family firm, family members may also offer personal resources
like free labor, equity investments, and financial loans. Many family
firms survive difficult times because family members are willing to work
without pay or offer their personal assets to secure loans for the business.[38]
Therefore, a strong family-firm identity can create a sense of oneness and
shared destiny among family members that lead them to work toward
organizational goals and to uphold the values of the family firm.

Another way family firms can see the benefit of building a strong
family-firm identity is through an involved and participative workforce.
Firms with much family member exchange, characterized as having family
employees who share ideas, feedback, and expectations of one another, are
more successful than those firms where family members do not communicate or exchange information.[39] Frequent and close social interactions
allow family members to create a common point of view regarding their
family business.[40] Specifically, family member exchange seems to be associated with a strong sense of shared ownership and organizational identity.
Family firms that foster family member exchange understand that family
relationships are the building blocks of their organization.[41] Study results
show that family member exchange helps to ensure that employees are
matched with the appropriate work tasks based on their abilities, thereby
strengthening family firm performance.[42] Similarly, another study demonstrated that despite lacking human capital, a family firm can successfully
pursue entrepreneurial ventures if the family possesses much pride and
unity toward the firm. As such, family firms may be able to compensate for
a lack of human capital with family dedication and commitment.[43] Since
family firms are often criticized for hiring family members regardless of
their qualifications,[44] factors that ensure family members contribute to the
firm may certainly distinguish the most successful family firms.

Likewise, family firms that implement a participative strategy process
are most successful.[45] A participative strategy process enhances family
members' identification with the firm, helping them to understand the
challenges facing the firm as well as the firm's strengths, weaknesses,
resources, and capabilities.[46] Encouraging family members to participate
in strategic decision-making may be especially important for family firms

because in order to remain competitive, family firms should generate new strategies for each generation that joins the firm.[47] Furthermore, participation in the strategy-making process seems to increase commitment to a course of action and improve the decision-making quality of family firms.[48] Additionally, family firms that encourage participation and collaboration support ethical norms that assist family firm performance through the accumulation of goodwill, loyalty, and social support.[49] Therefore, family members who strongly identify with their organizations will view their role in the family firm with pride and see their employment as a type of family obligation that provides a common rallying ground for the family.

The Family as an External Resource

Organizations tend to manage internal and external relationships according to the same principles, values, and goals.[50] Organizational identity influences external audiences' perception of the firm's image and branding practices,[51] thereby affecting the public's acceptance of the firm's products, strategies, and employees.[52] Since a family's identity is unique, it may be an important source of competitive advantage in the marketplace.[53] Families go to great lengths to maintain a positive reputation in their communities,[54] and the family often becomes a significant image of the firm in the eyes of external stakeholders. In this way, the family comes to personify the business, becoming an external resource for the family firm.

Being known as a "family firm" may be perceived as a positive and distinct feature in the minds of consumers, thus contributing to firm performance. Through image-making activity, firm leaders publicize what is special, unique, and distinctive about their business.[55] Because family firm members are likely to view their business as extensions of themselves and their family, they go to great lengths to create and maintain a positive organizational identity.[56] They understand that switching families if their family firm's reputation is damaged is not an option for them. Many family firms also understand that capitalizing on their family firm status may be a way to build a distinct corporate brand. For example, developing a family-based brand identity positively contributes to firm growth and profitability by influencing customer-centered values.[57] Promoting a business as a family business to external stakeholders such as customers, suppliers, and financiers capitalizes on their positive perception of family firms as trustworthy, customer-focused, and quality-driven.[58,59] In this way the family firm can establish an "extended family" of stakeholders who uphold the principles of loyalty, fairness, and respect, and thus build social support for the business.[60] A firm's close association with a prominent family can also help the firm to raise money and to attract and retain customers.[61]

Businesses such as S.C. Johnson, which portrays itself as "A Family Company," may have a competitive advantage. Indeed, a recent study by Zellweger and colleagues showed that firms that make their family-firm identity known to external stakeholders reap performance benefits.[62] As such, the family-firm identity can become a sustainable legacy passed down from one generation to the next, enabling the firm to build a competitive advantage that improves growth and performance expectations.[63]

Emphasizing a family-firm identity can also lead to the accumulation of community-level social capital – a resource that embodies the information, contacts, and reciprocity that family businesses appear to share through a community of family-controlled organizations.[64] Family businesses often possess a sense of community that encourages the businesses to provide social support and information to each other. The information gained from other family firms is likely to be inexpensive, trustworthy, and credible, improving decision-making.[65] Family firms also help one another navigate uncertainty in their environments, providing business tips and access to new markets.[66] For example, many family firms successfully use alliances and cooperative arrangements when pursuing international ventures.[67] Therefore, firms that nurture their family-firm identity may be able to gain access to community-level social capital that assists with their operations and performance.

While an organizational identity can cultivate a family that is an internal and external resource to a family firm, not all family firms choose to foster a family-firm identity. Recent research applying organizational identity theory acknowledges that family firms have two relevant identities – the family and the business – that can be segmented or integrated to different degrees.[68] Sorenson and colleagues note that "the creation of a family business does not guarantee the development of a family point of view."[69] Some family firms may choose to ignore or downplay their family firm status and thus resemble non-family firms to stakeholders. Perhaps the (mis)perception that family firms are resistant to change, stagnant,[70] or not professionally managed[71] leads these firms to avoid building a family-firm identity. Therefore, organizational identity is just one piece of the puzzle as to why some family firms are more successful than others.

INTEGRATING ORGANIZATIONAL IDENTITY WITH THE INVOLVEMENT AND ESSENCE APPROACHES

Figure 15.1 illustrates the integration of organizational identity with the components of involvement and essence approaches, offering a three-dimensional conceptualization of family firms. While the components approach reflects what the firm objectively looks like (i.e., family share-holders, managers, owners), the essence approach captures the family's influence on the business, and organizational identity assesses the degree to which firm leaders view the firm as a family firm. Where a firm is located on the model will have a profound impact on the firm's values and behaviors. For example, if we consider each component separately, the components of involvement approach, with its emphasis on ownership and control, should have the greatest impact on factors related to earnings and profit-sharing. An example of a solely "components of family involvement" firm would be a real-estate holding company with family ownership but professional management. The family is rarely involved in the management of the business and does not see the business as a "family business." The firm is merely a source of wealth for family members.

In contrast, the essence approach, with its emphasis on influence, should reflect the family's support for the business. An example of a solely "essence-oriented" firm would be one in which a business owner uses family labor, perhaps unpaid, yet the owner does not view the business as a family firm nor do family members share ownership of the firm. Perhaps the business owner's husband assists with bookkeeping or her children periodically stuff envelopes. But to the owner, it is *her* business.

Lastly, the organizational identity approach, with its emphasis on family-firm identity, captures the firm leaders' perception of the business – are we a family firm? Thus, organizational identity should have a significant impact on factors at the interface of the family and the firm such as issues related to family members' role in the business, the image and reputation of the firm as family-related, and the methods family members will use to accomplish and create firm goals. An example of a solely "identity-oriented" firm would be one in which an entrepreneur starts the business with the goal of his sons some day becoming partners – hoping to build a legacy for his family. No family members may currently work in the firm or share ownership, yet the entrepreneur still sees his firm as a "family firm." Another example would be a business owner who follows in her father's professional footsteps (i.e., lawyer, CPA, architect) and takes over his practice. But it is a sole proprietorship where she is the only owner and employee. She may still view her business as a "family firm" since she did acquire her father's business. However, from the components and essence approaches, her business would not be defined as a family firm.

As the approaches overlap, one can see how difficult it may become to understand and predict family firm behavior. The model clearly depicts why the goals and values among family firms may differ and why the concerns of family firms can be quite different from those of non-family firms. Therefore, this three-dimensional model explains how family businesses differ from non-family firms and also the variation among family firms. By combining organizational identity with the components of involvement and essence approaches, we begin to see how a family-firm identity may provide a sense of meaning and purpose to family members that directs their behavior. In turn, understanding these differences is key to explaining the various goals and behaviors that distinguish these firms.

DISCUSSION

Organizational identity offers a complementary yet unique approach to the components of involvement and essence approaches to defining family firms. As indicated by organizational identity theory, defining one's firm as a "family firm" may create internal as well as external consequences for the firm. Family-firm identity guides both sense-making and sense-giving functions. It depicts family members' consensual view of the business as a family firm (or not) and reflects a sense-making perspective that helps members make sense of what they do and why. Organizational identity also helps firm leaders provide a coherent guide for how firm members should behave and how external parties should relate to them.[72]

Given that research has begun to highlight the important role that families can play in helping or hindering the entrepreneurial efforts of family and non-family firm leaders alike,[73] understanding the direct influence of the family on the firm is important. Furthermore, it is important to understand if the family is a substantive component of the firm or merely symbolic. Succession problems are common in family firms – heirs are not always apparent or eager.[74] Since organizational identity highlights the *consensual* view of firm members that addresses "who we are" as an organization and guiding the behaviors of family members, family-firm identity may be key to explaining differences among family firms as well as differences between family and non-family firms. Organizational identity may also explain why some firms under family control behave more like non-family firms. For example, in industries where family firms are uncommon, these firms may feel pressure to hide their family involvement in order to make the firm seem more similar to others.[75] Therefore, organizational identity may be an important component in understanding family firm behavior – a component that complements the involvement and essence approaches to defining the family firm and explaining how the family can be a resource to the family firm.

Implications for Practice

Asking leaders to determine whether their business is a family firm and to explain what that means may be beneficial because it forces these leaders to define the role of the family in the firm. What the family would like to see accomplished through the business – the "family agenda" – could then be explored in terms of family wealth, career opportunities for family members, and reputation in the community.[76] In turn, what the business can accomplish through the family – "the business agenda" – can also be explored, examining the family's utility function and caretaking role in the business. An effective family-firm identity should therefore be seen as one in which the family and business are interdependent and collaborative, whereby one contributes to the other.

While the positive aspects of family-firm identity have been the focus here, a darker side should also be acknowledged. Sometimes family business leaders can be so embedded in the family that they pursue limited, self-serving family concerns at the expense of the business.[77] Some leaders must grapple with contradictory needs between the family and the business.[78] Conflicting expectations arising from family and business roles can cause leaders to question whether they need to interpret an issue from the point of view of a "boss," "mother," "entrepreneur," or "spouse." Such ambiguity can cause leaders to wonder which should come first: the family or the business. Furthermore, too much preference for the family can lead non-family employees to perceive family firm leaders as unfair and untrustworthy.[79] Since organizational identity is strengthened through social categorization and comparisons, family firms must work to integrate non-family employees into the business, or face problems stemming from the development of in-groups and out-groups. Thus, the cultivation of an effective family-firm identity is often a balancing act.

In closing, cultivating a family-firm identity may provide a family firm with a competitive advantage in the marketplace by establishing both internal and external social capital. In conjunction with the components of involvement and essence approaches, organizational identity helps explain how family firms are different from non-family firms as well as why some family firms are better able to harness the benefits of familiness than others. Although there are some caveats regarding the benefits of a family-firm identity, when nurtured to reflect the interdependent and symbiotic relationship between the family and the business, a family-firm identity allows a family firm to build on its unique heritage and provides direction for the business's future. It is a substantive force for family firms – guiding family members' behavior in the firm and offering the firm a distinctive edge when communicating with external stakeholders.

NOTES

1.   Chrisman et al. (2006).
2.   Chrisman et al. (2005).
3.   Ibid.
4.   Ibid.
5.   Goffee and Scase (1985).
6.   Parasuraman et al. (1986).
7.   Fock (1998).
8.   Redding (1991).
9.   Brush (1992).
10. Ashforth and Mael (1996).
11. Albert and Whetten (1985).
12. Nag et al. (2007).
13. Ashforth and Mael (1996).
14. Gioia et al. (2000).
15. Gioia (1998).
16. Ravasi and Schultz (2006).
17. Fiol (1991).
18. Ravasi and Schultz (2006).
19. Ibid., p. 435.
20. Ibid.
21. Sundaramurthy and Kreiner (2008).
22. Sorenson and Bierman (2009).
23. Muzellec (2006).
24. Reay (2009).
25. Shepherd and Haynie (2009).
26. Sundaramurthy and Kreiner (2008).
27. Lansberg (1983).
28. Shepherd and Haynie (2009).
29. Ibid.
30. Reay (2009).
31. Sundaramurthy and Kreiner (2008).
32. Ward and Aronoff (1995).
33. Sundaramurthy and Kreiner (2008).
34. Ibid.
35. Ibid., p. 425.
36. Eddleston and Kellermanns (2007).
37. Eddleston et al. (2008a).
38. Danes et al. (2009a).
39. Kellermanns and Eddleston (2007).
40. Sorenson et al. (2009).
41. Kellermanns and Eddleston (2007).
42. Ibid.
43. Eddleston et al. (2008b).
44. Schulze et al. (2001).
45. Eddleston and Kellermanns (2007).
46. Ibid.
47. Post (1993).
48. Kellermanns and Eddleston (2007).
49. Sorenson et al. (2009).
50. Rousseau and Wade-Benzoni (1994).
51. Karreman and Rylander (2008).
52. Fombrun and Shanley (1990).
53. Sundaramurthy and Kreiner (2008).

54. Dyer and Whetten (2006).
55. Scott and Lane (2000).
56. Dyer and Whetten (2006).
57. Craig et al. (2008).
58. Ibid.
59. Ward and Aronoff (1995).
60. Sorenson et al. (2009).
61. Sundaramurthy and Kreiner (2008).
62. Zellweger et al. (2010).
63. Craig et al. (2008).
64. Lester and Cannella (2006).
65. Haunschild and Beckman (1998).
66. Lester and Cannella (2006)
67. Gallo and García-Pont (1996).
68. Sundaramurthy and Kreiner (2008).
69. Sorenson et al. (2009, p. 250).
70. Miller et al. (2008).
71. Schulze et al. (2001).
72. Albert and Whetten (1985).
73. Jennings and McDougald (2007).
74. Stavrou (1999).
75. Reay (2009).
76. Villanueva and Sapienza (2009).
77. Le Breton-Miller and Miller (2009).
78. Shepherd and Haynie (2009).
79. Sundaramurthy and Kreiner (2008).

16. Reclaiming our identity as a business-owning family

Sylvia Shepard

INTRODUCTION

In her paper, "The family as an internal and external resource of the firm: the importance of building family-firm identity," (Chapter 15) Kimberly Eddleston presents a convincing argument that when employees and family leaders embrace their identity as a family firm,[1] their behaviors and decisions will be more likely to lead to the competitive advantages that often accrue to family businesses. While I agree with much of Eddleston's paper, she has not captured the dynamic nature of the family-firm identity in multi-generational family firms. She accurately notes that the organizational identity of a family firm is closely tied to the family, but she has not adequately considered the impact of the identity of the family itself on the family identity of the firm. From the perspective of a fifth-generation owner of a family firm, it is clear to me that a family-firm identity changes as each generation assumes ownership and leadership roles, with the early generations building the identity, and the later generations modifying, sustaining, or neglecting it. If the family-firm identity is to survive over the generations, the family's identity must remain strong. The multi-generational family in particular must resist the forces that pull it apart into multiple branches and nuclear family groups, actively nurturing its own identity as a single business-owning family.

THE DYNAMIC NATURE OF THE RELATIONSHIP BETWEEN THE FAMILY AND THEIR BUSINESS

Eddleston identifies three different ways to conceptualize a family firm: components of involvement, essence-oriented approach, and the organizational identity approach. In the components of involvement approach, family members own the firm, but utilize mostly professional managers and view their ownership stake as an investment alone. The family's perspective is that they own a firm together, but they have nothing to do with it, and the company does not identify itself as a family firm. In the essence-oriented approach, the family members may work in the firm, but they do not share in the ownership or the decision-making, and the owner does not identify the firm as a family business. Finally, the organizational-identity-oriented family-owned firm is one in which the family members and firm leaders celebrate the familiness of the firm. The firm is part of the family's identity, and the family is part of the firm's identity. The family identity infuses the organization internally, affecting behavior, strategy, and decision-making, and is projected externally, in a deliberate effort to shape outside perceptions of the organization.

Eddleston uses the family's role and its impact on the business as the criteria for defining a family firm, and I can see how a firm might clearly fall into one of the three categories described above. However, it is instructive to analyze firms that are clearly identified as family firms, according to Eddleston's criteria, in terms of the degree to which they reveal characteristics of an essence-oriented or component-oriented firm. Furthermore, firms that may appear to be purely essence-oriented may not be. For example, while most start-up firms tend to be essence-oriented, many can be identified as family firms, even in the start-up phase. Family capital is often used to finance the early years of the business, and this use of family resources might mean that the business would fall into the family firm category from the very start. Although the founder may be making all of the decisions, the family investors may have an influence that is not readily apparent.

In addition, the relationship between family members and their family-owned business may have a tendency to move toward a components orientation as the business matures, even when the firm retains its family-firm identity. For example, a multi-generational firm may have no family members in the business, no family governance system, a holding company structure and family members who view the company as an investment. Yet, it has established a reputation over the generations as a family firm. While the family identity is relatively weak in this scenario, this must still be considered a firm with a family identity. My family's story demonstrates how family-firm identities develop and change from generation to generation, and how a family-firm identity tends toward a components orientation as the family and its business matures.

THE FOUNDING GENERATION: CHRISTIAN VALUES

The founder of our family business, Elisha, was not only an entrepreneur, he was a pioneer.[2] He and his young wife left the East Coast in the mid-1800s and travelled to the Midwest to begin a new life. As one of the few businesses in a sparsely settled area, the growth of the company was integrally related to the growth of the community. In the 20 years following the purchase of a tiny struggling pail factory, the company grew to become the largest woodenware manufacturer in the Midwest. This company was a family firm from the start. Unlike a pure essence-oriented business, Elisha's business endeavors were financed by his father-in-law, who was involved not only as an investor, but at one point, as an owner. In fact, he saved the company from bankruptcy, buying 90 percent of the stock, and insisting that my great-great grandfather step aside and allow a non-family CEO, selected by his father-in-law, to run the company for ten years. Fortunately, the firm had already built a family-firm identity over the 20 years preceding the buyout, which was sustained during this early period of non-family leadership. After he resumed control of the company, Elisha was able to improve revenues and profitability enough so that the bank was willing to lend him the capital to buy back the business from his father-in-law. This early period of successful non-family leadership was important in rescuing a failing family firm, but it also established an unusual aspect of our family-firm identity – an acceptance of outside leadership.

Elisha was known to be generous and honest and provided inspirational leadership to the business as well as the community, becoming the town's greatest benefactor. Elisha was also a devout Christian and ran his business based on his Christian principles. He closed his factories on Sundays and sent horse-drawn wagons through town to pick up anyone who needed a ride to any church in town. He sometimes ended meetings by launching into a discussion of the joys of Christian service to the community, and even put Christian-oriented leaflets in the pails and tubs shipped from his factory. His passion for philanthropy, which came out of his evangelical fervor, was so all-consuming in his later years that he hired an agent to find worthy causes for his charitable dollars. In the third generation, this philanthropic legacy was institutionalized in a corporate foundation that is still giving away 1.5 percent of earnings. Elisha is quoted as saying, "Let me say to you, my friends, that it is a grand thing to do for those who are needy. I think any person will live longer and happier in this world by doing something to help mankind." These values became the core of our family-firm identity.

THE SECOND GENERATION: THE CALVINIST WORK ETHIC

While these early values remain important to this day, the second-generation leader, Charles, contributed another element to our family-firm identity. Charles was mainly remembered for his business acumen, and for being a relentless taskmaster. He was a workaholic and set a high standard for his employees. According to one oft-told story, he was in the barbershop and overheard one of his employees remark that there was no work at the pail factory because the staves were drying. Charles was appalled that he hadn't found something else to do at the plant. He asked the man what he was planning to do that day, and the man said that he was going to go get some firewood. Charles told him, "Save your shoe leather. I'll see that a load is delivered to you." That afternoon the man received a cord of oak logs that took him two days to split. For a man whose favorite saying was, "He who cuts his own wood warms himself twice," this was a just response to what he perceived as laziness. It was during his tenure that our family-firm identity became associated with having a highly skilled and productive workforce.

When Charles died suddenly at the age of 61, his sons were just out of college and not prepared to take over. Once again, an outsider, Willis Miner, took over and led the company for 15 years, as it transitioned from a woodenware company to a corrugated box manufacturer. During this difficult transition, Miner, who had been a long-time employee, managed the business well. Known for his honesty and integrity, he was the perfect successor to Charles. Miner was a long-time friend of the family, and he knew that his role was to provide a bridge between two generations of family leadership. Charles's two sons, Mowry and Carlton, were active in the business while Miner was president, having input into the strategic direction of the company. In fact, it was Mowry who convinced his father and Miner to move into corrugated packaging.

THE THIRD GENERATION: EMPLOYEE WELFARE

Mowry, and his brother Carlton, represented the third generation of leadership, with Mowry taking over as the president of the manufacturing company, and Carlton managing a newly-formed investment company. Unlike his father, Mowry believed that one should always balance work with play. In the winter he was known to come in early, and then take a long lunch and go ice-boating before returning to work. Yet, Mowry had inherited his father's business acumen and was a brilliant strategic thinker.

He was also a charismatic leader with a vision that motivated and inspired his workers.

Mowry loved being the president of his family firm, and his kind, genial nature made him the most beloved of all the family leaders. He went into the factory every day to chat with the workers and got to know them by maintaining a set of file cards with the name, photo, and family information of every employee. He cared deeply for the welfare of his employees and their families. In fact, he was known as the "welfare president." In one instance, the state welfare agency came to take the children away from one of Mowry's employees because the father was not feeding or clothing them properly. Mowry intervened, offering to turn over part of the father's salary to the welfare agency, to provide food and clothing for the children, as long as the children could stay with their father. Unfortunately, this was a lazy, unproductive worker, who openly disobeyed company rules. When his supervisor wanted to fire him, Mowry intervened because of the impact it would have on the employee's children. While incidents like this were unusual, under Mowry's leadership there was a relaxation of the internal controls and discipline that had been such an important element in the work ethic and in building a skilled workforce that had been essential to the company's success.

In what seemed to have become a pattern, the fourth generation of leadership was not ready to take over when Mowry retired. Anticipating this situation and understanding that the company needed to professionalize, Mowry brought in his successor six years before his retirement and groomed him for the job. Dick Johnson, who was hired as the CFO, had already begun to utilize more stringent accounting practices when he took over the leadership position. Where Mowry had spent his 25 years growing the company, Johnson was more concerned with operational discipline and financial oversight and control. He convinced Mowry to bring in independent board members, and he introduced performance reviews, which led to the removal of employees who fell short of the high standards he set. Many employees found him intimidating and demanding, and missed the more relaxed atmosphere under family leadership. However, the family supported and trusted him, understanding that the professionalization process was essential to the survival of the firm. Following the tradition, this non-family leader understood that his role was not only to professionalize the firm, but also to mentor the next-generation leader. Because this had become a common scenario in the transition from generation to generation, the strength of the family-firm identity never faltered during these periods of non-family leadership.

THE FOURTH GENERATION: PROFESSIONALIZATION

By the time the fourth-generation leader, Tad, assumed the position of CEO, the number of adult family owners had grown to 75, which meant that most of the family was not working in the business. While Mowry had occasionally asked his cousins for input, the company had never made a systematic effort to survey the family about their needs and expectations. Tad decided that it was time to do that, and so he travelled around the country, meeting with small groups of shareholders to discuss their thoughts about the family, its business, and the plan for the future. He was pleased to find that shareholders were proud of their family heritage and wanted to retain ownership. They also wanted an increased dividend and a more diversified company. With this in mind, Tad and his team developed the company's first strategic plan.

This initiative was a critical factor in sustaining the family-business identity in the fourth generation. As families grow, their family-firm identity is more and more dependent on a sense of connectedness to each other as well as the business. The centrifugal force of a growing family pushing toward individuation and self-determination necessarily strains the ties between the family members and their connection to the business. To counteract this natural tendency, the family must exert pressure in the other direction.[3] Unfortunately, while Tad recognized the need to reach out to the family, he didn't realize that this was not enough. He also needed to engage them in an ongoing process of communication and information exchange. This first initiative was not followed up with other family meetings, and the family continued to drift apart.

Tad was faced with another dilemma. While he felt strongly about his family's legacy and was devoted to the business, the prevailing view on family businesses in the 1970s and early 1980s led him to believe that a family business was more successful if it was run like a public company. Seeking to continue the professionalization process begun by Johnson, Tad began his tenure by attending one of the first executive education programs at Harvard. At that program he was exposed to the current literature on family businesses, which tended to focus on the evils of nepotism and challenges that confront family business owners. Convinced by the experts that having family members in operating positions was not necessarily an advantage, neither Tad nor his fourth-generation cousins encouraged the next generation to go into the family business.

Unfortunately, they also did not prepare the fifth generation to be owners. While the period of professionalization led to regular financial reports and annual meetings, most of the fifth-generation family members were ill-equipped to understand these business communications. Also, except for his "listening tour" in the early 1980s, the communication stream was unidirectional. Family members were expected to support the management team and stay quiet. Because the company was enjoying unprecedented growth, and the family shareholders were treated to increasing dividends and liquidity events, the shareholders were happy with this arrangement. In most cases, the income from the family company was viewed as an annuity with no responsibilities or requirements attached.

The company flourished under Tad's charismatic leadership, and the family values and legacy that had sustained it for more than 100 years were promoted within the company, as well as outside. But the family as a whole was less and less identified with the business, and the family-firm identity came to depend on just one person. When Tad retired, after a period of remarkable growth in revenue and earnings, the company began to falter.

At this time there were nine operating businesses, each one managed with little guidance from the corporate office. Without family members in key leadership positions, and without a concerted effort on the part of management and board to nurture the family-firm identity, there was no overall corporate identity – merely the identities of the different businesses that had been acquired over the previous 15 years. During the next ten years following Tad's retirement, the business went through four CEOs. With the family-firm identity in such a weakened state, there seemed to be no "consensual view of 'who we are as an organization' or 'what we do as a collective,'"[4] so it is not surprising that the board was unable to choose the right CEO. For the most part, shareholders could not even describe this conglomeration of businesses, much less identify with it. This relates to Eddleston's notion that the family-firm identity is a two-way street. The firm must be as much a part of the family's identity as the family is a part of the firm's identity. If the family members do not feel the connection to the business, the business loses the connection to its family owners.

In 2001, the process of becoming a components-oriented firm was accelerated when the business restructured into a holding company. That year, EBIT (earnings before interest and taxes) fell 92 percent from the previous year, and ROE (return on equity) was 0.2 percent. The next year, a fifth-generation family member, who was the president of the largest operating business, was removed from his position by the firm's non-family CEO. Two months later this CEO, who was the third to have been hired since Tad had retired, was fired. Even though the firm's family identity was severely strained by this point, the presence of a well-liked and visionary family leader provided the illusion of a family firm. However, when he left, that illusion was shattered, both inside and outside the company.

THE FIFTH GENERATION: FAMILY REUNIFICATION AND IDENTIFICATION

The fifth generation had grown up during the transition to the components-oriented model of family–business interaction. We were mostly uninvolved with the company, spread out around the country, developing our own careers and occasionally showing up for shareholder meetings. The cousins did not know each other, and did not care to.

The process of reviving our family-firm identity had actually begun ten years earlier with an effort by a fifth-generation family board member who began a process to reunite and re-engage the family. She started an annual family picnic, which provided an opportunity for family members to get together socially on the night before the annual shareholder meeting. She also arranged for printing and distributing a family tree to all shareholders, and sending out company-related birthday gifts to the young children of the fifth-generation shareholders. This included a children's book about the company. At the same time, Tad, who had recently retired as chairman of the board, decided that we should hire someone to write a family history book to be published in 1999 to commemorate our company's 150th anniversary. The project was pivotal in reminding him and others at the company and on the board, who were involved in the research and development of the book, that we had a legacy that we needed to nurture. In this same anniversary year, the corporate foundation board began recruiting from all six branches and instituted term limits to cycle more family members through the board. This was an essential ingredient in laying the groundwork for the family council.

Ironically, it was our non-family CEO who suggested that we needed a family council. Having worked at a family company previously, he realized the value to the company as well as to the family of having a family governance system. A few family members took on the task of creating a proposal for the council and planning the first family meeting. In the process, everyone in the family was contacted by phone by people on the task force urging them to attend the meeting. One family member, who was a documentary film maker, created a film about the family's history, which was shown at the inaugural family gathering. The release of the family history book, the showing of the family documentary, and the gathering of the family to celebrate their legacy energized everyone. It made them feel they were not only a part of the family, but also a legacy that involved owning a business together for 150 years. At the end of the film there were tears and hugs. We had arrested the forces pushing the family apart and there was a palpable feeling of longing for reunification and family identification. The process had begun.

It took two years, but when we finally got the council up and running, we had representatives from all six branches of the family, and decided that our first task was to re-establish our own identity as a business-owning family. To that end, we developed the following Purpose Statement:

To ensure the ongoing success of our businesses and the prosperity of our family, the Smith Family Council shall:

1. structure and facilitate dialogue within the family and between family members and the board
2. foster a community that nurtures strong and effective leadership, respects individual perspectives and works together toward shared goals;
3. engage family and other stakeholders in a continuing educational process;
4. identify, communicate and uphold our family's values; and
5. create an atmosphere in which family ties and affection can grow and flourish.

Just one year after the council was formed the family decided that after having a non-family chair for the previous five years, they must have a family chair of the board. The company also created a full-time position designated to coordinate shareholder communications. This same year brought about another major restructuring that led to divestitures in businesses unrelated to our core competencies, and reduced our holdings from nine operating companies to two, in the industry that our family knows and understands. This restructuring process, along with the creation of the family council, provided the basis for our family to move away from a components-orientation, rediscovering our connection to the business and to each other.

As a council, we worked hard to strengthen our identity as a business-owning family. The first project tackled by the council was the development of a family handbook. Many families start with a family constitution, but we weren't ready for this. Instead, we felt that the family needed to have ready access to information about the family and its businesses. One of the sections in this handbook was our family directory, including an updated list of all family members' mailing addresses, e-mail addresses and phone numbers. This directory proved to be one of the most effective tools in our family reconnection process. Second, we implemented our first family survey, which was designed to identify a shared vision for the future and long-term goals for the family enterprise. This project was done in collaboration with the board and a family business consultant, and it was the first time since Tad's listening tour 20 years earlier that feedback was solicited from the shareholders. The results of the survey indicated a desire for less formal communications between the business and the shareholders. It was felt that the quarterly reports were too difficult to understand, and that there was no forum for shareholders to ask questions. In response, the board and management began a series of quarterly teleconferences where family members would listen to a less formal discussion of the progress of the business and have an opportunity to ask questions on the call. The council also facilitated communication between family members by creating a family website, sending out newsletters, and planning and implementing annual family meetings.

To counteract the divisive effects of the in-group/out-group dynamic, the council chair has regular conversations with the board chair, which are shared with other council members. Council members are encouraged to talk to their branch members and share these interactions and conversations. In this way, we have developed a sense that there is a constant flow of information, between the board and the family members, and that there are no barriers to communication. Family members are encouraged to contact the council members and/or the family directors at any time.

Also, individual family members have become a much more visible presence in the business. The family council interacts regularly with the board and management. We have planning meetings at different sites so that we can meet the employees and work together on a variety of initiatives. We have worked with our communications director to have our website clearly indicate that we are a family business. We have recently discussed the possibility of sending family members to trade shows to not only learn more about the industries in which we operate, but also to promote our identity as a "family business."

CONCLUSION

As our family has reclaimed its identity as a business-owning family, we have made an effort to ensure that our family's vision and values are reflected in the company's mission statement and on its website. Aside from actively working to revitalize our family-firm identity, we are convinced that the employees of our company are more likely to identify the firm as a family firm as a result of our renewed commitment, and regular interactions with a variety of family members. Ultimately, as we regain our sense of who we are, we believe that our company is once again finding a consensual view of who it is as an organization. We also believe that this renewal of our family-firm identity has helped our business weather this recession, performing better than its competitors, and growing market share. Our annual report says it best:

Much has changed with our company and the world since our milestone 150th anniversary 10 years ago. Opportunities and challenges provided circumstances that motivated the company to divest of some businesses and make decisions to grow others. The unwavering efforts and solid values of the employees and shareholders that protect the company's legacy have never changed. As the third-oldest privately held manufacturing company in the US, our company holds a unique position in business history. We've been a good employer and a responsible, active corporate citizen for 160 years, holding firm to the values on which the company was founded. It is clear that the same values that have served the company so well in its first 160 years will sustain us far into the future.

What we have learned over the years is that these values will sustain us, but they must be nurtured and reinforced by our family. We have discovered that a family-firm identity, based on these values, evolves and changes from generation to generation, bearing the stamp of each successive family leader. To a certain degree, the family-firm identity can be sustained by a family presence in executive positions in the firm, regardless of the family's relationship to the firm. However, in the absence of family leadership, a robust family identity is an essential ingredient in maintaining the family-firm identity.

Unfortunately, just when the family identity is so important to the business, the centrifugal forces inherent in a growing family inevitably strain the ties between its members and erode the strength of the family's identity. This is when the family must make an effort to counteract these natural forces, establishing mechanisms designed to keep its members connected to each other and to their shared legacy. In our experience, both the family and its business benefit from this effort.

NOTES

1. Family firm, opposed to family-firm, is used in this paper when referring to family firm in general. Family-firm is used when referring to identity.
2. Blodgett (1999). This source was utilized to document the history in this section and the proceeding sections including (1) The Second Generation: The Calvinist Work Ethic; (2) The Third Generation: Employee Welfare; and (3) The Fourth Generation: Professionalization.
3. Lansberg (2002).
4. Kimberly Eddleston, Chapter 15 this volume, pp. 186–97.

17. Summary of dialogue: leveraging the family-business identity to access family and business resources

Trina S. Smith

Building upon the themes in the previous sections, Part III of the book highlights family-first enterprises and family-business identity as they relate to developing both the business and the family, and hence to family social capital. The discussion at the conference among the family business participants, advisors, and researchers centered on the following themes:

- Family-business identity:
  - to identify or not to identify as a family business;
  - potential negative impacts of identifying as a family business;
  - the positive landscape of family-business identity;
  - how to have a family-business identity;
- the problems with wealth and entitlement;
- gender;
- ethnic-minority families;
- development of the business and family structure;
- family business: What do we know? What do we need to know? Where do we go from here?

FAMILY-BUSINESS IDENTITY

Participants considered the pros and cons of identifying a business as a family business.

To identify or not to identify as a family business
A participant noted that a national study showed that many business owners indicated that they were family businesses, but almost half of them

never referred to theirs as family business. Another participant spoke to the mismatch commonly associated with family-business identity based on their experience with family business of the year award competitions:

> There are some firms that enter the competitions even though the firms are professionally managed, family members are not managers and are not involved in day-to-day operations. In addition, on their website they do not identify themselves as family businesses. However, family members are owners . . . *So, although some firms are family owned, their identities do not seem tied to the business.*

Another participant mentioned a similar dilemma, calling it a disjointed identity issue:

> We have done a case study of 32 families in business. Many of them didn't really see themselves as a family business. That is, being really family-oriented even though they had a family office and some centralized functions geared for the family. *So I think there's this disjointed identity issue.*

These issues lead into the question of *how* to identify yourself as a family in business. A participant summarized this in the following:

> I think that the idea of identity does add a very, very important element to the definition of a family business. I wonder how to integrate the identity of the family, the identity of the firm and the identity of individual family members? . . . How much is the family business a part of your identity? How do you keep the identity of the family separate from the business? How do you integrate all of the separate individual identities? . . . Since we created the family council, we now identify more with the family business. Nothing has changed in terms of the structure of the company, but a lot has changed in terms of the identities of the family members.

Potential negative impacts of identifying as a family business

Comments and discussions among participants centered on the potential negative impacts associated with a family-business identity. Two participants noted concerns with the concept of family identity when change happens. One stated:

> Our family business stops in the fifth generation because there's no succession plan . . . It's a 100-year-old business, so it's still in our family, although we've had many liquidity events. What happens with the family-business identity when transitions occur and liquidity transactions happen?

In direct relation, another participant discussed how environmental factors, such as taxes, impact the ability to transfer a family business to the next generation and keep a family-business identity:

> I think the second generation in our business always struggled with maintaining a long-term identity because of the US tax structure for transferring the business. We were not in a situation where we would be able transfer the family farm . . . There's no incentive to ensure that you can pass the family farm along easily.

Other participants discussed how a family-business identity may negatively impact the business, particularly in how non-family employees view entitlement of family employees:

> We are a family first-business . . . Sometimes the challenge in our company is that it can be too family-friendly, potentially at the expense of the business success . . . While employees like to work for our firm, they also see some problems with entitlement in the company.

Lastly, a participant noted concerns about perceptions about family businesses:

> In our city, which has a lot of technology firms, many businesses will downplay the notion that they are family firms because they think it helps in the marketplace. They think that if they're seen as a family business, they will be viewed as being less innovative and entrepreneurial.

The positive landscape of family-business identity
Participants discussed three positive aspects of family-business identity:

- family social capital;
- outside and inside perspective;
- role model for philanthropy and community.

Beginning with the idea of social capital, a participant commented:

> Some businesses may not be a true "family business," but they may be the result of a "family enterprise" or a family system. When you think that there was a family constellation, there's innovation within that family, and you're using family resources to some degree, whether it be financial or your network, your family background and system enables you to develop a business or some other opportunity. It influences you and enables you to do things that you otherwise wouldn't be able to do.

Another participant echoed this idea in relation to the agricultural industry:

> I came from the agricultural industry. They are all family businesses, regardless whether it's Cargill or a small farm with two sons and daughters. The farm identity is common to a very large group. Sometimes you had to tell them,

"Well you're running a business here." In America to say that your farm is a business is a bad word. They need to be a family farm, not a corporate farm. That kind of cultural view impacts their ability to keep their family healthy, recognize that they're a business, and take the steps they need to do to succeed.

And lastly, a family-business identity can serve as a philanthropic and community role model:

> There is a community focus in many family firms . . . So when you think about what is great about a family in business, [it] is not only the family and each individual family member, but the family has an influence on employees, and becomes a kind of an umbrella for their community, where they become this incredible support within their community.

How to have a family-business identity

Participants discussed both strategies for building a family-business identity and the evolution of a family-business identity. In the following story, we learn about how a family identity has developed and how pervasive it is:

> I am currently working for our family's company, . . . and we've been family owned and operated since 1913. So it's been passed down from generation to generation . . . As far as identity goes, our family put our name into the logo just five years ago, when we expanded. My mother developed the logo and now that's actually an identifying characteristic not only for our company, but for us. That is something that we pride ourselves in . . . It is not just an identifying characteristic for our family, but for our employees and for family who aren't even involved with the company . . . The logo represents our family identity.

Another participant, who claims not to be in a family business, tells us how a business gave them a family identity in the community:

> We also have a car dealership and it was our family identity. It wasn't a family business, but this is who we were in the community.

From a research view we learn about how family rituals that lead to happy functioning families may be a strategy to implement a family identity:

> Much of our family social science literature and family communication literature indicates that the many rituals emerge in our daily interaction . . . Much of our literature is starting to focus on intentionality – families trying to shape and change their culture by changing their patterns. Some highly effective and happy families talk about turning points where they decided to do things differently and it changed their family identity. It is helpful to be intentional and mindful about ritual.

Even more specific on the strategies is another participant's suggestions for providing roles for family members:

> Especially in a large family, if you provide as many opportunities as possible for family members to become involved, whether it be on a foundation board or family council or an owner's council or the board of directors or task groups or whatever, they can take on the family-business identity.

Furthermore, tied into this theme is a call for more research on this area, especially regarding social identity theory by one of the participants.

However, there are caveats to this in that one participant mentioned that maybe not all family members should be involved officially in the business:

> Just because family members aren't actively involved in management doesn't make businesses non-family businesses. They're still family enterprises. There may be a continuum of family impact, roles, and responsibilities that transforms both the family and the business . . . I question that family involvement in the business necessarily leads to a happier family. Families that are already more functional may stay involved with the business, so they look happier. But it's not necessarily because they are in the business. They are involved in the business because they are a functional family – that's why they are in the business. In the model where family is separate from the business, the family may not have the family skills to be involved.

THE PROBLEMS WITH WEALTH AND ENTITLEMENT

In this section we see some of the issues family businesses struggle with in terms of wealth and entitlement. One participant succinctly stated these central issues in the following questions and comments:

> How can we transfer wealth to the next generation and family business shares without creating a sense of entitlement? A fixation on entitlement can lead to the distraction of the family system and also impact the business. Can family governance possibly provide ritual or a sense of family identity that would provide the antidote to a sense of entitlement?

Participants also honed in on the emotions associated with wealth and entitlement. One person stated:

> I wonder about the corrosive effects of wealth in very wealthy families that are just living off the wealth – whether that contributes to a lower level of satisfaction and happiness.

This relates to an advisor's perspective stated in the following:

> I work with a lot of families who have wealth and in the third or fourth generation, the adults no longer feel an identity with the business. They're very wealthy from an inheritance, but have lost meaning. Somehow the values have been lost. They didn't grow up in the business. They didn't earn it. There's a lot of entitlement.

While the perspectives presented above talk about the disconnect between identity, wealth, and generations, others spoke of ways to help solve these issues. As such one participant noted:

> There is a disjointed lack of connectivity between legacy and wealth in the families we have studied. The wealth doesn't really kind of have the same meaning or purpose or identity, especially as it impacts more generations. So over time for more and more wealthy families there is a separation between family and business. A lot of families create family councils to create a sense of purpose and connection to the wealth on the family side.

And another person stated:

> In the families we studied that were really successful with managing business and wealth, they had engrained culturally in the family and in business practices no sense of entitlement around coming into the family business. It was a competitive landscape, and you really had to prove yourself that you were worthy. So we saw a different mindset and a sense of humility when the successive generation knew that it wasn't guaranteed they could come into business. Governance was oftentimes a huge component to help them identify with boundaries and rules and come to experience the family business or the enterprise.

GENDER

Two participants noted issues they faced in family businesses related to gender. One participant noted:

> I was in the family of a fourth-generation printing business in Chicago. I was told that there's no way a woman is every going to work in this business. I was kind of blown away. I thought I had a lot to offer. Then, I found out that only the men got the shares in the business.

Another participant stated:

> For many generations in our fifth-generation business, women were not allowed to work in the company. Then, no males wanted to be involved, so the firm began hiring women. Now only women work in the family firm.

However, another participant noted that research about men and women indicates more similarities than differences:

> There are three studies that I have done in the last few years, one on women and wealth, one on men and wealth, and then there's a comparison study, looking at the two populations in comparison. The irony of these studies is that men and women think they're so different, but they actually are so much alike in their values and their core beliefs.

ETHNIC-MINORITY FAMILIES

Participants discussed family business in relation to minority families. One person stated:

> We're primarily talking about white, Caucasian families, here. Bridging and bonding social capital means different things in different cultures. The business literature on minorities would say that families bond with others like themselves, not just the family, but others that look like themselves and that come from their own culture. This is important when it comes to starting, maintaining, and growing a business. If you come from the African American community, you've got to get outside of that community to grow and sustain the business. So bridging and bonding social capital works differently outside of the Caucasian white culture.

However, gender norms and rules vary in ethnic-minority families. One participant noted:

> Norms and rules do differ across cultures. In many Asian families, women are actually the control person. They carry the checkbook. The accounts are in their names. The men have to get a stamp book that says they can get into family accounts.

Moreover, another participant centered on important issues in immigrant and ethnic families regarding future generations and the business:

> You've all been to Chinese restaurants and see kids working there busing tables and so forth. You've got family ownership, but in no way, shape or form did the parents want the children taking over the business. They wanted their children to go on as lawyers and doctors.

These comments on diversity relate to a comment by a participant about America's diverse cultures, the concept of family social capital, and the passion and vision for the entrepreneurial spirit:

[Y]ou're going to find immigrants from all over the world that are still coming here, you know and one of the things that they have in common is family and innovation and business . . . But it says something great about us, as a people. It isn't just about family, but it's about us as Americans. It says something really terrific about us that we can adapt to the values, beliefs, vision and all that. We do it instinctively, as a people. I'm just very optimistic listening to this conversation and reading this research about what is already going on in America that is part of the solution and not part of the problem.

DEVELOPMENT OF BUSINESS AND FAMILY STRUCTURE

This book has highlighted the importance for owners of family businesses to focus both on the family and the business. Within the framework of family social capital, we learn that healthy functioning families and businesses can exist to support each other, but it takes recognition of both to do so. In the following summary, participants describe their struggles, challenges, and solutions for dealing with the development and structure of both family and business. One participant commented:

> In our family business center, we have businesses apply for awards, and we ask how owners are connected to the business. They just own it . . . and the families' role is just they basically own it. So they're not a resource for the business. The business is a resource for the family.

Another person made mention of the focus on the business when a formal board was created:

> Our family business had an advisory board and then transition[ed] to a formal board of directors. When we made that transition, even though two family members sit on the board, the board is not very involved with the family. The focus is only on the business.

This comment connects with another participant's candid questions and comments on strategies used by family businesses:

> How can the business also help the family? How can it be more family friendly? The family is always helping the business.

Most participants gave examples and comments centering on how to develop the structure of the family. Here are some strategies that have been used:

Communication rituals

You said you started to identify with the family when you started having family council meetings. Perhaps, we ought to encourage family business owners, those who want to pass the business onto the next generation, to start a set of communication rituals. It could be a consistent discussion around the dinner table every night, it could be family meetings focused on the business, or it could be a regular visit to the business on a regular basis. In other words, you establish a set of rituals that enable you to own an identity related to family business.

Utilizing business practices in the family

The business can provide a focus and a mechanism, by which some family conflicts can be overcome. It can provide some focus that develops unity, which can build social capital and then trust can grow out of that. I also think that the reverse is true. When the family becomes engaged in the business, the business can be more successful. If the family is separated from the business, it's still a family business. The business may question where are we going? What is our goal? We are owned by this group and they're not directing us. They're not telling us where the ship is going. The business may flounder, because it doesn't have a clear vision. The family can provide that clear vision when the family does become more involved.

In business, there are specific departments created for thinking about R&D, IT, and other things. The same doesn't happen in a family setting . . . So families need the foresight to think ahead and set up some provisions. Businesses use available time, resources, outside influence, classes, development, and third parties coming to prepare for change. In the family setting, we need to think of it that way. Families are reluctant to jump into something if they don't need to deal with something now. However, the business might influence families regarding the constant need to innovate, to find the next best thing, or the next best practice that can promote family development. However, families tend to assume that they're fine and then are faced with a huge conflict right in the moment. Families need to take some tips from the business part of our family business.

European models

A study in Spain indicated that boards there are involved in issues related to both the family and the business. Boards help govern family involvement in and preparation to work in the business. Boards stay in touch with the family and try to understand the family's needs. The model in Spain may be different than it is in the United States.

An owner of a large family business in Europe believed in developing the next generation for a career. The developmental path started in high school. Their attitude was that if you want to work in this business, we'll put resources into you, and we'll help you. However, there are things you need to do through high school, through college and all of these things are meant to develop you, as a potential leader for our business. They believe in family development.

One participant gave an example of a positive impact of using these kinds of strategies:

The families in business that I know who have done some development are impressive. I've been impressed, very impressed with the quality of those people . . . A lot of them suggest that they work together better as a family because of family development.

FAMILY BUSINESS: WHAT DO WE KNOW? WHAT DO WE NEED TO KNOW? WHERE DO WE GO FROM HERE?

One of the participants summarized the history of family business research and organizations:

A large movement started back in the 80s when things like the Family Firm Institute and a journal were started. The research that's being done in this area has grown, and conversations about this topic have grown also. So, there's evidence of institutional change. And, there are more organizations that are being developed. First, was an organization called Family Business Network in Europe that has done very well. That network is coming to the United States, but in the meantime there've been all kinds of initiatives in the United States and other places in the world regarding family business. There's a lot of interest that's coming from a variety of sectors.

For over 30 years, family business as a field has become institutionalized through research, education, and advocacy. What have we learned in these past 30 years? A lot, as this volume and works in family business journals and other books show. Yet, as the participants noted there are plenty of topics yet to be addressed that family businesses face. Yet, we can only do this by the connection of family businesses, advisors, and scholars.

PART III   QUESTIONS TO CONSIDER

1. Do you identify as a family business? Why or why not?
2. What can be done to create a family identity?
    (a)   How would this help with generational issues?

    (b)   How would this help with issues of wealth and entitlement?

3.   How has gender played a role in the history of your family business?

4.   How can the business be supportive of family members' participation in family life?

5.   How can you develop family structures that improve not only communication and relations in the family, but also in the business? Do you have a family council?

6.   What can we learn from ethnic and minority family businesses?
   - (a)   If you work with them as an advisor, are your approaches culturally relevant?
   - (b)   How can we invite them to join our learning and education in family business for mutually beneficial learning?
   - (c)   What studies can be done on these types of family businesses?

7.   What more do we need to learn about family businesses?
   - (a)   How can we continue the dialogue among family businesses, advisors, and researchers?
   - (b)   Who else can be included in the dialogue?
   - (c)   How might organizations devoted to family businesses help us?

PART IV

Concluding materials

18. Summary and conclusion: social capital in business families

Ritch L. Sorenson

This volume adds to our understanding of social capital in family business. Over the course of the three conference forum sessions, family business researchers, owners, and advisors heard presentations and engaged in dialogue to develop an understanding of social capital concepts and potential applications of those concepts to family business.

In very broad strokes, the conference participants seemed to agree on the following: (1) social capital concepts apply to business families; (2) family social capital gives family businesses a potential advantage; (3) to be an advantage, social capital must be developed and maintained; (4) dysfunctional family relationships can be a liability to business; and (5) business families can develop communication patterns and common identities that build trusting relationships and fulfill the potential for social capital in family firms.

At the beginning of the conference, based on the social capital literature we summarized social capital concepts as being made up of communication, common identity, moral infrastructure, reputation, and collective trust. Then, we discussed how those concepts might apply to family business. Below, based on contents of the conference and this book, I summarize the elements of social capital as they apply in family firms.

COMMUNICATION

Communication is the foundation for social capital. It provides for the transfer of information that enables individuals to understand one another and to establish cooperative relationships.

To develop *family* social capital, conference participants indicated that communication should be both positive and frequent. One cannot assume that being a blood relative is sufficient to maintain positive relationships among family members. Positive communication sustains good family relationships, while negative communication leads to poor relationships and even severed relationships.

In addition, communication should be frequent. As the number of family members increases and they become dispersed, communication frequency among family members tends to decline. In the second generation and beyond, it is less feasible to engage in the frequent informal communication required to maintain relationships. More formal or structured communication in the form of family meetings, newsletters, or e-mails helps to substitute for loss of informal contact. Communication not only helps sustain relationships, but also a common identity.

COMMON IDENTITY

A basic element of group cohesion is a common identity, which is made up of beliefs about "who we are and what we do." Without a set of common beliefs, it is difficult to engage in coordinated action.

To engage in coordinated action in relation to a business, family members need a common set of beliefs about "who we are and what we do as a family." In family businesses, these beliefs are often expressed as values, norms, and goals. When family members mature and become more independent, life pursuits, personal interests, and relationships outside the family lead to changes in perspectives and beliefs. To sustain a common set of working beliefs, families often need to re-engage and more formally agree on values and goals that represent the "family point of view."

MORAL INFRASTRUCTURE

In the social capital literature, the social and interpersonal interaction that sustains a common set of beliefs is called a moral infrastructure: what is morally or socially correct according to the group. At the conference and in this volume, we refer to this concept as social infrastructure.

The frequent interpersonal interaction in small, nuclear families, especially if all family members work in the business, maintains a common set of beliefs. However, when business ownership is dispersed among many family members who do not work in the business, families may find it very difficult to sustain a common set of beliefs. To sustain a common set of beliefs, the social infrastructure may need to become more formal, planned, and organized. For example, families can organize family councils and newsletters.

Another way of describing social infrastructure is in terms of communication patterns. Patterns of communication provide stability, but also should change over time. For example, when children become adults, the pattern of parent (superior) to child (subordinate) communication should give way to more of a peer-to-peer form of communication.

REPUTATION

A group's reputation is developed through behavior over time. Individuals and entities outside the group learn from observation what they can expect from the group. Consistent behavior is made possible through clarifying and reinforcing group norms and obligations, which requires that the group have sufficient interaction to insure the observance of norms.

Small families that work together in a business are typically able to sustain norms and behavior sufficiently to establish a reputation. Sustaining a reputation among a large and diverse group of family owners is more of a challenge. Nevertheless, through developing governance processes, it is possible for a large group to agree on values, norms, and obligations associated with the business.

COLLECTIVE TRUST

Collective trust means that individuals within the group can rely on the group to achieve its common goals. The elements of social capital described above help to produce collective trust.

Compared to non-related individuals, collective trust in families may be more easily established because families have a common history, strong emotional ties, and a commitment to their members. To establish and maintain trust, families need a social infrastructure that sustains a common identity and collective norms.

SUMMARY

All of the elements of social capital described above apply to families in business. In general, compared to non-related individuals, family members have more frequent communication, more commonly-held beliefs that form a common identity, a well-established social infrastructure, and a long-term common history of interaction that helps family members know the extent to which they can rely on one another. Thus, compared to non-related groups, families likely have immediate social capital, which makes it possible for the family to be an asset to a business, giving the business a potential advantage.

However, one cannot assume that the social relationships and infrastructure within all families will be an asset to a business. There are some families that have negative relationships and a dysfunctional social infrastructure. Such families would likely be a liability to a business. Even among families that have social capital, family members will likely need to make changes in the nature and patterns of communication to strengthen and sustain their social capital over time.

19. Recommendations for building family social capital

Ritch L. Sorenson, William Monson, and Trina S. Smith

Over three forum sessions, family business owners, advisors, and researchers discussed various elements of social capital and developed a common body of knowledge. Participants then met to apply what they had learned to family business. Before the discussion, William (Bill) Monson – a skilled facilitator – provided an overall summary of the forum sessions. Next, the participants made recommendations about developing social capital. Bill's summary is integrated into these recommendations.

Recommendations drawn from the summary and discussion, which was recorded, are provided below. Recommendations are divided into two topics that emerged: (1) how to build social capital in the family; and (2) how to build social capital between the family and the business.

HOW TO BUILD SOCIAL CAPITAL IN THE FAMILY

The following recommendations represent the collective thought of conference participants about how social capital concepts might be applied within a family.

Engage in inclusive communication   The foundation for social capital is communication. Every individual who is a relevant part of the group – for example, family members or family shareholders – should be included. When members of a group are left out, they feel disenfranchised; they don't feel they are a part of the group.

Promote positive and open communication patterns   Positive communication patterns strengthen relationships. Negative communication patterns weaken relationships. Openly addressing differences and issues may help to promote change to maintain positive communication patterns.

Develop a clear and unifying identity   A family identity comprises a common set of values and goals. In small, nuclear families the identity may be very clear. When children become adults, especially into the second generation and beyond, the family may need to engage in more formal conversations that enable them to agree on common values and goals.

Bridge identity across generation   The values that define a family's identity can be sustained across generations. For the identity to be a bridge across generations, families can instill and reinforce common values.

Collaborate about, don't impose values   Values are more likely to be accepted by the next generation when they have a voice in creating and molding values. Through collaboration, families can both honor the past and engage the rising generation in discussions about common values.

Celebrate family identity   The family identity might be celebrated and become vivid through telling stories that reinforce family values about living relatives or ancestors. The family could also draw attention and appreciate the social infrastructure (communication, reunions, and meetings) that sustains the identity. Symbols such as a logo or family crest might be used to clarify family identity.

Recognize that investing in social capital increases human and financial capital   Families with effective communication, a common identity, and collective trust expand human capital because family members are willing to commit to the family their knowledge, experience, and energy. Financial capital is also expanded. Family members who trust and support one another are more willing to share financial resources and contacts with financial capital and resources.

Organize and learn to work together   Family social capital increases when families learn that they can successfully work together. Many families in business learn that they can work together when doing community service projects. They gain confidence in their ability to work together, and they develop collective trust.

HOW TO BUILD SOCIAL CAPITAL BETWEEN THE FAMILY AND THE BUSINESS

The previous section provides suggestions for developing social capital *in* the family. This section provides recommendations for developing social capital *between* the family and the business.

Align the family and the business identity   For the alignment to occur, enterprise governance must encourage the family to define its values, goals, and strategy so that the business and family can become aligned. When the identities are aligned, the family and the business can be committed to one another.

Share information   Withholding relevant information from the family or the business creates distrust and limits the ability of the family and the business to be a resource to one another. The family and the business both benefit from openness and transparency.

Include stakeholders   Leaving family members and business stakeholders out of relevant communication and gatherings creates divisiveness and distrust. When appropriate, include family members who are not owners or blood relatives in gatherings. For example, some families in business invite spouses who are not owners to family business meetings. This inclusion can create broader understanding and a greater sense of unity.

Share resources   When functioning at its best, social capital yields resilient trust and confidence; family members believe that committing their financial and human capital will contribute to the common good of the family and the business. For example, family members may commit their own money, time, and effort to help family businesses get started; they may provide infusions of financial capital to take advantage of growth opportunities; or spouses who do not own or work in the business may share their expertise.

Make roles adaptable   Role rigidity limits growth and opportunities to contribute. Over time as family members change, the nature of roles should also change. For example, adult children may acquire capabilities to take on more responsibility. Aging family members may step back from leadership, but still provide perspective and mentoring. Role limitations based on gender constrain potential contributions. Thus, being adaptable can allow family members to make greater contributions.

Find ways to integrate work and family   Some owners choose to find ways that the overall enterprise can benefit both business and family. For example, boards of directors might become acquainted with family members, recognize their talents and abilities, and provide advice about ways to develop these individuals to participate in the business.

Articulate values and goals for both family and business   One way of uniting the family with the business is agreeing on common values and goals. Frequent reference to a common values and goals statement serves as a reminder of a common identity.

Promote attitudes and policies friendly to both family and business   Understanding and being responsive to family and business needs helps both the family and the business. Family members that do not work in the business can understand and support those who do. Likewise, business policies and practices can recognize the importance of family concerns and be supportive of those who care for and develop the family. Family members who have primary roles in the family and the business could be given a voice in developing policies that benefit both the family and the business.

Accept the uniqueness of being a family business   Realize that every organization is unique and that you don't have to be a public non-family corporation to be successful. In fact, much evidence suggests that family involvement in business provides many benefits including profitability, longevity, and investment in employees.

Clarify how family and business contribute to one another   For example, the family contributes human, financial, and social resources that sustain the business for the long term. The family also provides the core beliefs that make the business sustainable and unique. The business sustains the family economically and provides opportunities for family growth and development. To better understand potential benefits of combining family and business, the family might discuss the following kinds of questions with board members and business leaders:

- How does our business benefit from family ownership?
- How does my family help the business? How could my family be of greater help to the business?
- How does the business help my family? Are there additional ways that the business might help my family?

CONCLUSION

The recommendations provided above support the notion that family relationships do not automatically translate into social capital. Sustaining social capital in families and between families and businesses requires attention and effort. Families that have stores of resilient trust focus attention and effort on developing a social infrastructure that supports frequent and open communication and a common identity.

Appendix A Conference participant biographies

David Durenberger David Durenberger was elected to replace Hubert and Muriel Humphrey as senior US Senator from Minnesota in 1978. The only MN Republican in history elected to three terms in the Senate, Durenberger retired in 1995, having served 16 years on the Senate Finance Committee where he was chair on its Health subcommittee. He also served 12 years on Environment and Public Works, ten years on Health, Education, Labor and Pensions, four years on Government Affairs, and eight years on the Select Committee on Intelligence, which he chaired in 1985–86. David is founder and current Chair of the National Institute of Health Policy at the Opus College of Business of the University of St. Thomas, Minnesota. He has also served on various national health commissions and boards including the Medicare Payment Advisory Commission. He currently serves on the Board of the National Commission on Quality Assurance (NCQA) and the Kaiser Commission on Medicaid and the Uninsured. Durenberger has authored books on health policy and national security policy, is a nationally sought-after public speaker, and writes a popular bi-weekly national commentary on current events.

Rebecca Greene, MS Rebecca Greene graduated with her MS in Communication Studies from Texas Tech University. Her emphasis in the program was on family communication and her thesis was entitled "A contextual model of conflict in marriage." She has taught a wide variety of Communication courses at both Texas Tech University (TTU) and South Plains College, Texas, including Family Business at TTU. She has presented work at a conference based on a research project her Family Business students completed. Currently, Rebecca teaches Business and Professional Communication at South Plains College. She is planning to become certified to teach for the "Twogether in Texas" initiative, offering free premarital classes to couples in Texas.

Josephine Hubbard Josephine Hubbard is a professional working in the stewardship and management of donor and member constituencies, fund development, marketing, and project management. Jo managed the outreach and member activities at the Family Business Center, Opus College of Business, University of St. Thomas. She worked with business families in the community to build a member network to address their needs and interests. She also worked with advisors to build a community of multi-disciplinary professionals interested in learning and sharing information in the field of family business. Her expertise and interests are focused on collaboration and networking to strengthen organizations and community. Josephine is an active volunteer and member on non-profit boards and committees. She has a BA from the University of Minnesota and an MA from St. Mary's University of Minnesota.

John Hughes, MA John Hughes has worked both in and with family-owned and closely-held businesses and their owners for more than 30 years. The focus of his work is to support clients in the continual development of their family relationships, leadership talent, organization, and culture to create a sustainable business and a healthy family. John has extensive experience working with construction and real-estate-related clients and experience with financial institutions, manufacturers, transportation, retail, and service firms. John uses a holistic approach that balances the desire for maintaining strong, healthy family relationships with sound business structures and the development of a shared vision for the future of the business. Through the use of objective assessment tools, he helps companies identify, develop, and fully utilize their leadership talent to achieve their key business goals. When working with individuals, engagements focus on developing key leaders in the current or next-generation management team by helping them improve their emotional intelligence and maximizing their ability to capitalize on natural talents. When working with organizations, he addresses the ability of the leadership team to function effectively and to think together and to create a flexible and responsive structure that allows individuals to assume responsibility for their outcomes. Organizational projects have focused on leadership team and partnership effectiveness, conflict resolution, and communication and commitment enhancement.

Julia Kaemmer Julia Kaemmer is a member of the fifth generation of the Andersen Windows family. In 1996 Julia's family formed an independent family office called HRK Group Inc., and in 1997 the members of HRK Group Inc. sold their ownership of Andersen Windows. HRK is a full-service family office comprising an investment partnership, a private trust company, and a private foundation. Julia serves as the Vice-Chair of both the HRK Foundation Board and the HRK Family Council. Julia graduated from Carleton College, Minnesota in 1995 with a BA in Studio Art. For the past 14 years she has worked professionally as an artist and started a family. Julia has served as a Board member on the HRK Foundation Board, as a Trustee of the Science Museum of Minnesota, and as an advisor for the St. Croix Watershed Research Station.

Sophie Kelley, MBA Sophie Bell Kelley, President and CEO of Adler Management, LLC, serves the Rauenhorst family in the areas of financial services, investment management, estate planning, and philanthropy. Previously, Ms. Kelley was the CEO of Anchor Bank, NA, part of a multi-bank holding company, Anchor Bancorp, Inc., a privately owned Minnesota company. She has also served in senior executive positions with Norwest Bank Minnesota (now Wells Fargo) and First Bank System, Inc. (now US Bank). Earlier in her career she provided strategic and financial consulting to families and individuals in the area of wealth management planning as principal and CEO of Intrinzia Family Office. From 1997 to 2004, she was the president and CEO of a business and technology consulting company serving Fortune 500 companies in the Twin Cities. She is currently a member of the Metropolitan Economic Development Association (MEDA), Minnesota Women's Economic Roundtable, and the Minneapolis Club. Ms. Kelley has a BA degree in Psychology from Mount Holyoke College and an MBA in Marketing from the University of Minnesota.

Judy Rauenhorst Mahoney Judy Rauenhorst Mahoney is a member of the second generation of Opus Corporation, a family business founded by her father in 1953. She has participated in the University of St. Thomas Family Business program since its inception and serves on its advisory board. She is also a founding board member of Family Enterprise USA. In 2006 she earned a mini-MBA in Family Business from UST. She founded Teach Me Tapes, Inc. in 1984. When searching for foreign language materials to use with her young children, she discovered the need for a fun, educationally entertaining approach to language learning. The company has over one million books and audio in print, published in ten languages.

Jim Rockwell, JD Jim Rockwell graduated from the University of St. Thomas in 1971 and William Mitchell College of Law in 1976. He practiced law for 20 years with Robins Kaplan and Popham Haik law firms. As an attorney, he worked primarily with clients on estate planning and closely-held business planning. In 1995 he left the practice of law and joined Lowry Hill as a financial principal. Lowry Hill is an affiliate of Wells Fargo that provides investment management and financial planning services to a limited number of families. Jim has taught Wills and Trusts courses at William Mitchell and the University of St. Thomas Law Schools as an adjunct faculty member. He currently serves as a board advisor for the Family Business Center at St. Thomas, a board member of Catholic Charities, and is a past Trustee of the Minneapolis Foundation.

Kirby Rosplock, PhD Kirby Rosplock is Director of Research and Development at GenSpring Family Offices. Kirby has extensively researched family wealth and the family enterprise and is a published author and recognized speaker in the family office industry. She has conducted studies on women and wealth, men and wealth, and the intersection of the family business and the family office. She is the editor of GenSpring's *A Thought Leader's Guide to Family Wealth* (2009), which comprises insights from leading family wealth experts and was created in celebration of the firm's twentieth anniversary. She is a co-owner of a family business, and is a fifth-generation family member of a separate family enterprise. Kirby is the research director and co-researcher with Dr. Dianne H.B. Welsh, University of North Carolina at Greensboro, Dr. Juan Roure and Juan Luis Segurado, University of Navarra, IESE Business School, on a project exploring entrepreneurial orientation and governance practices in family businesses and family offices.

Michael Sullivan, Jr. Mike Sullivan, Jr. is a principal at Gray Plant Mooty and concentrates his practice on business/corporate law, with an emphasis on representing closely-held and emerging growth companies. He is currently the chair of the firm's Family Business Enterprise Advisory Team. Mike advises businesses on a broad range of business and legal issues. He acts as the outside general counsel for several of the firm's clients. Mike concentrates most of his time on mergers and acquisitions, venture capital financings, and private equity and debt offerings. He also spends time counseling clients with respect to control contests, shareholder disputes, corporate governance, and fiduciary duties. Mike has written and spoken on various corporate topics throughout his career. He has also been active in Minnesota's business law legislative reform.

Joan C. Thompson Joan Thompson is the Executive Vice-President/CFO and a Director of Minnesota Wire, a 42-year-old second-generation family business. The company is a custom design manufacturer in the medical, defense, and communication industries. She has been with the company since 1981, primarily working in administration, finance, and human resources. During that time, the company grew from seven to more than 200 employees. She is one of the seven family members who currently work for Minnesota Wire. "It is a long standing tradition but also an ongoing commitment that Minnesota Wire be involved in the community, especially when able to help those in need," according to Thompson. Joan has also served as a director on numerous boards in business, banking, healthcare, and non-profits. Her current participation on boards includes The Amherst H. Wilder Foundation, Allina Hospitals & Clinics and The United Hospital Foundation, where she previously served as chairperson. She speaks regularly to business, government, community, and civic organizations on a variety of subjects such as ethics, leadership, family business, and workforce development. She has received numerous awards including the *Minneapolis/St. Paul Business Journal* Women in Business/ Women to Watch, the United Hospital Foundation Trustee of the Year, the St. Paul Area Chamber Bravo, Deubner, and HERBIE Awards.

Peter Christian Ward Peter Ward started his business career after graduating from the University of St. Thomas, with his undergraduate degree in business, in May of 1998. Upon graduating he went to work as a consumer lender with TCF bank and quickly earned a consumer lending branch manager position. After leaving TCF Bank in 2000, he worked for a tax and estate planning firm that specialized in creative tax planning for high net worth individuals and families. Peter worked there until receiving the call from his father in April 2001, asking him to join the family business, which he did in June of 2001. Peter returned to the University of St. Thomas where he completed his MBA. Peter is now a partner in the family "angel" investment group and works with his father, mother, brother, and other family members. Peter and his family have won the "Family Business of the Year Award" through the University of St. Thomas.

Christine Warren Christine Warren started her professional career 40 years ago when she received her MSW (Master of Social Work) and subsequently became certified as an LICSW (Licensed Independent Clinical Social Worker) and LMFT (Licensed Marriage and Family Therapist). In her private practice she did long-term therapeutic work with individuals and families. She also established a training facility for seasoned therapists. This work grew to focus on family business consulting with emphasis on succession planning, leadership development, and organizational systems growth and health analysis. Christine established and became President of Organizational Development, Inc. Recently, Christine founded Oxygen Plus, Inc and is currently President. The company, a leader in this new category, manufactures and sells personal, portable recreational oxygen.

Appendix B The structured dialogue process

Ritch L. Sorenson

STRUCTURE

At the conference described in this book, family business owners, advisors, and researchers met to engage in a structured dialogue process about social capital in family business. Participants were invited because of professional or family business interests that heavily involved social capital in family business. The "structure" was designed to: (1) prepare participants to engage in dialogue; (2) provide equal access to dialogue during three forum sessions; (3) build continuity and a common body of knowledge across conference sessions; (4) summarize applications based on an accumulated body of knowledge; and (5) invite researchers to revise papers and practitioners to write papers applying the knowledge acquired during the conference. Below, I discuss and provide comments about each part of the process.

Prepare Participants to Engage in Dialogue

Because of their expertise in various topics associated with social capital, researchers were invited to write papers and give short presentations based on their papers at the beginning of one of the three forum sessions at the conference. For both their papers and presentations, researchers were asked to use language for a broad audience that included practitioners. To prepare for conference dialogue, participants were invited to read the papers prior to the conference.

Given the feedback during and after the conference, we learned that this preparation phase for the conference was helpful. However, the preparation phase could be improved by asking authors to write short summaries of their papers for practitioners. For some participants the language used by researchers was somewhat technical. In the future, we will ask researchers to include a practitioner-friendly summary, including definitions of concepts.

To prepare participants to engage in dialogue, each two-hour forum session began with two short presentations given by researchers. Researchers had been encouraged to treat presentations as a short introduction and overview. However, the researchers were passionate and knowledgeable about their subject matter, and some had a tendency to speak longer than the allotted time. In the future, we will reinforce the importance of keeping the presentations within the 15-minute time frame.

In general, the preparation process provided the necessary concepts and language that enabled participants to engage in dialogue. Participants did not require prompting to engage in dialogue after presentations were completed. And, they continued the dialogue until the end of each forum session.

Provide Equal Access to Dialogue

Immediately after the first set of presentations, conference participants were given the guidelines for structured dialogue: (1) everyone is encouraged to participate; (2) signal a desire to participate by turning your name block (names written and inserted onto a wood block) on its end; (3) as directed by the facilitator, speak in the order that name blocks were placed on end; (4) keep comments brief so that others can participate; and (5) raise your hand to offer a comment relevant to a topic currently being discussed, which should not occur often so that others can participate; and (6) the facilitator manages the entire process with the intent of giving all participants equal access.

The facilitator for this process, Josephine Hubbard, who was Associate Director of our Family Business Center, directed participants to comment in the order participants signaled a desire to make a comment. She also controlled access to the floor by allowing participants who raised their hands to interject comments relevant to a topic on the floor. This process worked very well. The facilitator was prepared with questions that could prompt discussion. However, those questions were not required because the participants were highly engaged in discussion. The participants asked questions, which provided them the opportunity to influence discussion.

In general, the facilitator managed to enable all to participate and to avoid domination by a few. In the future, we will encourage the facilitator to watch for opportunities to clarify understanding and define terms when necessary.

Overall, the guidelines for structured dialogue worked very well. Often, many name blocks were placed on end simultaneously. Occasionally, individuals raised their hands to comment about a topic being discussed. For the most part, individuals were satisfied to make their contributions in order. Assured that when their turn came they would have an opportunity to speak, participants listened to the ongoing dialogue.

Build Continuity and a Common Body of Knowledge across Conference Sessions

William (Bill) Monson, an expert facilitator and former Director of our Family Business Center, helped facilitate the conference. His primary role was to synthesize our discussions. To maintain continuity and to build on the thoughts expressed, Bill provided a brief summary of the previous session before we began the next one. This process helped retain continuity and build on the discussion from the previous session.

Some participants could not attend all forum sessions, which became somewhat of a problem when they missed an early session. Because the body of knowledge is built across sessions, participants who missed early sessions did not fully connect with the group; their understanding and ability to contribute was limited. In the future, we will emphasize the importance of attending all three forum sessions.

Comments in each forum session were recorded and transcribed. To encourage openness, we told participants that their identity would be confidential. For this reason and because summaries of dialogue represented the cumulative knowledge created by the group, participant names are not associated with quotes and comments in dialogue summaries.

Each stakeholder contributed to the dialogue from a different perspective. Family business owners spoke from personal experience. Women may be more likely to notice social relationships in their families and be motivated to discuss them. Therefore, primarily female owners were invited to participate in the conference. Notably, male owners who were invited and who read preconference materials chose not to attend.

Compared to owners, family business advisors brought a more independent and objective perspective. They worked with many family businesses and were likely to see social patterns and trends across families.

Researchers provided perhaps the most independent and objective perspectives. Researchers rely on methodologies designed to promote objectivity. And often, researchers gather information from many family businesses, which broadens their observations. Researchers provided language and conceptual tools that promoted understanding and facilitated communication. They also provided an overview of knowledge on a given topic.

Summarize Applications Based on Accumulated Body of Knowledge

By the end of the conference, the participants had developed a common body of knowledge that was informed by the perspectives of the three stakeholder groups. At the conclusion of the conference, Bill Monson, as part of his role as facilitator, provided an overall summary of the conference and led a discussion about potential applications of social capital concepts in family business. This closing discussion was recorded and transcribed. Recommendations that were derived from this discussion are included in this book Chapter 19.

After this discussion, the participants were invited to join one of four groups – owners, family members, advisors, or researchers – to discuss perspectives and possible applications for concepts in their areas of practice. These discussions were recorded and transcribed. A summary of these discussions is provided in Appendix C. These discussions helped participants find applications for social capital concepts in their fields of practice.

Researchers Revise and Practitioners Write Papers Applying Social Capital Concepts

The preparations for the conference, the dialogue during the conference, and the writing following the conference all contributed to the body of knowledge about family business and social capital. And, this body of knowledge informed and improved the practice of the three groups of stakeholders. Family business owners and advisors obtained conceptual tools and learned from the experiences of others. Four owners used social capital concepts to interpret their families' experiences when they wrote papers following the conference. In addition, two advisors wrote papers to illustrate how they use social capital concepts in their practice. These papers provide insightful applications for advisors' practices and for families and researchers to see processes that promote trust in families.

ORIGINS OF THE STRUCTURED DIALOGUE PROCESS

The structured dialogue process used in the conference emerged from the influence of and consultations with Professor Kenneth Goodpaster, Senator David Durenberger, and Family Business Center Director William (Bill) Monson. All three attended and participated in the conference.

Professor Kenneth Goodpaster conducts seminars and retreats at the University of St. Thomas based upon the world-renowned Aspen Institute Executive Seminars. Ken has added some of his own refinements to the Aspen Institute approach for his retreats and for his Great Books Seminars. Ken's approach includes having participants read materials before meeting and then expressing their reflections about the readings during a structured dialogue. Ken uses the practice of placing name blocks on their end as a place holder to make comments. He also provides a detailed summary of participant comments from the previous day before engaging in additional dialogue. Ken made the following comments about his approach:

> My approach to teaching has been influenced by two primary experiences: (1) ten years of teaching by the case method at Harvard Business School, and (2) 20 years of moderating Aspen Executive Seminars (for seven years at the Aspen Institute overlapping 18 years here at St. Thomas).
>
> From the Harvard Business School, I appreciated the critical importance of learner-centered classroom process: preparation of the materials and careful attention to framing questions and follow-ups that are "fertile" in relation to the materials. Also crucial are listening and recording skills.
>
> The latter served me well in my Aspen Executive Seminar experience, where the materials are not case studies but classical and contemporary readings in philosophy, politics, economics, history, and literature. As an Aspen moderator for many years, I learned the value of re-stating and clarifying participant contributions – for the sake of the individuals contributing and the others around the (circular) seminar table.
>
> I also learned (and today use regularly) the technique of having participants set their name blocks (or tents) on end vertically – as a surrogate for raising their hands constantly to get into the seminar conversation. This simple process tool has an amazing influence on the capacity of participants to actually listen to one another, with concerns about "getting in" taken care of by the name block queue. When there are times that call for an "override" of the queue, this can be handled (and kept to a minimum) by allowing brief hand-raising interruptions.
>
> Another technique that I originated at Aspen is the idea of a "Midnight Journal." In the late evening at the end of a seminar day that might have included two or three long sessions, I write a fairly detailed narrative of the content of the discussions, right down to specific language used by participants. I then read this narrative to the participants the next morning – using it as a springboard for the next day's discussion. This journal writing does take three or more hours each evening – and for this reason I often salt it with wit and fiction to keep it entertaining – but it seems worth it when participants indicate that it has value to them, creating continuity across the week-long seminar.
>
> A few days after the seminar, I assemble these narratives into a "Midnight Journal" document that represents a good record of the actual flow of the seminar conversation, beginning to end. Participants tell me that they save the journal and revisit the seminar months and years later. These journals have also been used as tools for mentoring in new moderators at Aspen and at St. Thomas. So they serve multiple purposes.

David Durenberger consulted with us about developing a format that encourages active involvement in discussion. David served as a US Senator from the State of Minnesota for 16 years and is founder and current Chair of the National Institute of Health Policy at the University of St. Thomas.

For ten years, David led the Medical Technology Leadership Forum designed to define and develop consensus about policy related to medical technology. He made these comments about his approach:

[My approach to collaborative stakeholder conferences] was the product of experimentation in the public policy arena. I participated in congressional hearings to learn something. From Ted Kennedy I learned a hearing was a legislative means to an end – his witnesses were always "victims" of a lack of a national policy he advocated. From Russell Long I learned hearings were a means to sort out national interests from local/regional.

From Pat Moynihan I just learned and learned and learned because he called interesting witnesses and the two of us stayed two hours beyond the scheduled ending quizzing experts. Abe Ribicoff set aside two full days in 1979 for his committee to hear from anyone who had an opinion on what is now called climate change. I called witnesses with reputations for seeing the future; when they finished testifying, I called them to sit with Senators and ask their own questions of the other witnesses.

From all of this I learned the value of listening and learning and the need to stimulate both. Put stakeholders in the room with experts like themselves challenging them to think differently and the "conversation" began to shape some, if not unanimous, consensus. From there the staff would go off finding other expertise and at some point I would put out a draft of legislation for comment before it was introduced. This allowed the extremes to hammer away at it and those who wanted a consensus to firm up their positions to the point I felt confident in taking the proposal to Senate and House policy colleagues to enlist their co-sponsorship since I'd already done a lot of their political "vetting."

This was used for ten years by the Medical Technology Leadership Forum (MTLF) of 40 leaders in med tech and related policy to explore policy issues and technology capacity no one had thought had legislative potential. We used the format I described to you to write a report on defining the problem agreement, and what consensus came out of the forum on alternative policy approaches to reduce or eliminate or anticipate the problem. It worked.

Key ingredients: people in leadership positions whose feet are always to some fire; a changing environment in which all must make some adjustments to take advantage of change; knowledgeable and respected academics/researchers/ clinicians who can source their conclusions and identify their bias; social folk who like to be with each other and have no need to "hold back" from the learning process, that is, "there is no such thing as a dumb question"; willingness to leave distractions at the door.

Bill Monson, former Director of our Family Business Center, collaborated with me in designing and managing our conference. Bill directed the university's Executive MBA program for 16 years and had considerable experience in group facilitation. He has an exceptional ability to listen to a group, and to integrate and synthesize comments both verbally and visually. Bill made the following comments about experiences that helped prepare him for his role in the conference:

> My professional and academic interests are organized around how owner/ manager teams run their organizations in situations where, as the expression suggests, "none of us is as smart as all of us." Increasing complexity along with pervasive and rapid change beg for a more systemic approach to managerial leadership. Thus, I'm interested in how to best manage in cross-functional teams so as to optimize the whole organization when there are multiple stake-holders with particular (and often competing) claims on how the organization ought to be run. So, this multi-stakeholder conference, and my role in it, reflect the core of my work.

> Synthesis and coherence of thinking are often illusive when we have conversations with ourselves let alone when we have conversations with others who share a role or perspective. Integrating the diverse threads of thought among people who have different stakeholder perspectives, language, methods, and interests is, of course, not always possible. As you've already read, this conference did approximate some agreement on a number of common interests and themes. We both studied and successfully experienced the conference topic of building social capital.

> The particular processes used to promote respectful, adult dialogue reflect the work of Reg Revens, Malcolm Knowles, and Stephen Brookfield. Principles of mind mapping from the work of Tony Buzan informed my approach to synthe-sizing multiple ideas and threads from dialogue. The multi-stakeholder learning process was further grounded in the work of Russ Ackoff, Chris Argyris, and Peter Senge.

Appendix C Summary of comments from owner, advisor, family member, and research breakout groups

Trina S. Smith and Ritch L. Sorenson

Following the three forum sessions and the conference summary, participants were invited to join owner, family member, advisor, or research stakeholder groups to discuss implications and applications for what they had learned. These discussions were intended to develop a link between conference dialogue and practice. Below, we summarize comments from the four groups.

FAMILY BUSINESS OWNERS

In their discussions, family business owners focused on using social capital concepts to involve family members and to create a common identity across generations. Each idea is provided as a numbered statement followed by a brief explanation and/or illustrative quote:

1. Identity should fit the family:
   - "There's no one way, . . . we're all very different."
   - "We all do it differently."

2. Involve the next generation:
   - "The overarching takeaway for us was . . . how do we involve the next generation?"

3. Create a unique succession plan for each family:
   Each family should answer these two questions:
   - What does succession mean for our family?
   - What is it going to look like?

4. Clarify expectations, be transparent, and transfer information:
   - "[to involve the next generation] it's critical to have clear expectations [and] transparent information of transfer. The governing bodies need to really articulate and with advisors help . . . to crystallize what is really important."

5. Develop a plan for transferring identity:
   - What is important to pass down?
   - How should it be articulated?
   - How do you see the next generation being involved?

6. Share information early:
   - Younger family members desired earlier conversations about the family business to build social capital and cultivate interest.
   - Older members asked, "How do you start the information transfer?"

7. Increase communication:
   - "The quantity of social capital is equal to the quantity of communication."

8. Determine how to communicate and the process of communication:
   - What should be included in content?
   - What should be the process for communication?
     - How much?
     - When?
     - Who to?

9. Use logos, pictures, and other symbols to develop common identity:
   - "If we were to draw a picture of our own family, what would that be?"
   - "What do we look like?"

FAMILY MEMBERS

Family members focused on: (a) the well-being and development of the family; (b) the elements of social capital, especially identity, that strengthen the family; and (c) how family social capital relates to the larger community and contributes to the common good:

1. Determine if the business is good for the family:
   - "But I often wonder, they're [family businesses] good for the US and they're good for the employees, but are they always good for the family?"
   - "That's hard; when do you let go?"

2. What is the role of faith in families?
   - Is there a connection between successful family businesses and strong faith?
   - What are the challenges families face when spouses are from different faiths?

3. A common family identity creates a sense of safety and security:
   - When the family is seen as a unit, a family identity gives "that sense of security, feeling more confident in yourself, feeling safe, because you have a sense of security with your family."

4. Use advisors to develop the family:
   - Use advisors for both the prevention and solving of problems.
   - "To plan, rather than react when a crisis comes up and to get training for communication and things, rather than just muddling through."
   - "[U]sing an advisor in a preventative way is important in planning."

5. Social capital in the family is related to the larger community and to the common good, and creates legacy for the family:
   - Family participants spoke to the importance of outside sources on leadership in relation to "the impact that others can have on your family."
   - We should see the "family as community" and "teach the family about what's the common good." Questions and ideas to consider in doing this are:
     - What's bigger than us?
     - What's bigger than me?
     - What's bigger than our family?
     - What's bigger than our community?
     - "Think of yourself as a resource for others, instead of always 'what can I get?'"

6. Changes in the business and the family can negatively affect identity:
   - Family members, especially when young, may need help and

support when something negative happens in the business or the family.

- "[A]nd things all of a sudden aren't going so rosy . . . and all of sudden people feel like because I'm in this family all of a sudden our life or my life is up on a billboard somewhere."
- What happens to the family and younger generations when something negative happens?

ADVISORS

Advisors were concerned about disconnect between academic language and research, and the language and experience of their clients. Nevertheless, a major contribution researchers can make is offering language and concepts that give families options. For the sake of the family, one option might be not to keep the business in the family.

1. A disconnect between academic and useful language:
   - "[T]here's a disconnect between the language researchers use and the language that you need to use with the family or your clients."
   - There should "be a language more familiar to everyone."

2. Difficulty in translating academic research to practice:
   - The "application of research to practice" is difficult when "the constructs are so nestled in the research framework."
   - There is "a disconnect to how we think about the terms and how they think about it."

3. Families are more complex, less matter of fact than research portrays:
   - "And the family I meet is so much more complex than the family we talked about today in the concepts and so it gets hard to translate for me."

4. Money is missing from the discussion:
   - "[W]e need to talk about money, because it runs our world."
   - "[W]e're in the trenches with these guys [*sic*] and that's what we're talking about most of the time."

5. Questions about the necessity of keeping a family business:
   - "Why are we perpetuating family businesses or the concept that a family business is so important to carry on?"

- "What is the mindset of the patriarch or matriarch that feels this is the most important thing for a family to hold on to?"
- "[I]t's often the worst thing that a family patriarch or matriarch could do is to try to hold on the business for future generations when it stifles them, it hurts them socially."
- Advisors referred to the philosophy of Chinese families: "Teach your kids how to work hard; don't promise them anything; encourage them to go and do what they want to do later in life."

6. Families need to know their options:
    - "They [family/family business] are tied into a way that's not healthy for the individual or even for the family businesses and that means a vehicle for discussion."
    - Research can provide language and concepts that provide families options that can "break down barriers" and change their "standard operating procedures."

FAMILY BUSINESS RESEARCHERS

Family business researchers raised many issues related to researching family social capital that are categorized below in terms of what could be studied, how it could be studied, and who would do the studies.

What could be studied?
1. Wealth:
    - Attitudinal effects.
    - Emotional effects.
    - Behavioral effects.

2. Generations:
    - "How different generational just interpret things differently."

3. Organizational identity of family businesses:
    - What will be passed on from one generation to the next?
    - What is critical and valued?
    - How it is communicated?

4. History of business families:
    - Rituals.

- Stories and histories of matriarchs and patriarchs, particularly those shared in the business.
- Ethnographies.

5. Generational differences and similarities:
    - Longitudinal studies of dialogue across generations one, two, three, and four.
    - Determine what and what does not transcend generations.
    - Start with the ideas of founders and determine what kinds of ideas persist and how ideas are interpreted in succeeding generations.

6. Multi-informant studies:
    - Capture a holistic view of what's going on with social capital.

How could it be studied?
1. Methods:
    - Experiential action research.
    - Case studies.
    - Multilevel analyses.
    - Advanced statistical procedures.
    - Aggregating individual perceptions to family and organizational levels.

2. Measurement:
    - To create a common body of knowledge, we need a common unit of measurement across academic disciplines so that knowledge is transferable.

Who could do the studies?
Consortia could bring together scholars from different disciplines, including psychology and sociology, who could work toward using common measures and methods, and eliminating duplication of research.

References

Adams, G.A., L.A. King, and D.W. King (1996), "Relationships of job and family involvement, family social support, and work–family conflict with job and life satisfaction," *Journal of Applied Psychology*, **81** (4), 411–20.

Adler, P.S. and S.W. Kwon (2002), "Social capital: Prospects for a new concept," *Academy of Management Review*, **27** (1), 17–40.

Albert, S. and D.A. Whetten (1985), "Organizational identity," in L.L. Cummings and B.M. Staw (eds), *Research in Organizational Behavior*, Volume **7**, Greenwich, CT: JAI Press, pp. 263–95.

Arregle, J.L., M.A. Hitt, D.G. Sirmon, and P. Very (2007), "The development of organizational social capital: Attributes of family firms," *Journal of Management Studies*, **44** (1), 73–95.

Ashforth, B.E. and F.A. Mael (1996), "Organizational identity and strategy as a context for the individual," in J. Baum and J. Dutton (eds), *Advances in Strategic Management*, Volume **13**, Greenwich, CT: JAI Press, pp. 17–62.

Aylor, B. and M. Dainton (2004), "Biological sex and psychological gender as predictors of routine and strategic relational maintenance," *Sex Roles*, **50** (9/10), 689–97.

Barnett, R.C. (1998), "Toward a review and reconceptualization of the work/family literature," *Genetic, Social, and General Psychology Monographs*, **124** (2), 125–82.

Barnett, R.C. and J.S. Hyde (2001), "Women, men, work, and family: An expansionist theory," *American Psychologist*, **56** (10), 781–96.

Basco, R. and M.J.P. Rodriquez (2009), "Studying family enterprise holistically: Evidence for integrated family and business systems," *Family Business Review*, **22** (1), 82–95.

Baxter, L.A. (1987), "Symbols of relationship identity in relationship cultures," *Journal of Social and Personal Relationships*, **4** (3), 261–80.

Baxter, L.A. (2004), "Relationships as dialogues," *Personal Relationships*, **11**, 1–22.

Baxter, L.A. and D.O. Braithwaite (2006), "Family rituals," in L. Turner and R. West (eds), *The Family Communication Sourcebook*, Thousand Oaks, CA: Sage, pp. 259–80.

Baxter, L.A. and C. Clark (1996), "Perceptions of family communication patterns and the enactment of family rituals," *Western Journal of Communication*, **60**, 254–68.

Baxter, L.A., D.O. Braithwaite, J. Kellas, C. LeClair-Underberg, E. Lamb-Normand, T. Routsong and M. Thatcher (2009), "Empty ritual: Young-adult stepchildren's perceptions of the remarriage ceremony," *Journal of Social and Personal Relationships*, **26** (4), 467–87.

Bennett, L.A., S.J. Wolin, D. Reiss, and M.A. Teitelbaum (1987), "Couples at risk for transmission of alcoholism: Protective influences," *Family Process*, **26** (1), 111–29.

Bennis, W.G. and J. Goldsmith (1997), *Learning to Lead*, Reading, MA: Perseus Books.

Black, C. (2000), "Don't talk: Communication rules in the alcoholic family," in K. Galvin and P. Cooper (eds), *Making Connections: Readings in Relational Communication*, Los Angeles, CA: Roxbury.

Blanchard, B. (2007), "Mattel apologizes to China," *Wall Street Journal*, 22–23 September.

Blodgett, R. (1999), *Menasha Corporation: An Odyssey of Five Generations*, Lyme, CT: Greenwich Publishing Group, Inc.

Bossard, J.H.S. and E.S. Boll (1950), "Ritual in family living," *American Sociological Review*, **14**, 463–69.

Bossard, J.H.S. and E.S. Boll (1950a), *Ritual in Family Living: A Contemporary Study*, Philadelphia: Philadelphia University Press.

Bruess, C.J. and A. Hoefs (2006), "The cat puzzle recovered: Composing relationships through family ritual," in J. Wood and S. Duck (eds), *Composing Relationships*, Belmont, CA: Wadsworth.

Bruess, C.J. and J.C. Pearson (1997), "Interpersonal rituals in marriage and adult friendship," *Communication Monographs*, **64**, 25–46.

Bruess, C.J.S. and J.C. Pearson (2002), "The function of mundane ritualizing in adult friendship and marriage," *Communication Research Reports*, **19** (4), 314–26.

Brush, C.G. (1992), "Research on women business owners: Past trends, a new perspective and future directions," *Entrepreneurship Theory and Practice*, **16** (4), 5–30.

Carlson, D.S., K.M. Kacmar, J.H. Wayne, and J.G. Grzywacz (2006), "Measuring the positive side of the work–family interface: Development and validation of a work–family enrichment scale," *Journal of Vocational Behavior*, **68** (1), 131–64.

Chan, K.W. and R. Mauborgne (2005), *Blue Ocean Strategy: How to Create Uncontested Market Space and Make the Competition Irrelevant*, Boston, MA: Harvard Business Press.

Chrisman, J.J., J.H. Chua, and P. Sharma (2005), "Trends and directions in the development of a strategic management theory of the family firm," *Entrepreneurship Theory and* Practice, **29** (5), 555–75.

Chrisman, J.J., L.P. Steier, and J.H. Chua (2006), "Personalism, particularism, and the competitive behaviors and advantages of family firms: an introduction," *Entrepreneurship Theory and Practice*, **30** (6), 719–29.

Cicourel, A.V. (1973), *Cognitive Sociology*, Harmondsworth: Penguin.

Cohen, S. and T.A. Wills (1985), "Stress, social support, and the buffering hypothesis," *Psychological Bulletin*, **98** (2), 310–57.

Coleman, J.S. (1988), "Social capital in the creation of human capital," *American Journal of Sociology*, **94**, S94–S120.

Coleman, J.S. (1990), *Foundations of Social Theory*, Cambridge, MA: Harvard University Press.

Columbia Accident Investigation Report (CAIB) (2003), Volume 1, chapter 7, p. 177, available at: http://www.nasa.gov/columbia/home/CAIB_Vol1.html; accessed 8 June 2011.

Compan, E., J. Moreno, M.T. Ruiz, and E. Pascual (2002), "Doing things together: Adolescent health and family rituals," *Journal of Epidemiology and Community Health*, **56** (2), 89–94.

Cook, J. and T.D. Wall (1980), "New work attitude measure of trust, organizational commitment and personal need non-fulfillment," *Journal of Occupational Psychology*, **53** (1), 39–52.

Craig, J.B., C. Dibrell, and P.S. Davis (2008), "Leveraging family-based brand identity to enhance firm competitiveness and performance in family businesses," *Journal of Small Business Management*, **46** (3), 331–50.

Danes, S.M. (2006), "Tensions within family business-owning couples over time," *Stress, Trauma and Crisis*, **9** (3–4), 227–46.

Danes, S.M. and S. Amarapurkar (2001), "Business tensions and success in farm family businesses," *Family Economics and Resource Management Biennial*, **4**, 178–90.

Danes, S.M. and Y.G. Lee (2004), "Tensions generated by business issues in farm business-owning couples," *Family Relations*, **53** (4), 357–66.

Danes, S.M. and E.A. Morgan (2004), "Family business-owning couples: An EFT view into their unique conflict culture," *Contemporary Family Therapy*, **26** (3), 241–60.

Danes, S.M. and P.D. Olson (2003), "Women's role involvement in family businesses, business tensions, and business success," *Family Business Review*, **16** (1), 53–68.

Danes, S.M., V. Zuiker, R. Kean, and J. Arbuthnot (1999), "Predictors of family business tensions and goal achievements," *Family Business Review*, **12** (3), 241–52.

Danes, S.M., N. Fitzgerald, and K.C. Doll (2000a), "Financial and relationship predictors of family business goal achievement," *Financial Counseling and Planning*, **11** (2), 43–53.

Danes, S.M., R. Leichtentritt, and M. Metz (2000b), "Effects of conflict severity on quality of life of men and women in family businesses," *Journal of Family and Economic Issues*, **21** (3), 259–86.

Danes, S.M., M.A. Rueter, H.K. Kwon, and W. Doherty (2002), "Family FIRO model: An application to family business," *Family Business Review*, **15** (1), 31–43.

Danes, S.M., H.R. Haberman, and D. McTavish (2005), "Gendered discourse about family business," *Family Relations*, **54** (1), 116–30.

Danes, S.M., K. Stafford, and J.T. Loy (2007), "Family business performance: The effects of gender and management," *Journal of Business Research*, **60** (10), 1058–69.

Danes, S.M., J.T. Loy and K. Stafford (2008a), "Business planning practices of family-owned firms within a quality framework," *Journal of Small Business Management*, **46** (3), 395–421.

Danes, S.M., J. Lee, K. Stafford, and R.K.Z. Heck (2008b), "The effects of ethnicity, families and culture on entrepreneurial experience: An extension of sustainable family business theory," invited article for *Journal of Developmental Entrepreneurship, Special Issue* titled *Empirical Research on Ethnicity and Entrepreneurship in the U.S.*, **13** (3), 229–68.

Danes, S.M., K. Stafford, G. Haynes, and S.S. Amarapurkar (2009a), "Family capital of family firms: Bridging human, social, and financial capital," *Family Business Review*, **22** (3), 199–215.

Danes, S.M., J. Lee, S. Amarapurkar, K. Stafford, G. Haynes, and K. Brewton (2009b), "Determinants of family business resilience after a natural disaster by gender or business owner," *Journal of Developmental Entrepreneurship*, **14** (4), 333–54.

den Dulk, L. (2005), "Workplace work–family arrangements: A study and explanatory framework of differences between organizational provisions in different welfare states," in S.A.Y. Poelmans (ed.), *Work and Family: An International Research Perspective*, Mahwah, NJ: Lawrence Erlbaum Associates, pp. 211–38.

Department of Defense Human Factors Analysis and Classification System (DODHFACS) (2005), 11 January, Attachment 1, p. 7; available at: http://www.useg.mis/safety/docs/ergo_hfacs/hfacs.pdf; accessed 8 June 2011.

Dess, G.G. and J.D. Shaw (2001), "Voluntary turnover, social capital, and organizational performance," *Academy of Management Review*, **26** (3), 446–56.

Driver, J.L. and J.M. Gottman (2004), "Daily marital interactions and positive affect during marital conflict among newlywed couples," *Family Process*, **43** (3), 301–14.

Drucker, P. (1994), "The age of social transformation," *The Atlantic Monthly*, **274** (5), 53–80.

Dyer, W.G. (1988), "Culture and continuity in family firms," *Family Business Review*, **1**, 37–50.

Dyer, G. and D.A. Whetten (2006), "Family firms and social responsibility: Preliminary evidence from the SP 500," *Entrepreneurship Theory & Practice*, **30** (6), 785–802.

Eddleston, K. and F.W. Kellermanns (2007), "Destructive and productive family relationships: A stewardship theory perspective," *Journal of Business Venturing*, **22** (4), 545–65.

Eddleston, K., F.W. Kellermanns, and R. Sarathy (2008a), "Resource configuration in family firms: Linking resources, strategic planning and environmental dynamism to performance," *Journal of Management Studies*, **45** (1), 26–50.

Eddleston, K.A., F.W. Kellermanns, and T. Zellweger (2008b), "Family harmony: A facilitator of corporate entrepreneurship in family firms," paper presented at the Family Enterprise Research Conference, Milwaukee, Wisconsin.

Field, J. (2003), *Social Capital*, London: Routledge.

Fiese, B.H. (2006), *Family Routines and Rituals*, New Haven, CT: Yale University Press.

Fiese, B., T. Tomcho, M. Douglas, K. Josephs, S. Poltrock, and T. Baker (2002), "A review of 50 years of research on naturally occurring routines and rituals: Cause for celebration?," *Journal of Family Psychology*, **16** (4), 381–90.

Fiol, C.M. (1991), "Managing culture as a competitive resource: An identity-based view of sustainable competitive advantage," *Journal of Management*, **17** (1), 191–211.

Fletcher, J.K. and L. Bailyn (2005), "The equity imperative: Redesigning work for work–family integration," in E.E. Kossek and S.J. Lambert (eds), *Work and Life Integration: Organizational, Cultural, and Individual Perspectives*, Mahwah, NJ: Lawrence Erlbaum Associates, pp. 171–89.

Fock, Siew-Tong (1998), "The impact of family conflicts on the development of the Chinese entrepreneurially managed family business: The Yeo Hiap Seng Case in Singapore," *Journal of Small Business and Entrepreneurship*, **15** (2), 88–103.

Fombrun, C. and M. Shanley (1990), "What's in a name? Reputation building and corporate strategy," *Academy of Management Journal*, **33** (2), 233–58.

Fukuyama, F. (1995), *Trust: The Social Virtues And the Creation of Prosperity*, New York: Free Press.

Gallo, M.A. and C. García-Pont (1996), "Important factors in family business internationalization," *Family Business Review*, **9** (1), 45–59.

Galvin, K., C. Bylund, and B. Brommel (2004), *Family Communication: Cohesion and Change*, 6th edition, Boston, MA: Allyn and Bacon.

Ganster, D.C., M.R. Fusilier, and B.T. Mayes (1986), "Role of social support in the experience of stress at work," *Journal of Applied Psychology*, **71** (1), 102–10.

Gimeno-Sandig, A. (2005), "Performance in the family business: A causal study of internal factors and variables," doctoral dissertation, ESADE Universitat Ramon Llull, Spain.

Gioia, D. (1998), "From individual to organizational identity," in D. Whetten and P. Godfrey (eds), *Identity in Organizations: Building Theory Through Conversations*, Thousand Oaks, CA: Sage, pp. 17–31.

Gioia, D.A., M. Schultz, and K.G. Corley, (2000), "Organizational identity, image, and adaptive instability," *Academy of Management Review*, **25** (1), 63–81.

Goffee, R. and R. Scase (1985), *Women in Charge*, London: Allen and Unwin.

Goffman, E. (1967), *Interaction Ritual: Essays on Face-to-face Behavior*, Garden City, NY: Anchor.

Gordon, J.R., K.S. Whelan-Berry, and E.A. Hamilton (2007), "The relationship among work–family conflict and enhancement, organizational work–family culture, and work outcomes for older working women," *Journal of Occupational Health Psychology*, **12** (4), 350–64.

Gottman, J. (1994), *Why Marriages Succeed or Fail . . . And How You Can Make Yours Last*, New York: Simon and Schuster.

Gottman, J.M. and J. DeClaire (2001), *The Relationship Cure*, New York: Crown Publishing.

Gottman, J.M. and J.L. Driver (2005), "Dysfunctional marital conflict and everyday marital interaction," *Journal of Divorce and Remarriage*, **43** (3/4), 63–78.

Gottman, J.M. and J.S. Gottman (2007), *And Baby Makes Three: The Six-Step Plan for Preserving Marital Intimacy and Rekindling Romance After Baby Arrives*, New York: Crown Publishing.

Gottman, J.M. and C.I. Notarius (2000), "Decade review: Observing marital interaction," *Journal of Marriage and the Family*, **62** (4), 927–47.

Gottman, J.M. and N. Silver (1999), *The Seven Principles for Making Marriage Work*, New York: Crown Publishing.

Gottman, J.M., J.S. Gottman, and J. DeClaire (2006), *Ten Lessons to Transform Your Marriage: America's Love Lab Experts Share Their*

Strategies for Strengthening Your Relationship, New York: Crown Publishing.

Grandey, A.A., B.L. Cordeiro, and J.H. Michael (2007), "Work–family supportiveness organizational perceptions: Important for the well-being of male blue-collar hourly workers?," *Journal of Vocational Behavior*, **71** (3), 460–78.

Haberman, H.R. and S.M. Danes (2007), "Father–daughter and father–son family business management transfer comparison: Family FIRO model application," *Family Business Review*, **20** (2), 163–84.

Haidt, J. and C. Joseph (2007), "The moral mind: How five sets of innate moral intuitions guide the development of many culture-specific virtues, and perhaps even modules," in P. Carruthers, S. Laurence, and S. Stich (eds), *The Innate Mind*, Volume 3, New York: Oxford, pp. 367–91.

Handy, Charies (2002), "What's a business for?" *Harvard Business Reviews*, December.

Hanson, G.C., L.B. Hammer, and C.L. Colton (2006), "Development and validation of a multidimensional scale of perceived work–family positive spillover," *Journal of Occupational Health Psychology*, **11** (3), 249–65.

Harrison, T., "Teleopathy – target fixation and how to combat it" unpublished class journal.

Haunschild, P.R. and C.M. Beckman (1998), "When do interlocks matter? Alternate sources of information and interlock influence," *Administrative Science Quarterly*, **43** (4), 815–44.

Heck, R.K.Z., S.M. Danes, M.A. Fitzgerald, G.W. Haynes, C.R. Jasper, H.L. Schrank, K. Stafford, and M. Winter (2006), "Role of family in family business entrepreneurship," in P.A. Poutziouris, K.X. Smyrnios, and S. Klein (eds), *Family Business Research Handbook*, Cheltenham, UK and Northampton, MA, USA: International Family Enterprise Research Academy (IFERA) and Edward Elgar, pp. 80–105.

Hobfoll, S.E. (1989), "Conservation of resources," *American Psychologist*, **44** (3), 513–24.

Hoffman, J., M. Hoelscher and R. Sorenson (2006), "Achieving sustained competitive advantage: A family capital theory," *Family Business Review*, **24** (2), 137–46.

Homer, M.M., P.A. Freeman, R.B. Zabriskie, and D.L. Eggett (2007), "Rituals and relationships: Examining the relationship between family of origin rituals and young adult attachment," *Marriage and Family Review*, **42** (1), 5–28.

Hubler, T.M. (2005), "Forgiveness as an intervention in family-owned business: A new beginning," *Family Business Review*, **18** (2), 95–103.

Jacobs, J. (1965), *The Death and Life of Great American Cities*, London: Penguin Books.

Janis, I.L. (1982), *Groupthink: Psychological Studies of Policy Decisions and Fiascos*, Boston: Houghton-Mifflin.

Jennings, J.E. and M.S. McDougald (2007), "Work–family interface experiences and coping strategies: Implications for entrepreneurship research and practice," *Academy of Management Review*, **32** (3), 747–60.

John Paul II (1991), Encyclical Letter, *Centesismus Annus*, section 36.

Jorgenson, J. and A. Bochner (2004), "Imagining families through stories and rituals," in A. Vangelisti (ed.), *Handbook of Family Communication*, New Jersey: Lawrence Erlbaum, pp. 513–38.

Karreman, D. and A. Rylander (2008), "Managing meaning through branding – the case of a consulting firm," *Organization Studies*, **29** (1), 103–25.

Kaye, K. (2002). "Penetrating the cycle of sustained conflict," in C.E. Aronoff, J.H Astrachan and J.L. Ward (eds), *Family and Business Sourcebook III*, Marietta, GA: Family Enterprise Publishers, pp. 382–97.

Kaye, K. (2009), "Incompatible Stories," available at: http://www.kaye.com/fambz/Trust1.pdf; accessed 20 May 2011.

Kellermanns, F.W. and K.A. Eddleston (2007), "A family perspective on when conflict benefits family firm performance," *Journal of Business Research*, **60** (10), 1048–57.

Kirchmeyer, C. (1992), "Nonwork participation and work attitudes: A test of scarcity vs. expansion models of personal resources," *Human Relation*, **45** (8), 775–95.

Krakauer, J. (1997), *Into Thin Air: A Personal Account of the Mt. Everest Disaster*, NY: Anchor-Doubleday, p. 233.

Lansberg, I. (1983), "Managing human resources in family firms: The problem of institutional overlap," *Organizational Dynamics*, **12** (1), 39–46.

Lansberg, I. (1999), *Succeeding Generations*, Boston, MA: Harvard Business School Press.

Lansberg, I. (2002), "A developmental model of how shareholder families evolve: What happens when siblings take over?," presentation at the Governing the Family Business program at Kellogg University, 27–30 October, 2002.

Leana, C.R. and H.J. Van Buren (1999), "Organizational social capital and employment practices," *Academy of Management Review*, **24** (3), 538–55.

Le Breton-Miller, I. and D. Miller (2009), "Agency vs. stewardship in public family firms: A social embeddedness reconciliation," *Entrepreneurship Theory and Practice*, **33** (6), 1169–91.

Lester, R.H. and A.A. Cannella (2006), "Interorganizational familiness: How family firms use interlocking directorates to build community-level social capital," *Entrepreneurship Theory and Practice*, **30** (6), 755–75.

Loehr, J. and T. Schwartz (2001), "The making of a corporate athlete," *Harvard Business Review*, **79** (1), 128.

MacDermid, S.M. (2005), "(Re)considering conflict between work and family," in E.E. Kossek and S.J. Jambert (eds), *Work and Life Integration: Organizational, Cultural, and Individual Perspectives*, Mahwah, NJ: Lawrence Erlbaum Associates, pp. 19–40.

Marchand, R. (2001), *Creating the Corporate Soul: The Rise of Public Relations and Corporate Imagery in American Big Business*, Berkeley: University of California Press.

McGee, D. and D.W. Kinhardt (Executive Producers) (2010), *This Emotional Life* [Television broadcast], NOVA/WGBH Science Unit and Vulcan Productions, Inc., Boston: Public Broadcasting Service.

Meredith, W.H. (1985), "The importance of family traditions," *Wellness Perspectives*, **2** (2), 17–19.

Meredith, W., D. Abbott, M. Lamanna, and G. Sanders (1989), "Rituals and family strengths," *Family Perspectives*, **23** (2), 75–83.

Miller, D. and M. Le Breton-Miller (2005), *Managing for the Long Run: Lessons in Competitive Advantage from Great Family Businesses*, Boston, MA: Harvard Business School Press.

Miller, D., I. Le Breton-Miller, and B. Scholnick (2008), "Stewardship vs. stagnation: An empirical comparison of small family and non-family businesses," *Journal of Management Studies*, **45** (1), 51–78.

Molm, L.D., D.R. Schaefer, and J.L. Collett (2009), "Fragile and resilient trust: Risk and uncertainty in negotiated and reciprocal exchange," *Sociological Theory*, **27** (1), 1–32.

Muzellec, L. (2006), "What is in a name change? Re-joycing corporate names to create corporate brands," *Corporate Reputation Review*, **8** (4), 305–21.

Nag, R., K.G. Corley, and D.A Gioia (2007), "The intersection of organizational identity, knowledge, and practice: Attempting strategic change via knowledge grafting," *Academy of Management Journal*, **50** (4), 821–47.

Nahapiet, J. and S. Ghoshal (1998), "Social capital, intellectual capital, and the organizational advantage," *Academy of Management Review*, **23** (2), 242–66.

Ngo, N. (2004), "Divorce running a restaurant," *St. Paul Pioneer Press*, 2 April, 2004.

Olson, P.D., V.S. Zuiker, S.M. Danes, K. Stafford, R.K.Z. Heck and K.A. Duncan (2003), "The impact of the family and business on family business sustainability," *Journal of Business Venturing*, **18** (5), 639–66.

Orbe, M. and C. Bruess (2005), *Contemporary Issues in Interpersonal Communication*, Los Angeles: Roxbury.

Parasuraman, S., Y.S. Purohit, V.M Godshalk, and N.J. Beutell (1986), "Work and family variables, entrepreneurial career success, and psychological well-being," *Journal of Vocational Behavior*, **48** (3), 275–300.

Pearson, A.W., J.C. Carr, and J.C. Shaw (2008), "Toward a theory of familiness: A social capital perspective," *Entrepreneurship Theory and Practice*, **32** (6), 949–69.

Portes, A. (1998), "Social capital: Its origins and applications in modern sociology," *Annual Review of Sociology*, **24**, 1–24.

Post, J.E. (1993), "The greening of the Boston Park Plaza Hotel," *Family Business Review*, **6** (2), 131–48.

Poza, E.J. (2010), *Family Business*, 3rd edition, Mason, OH: South-Western Centage Learning.

Poza, E.J. and T. Messer (2001), "Spousal leadership and continuity in the family firm," *Family Business Review*, **14** (1), 25–35.

Putnam, R.D. (1993), "The prosperous community: Social capital and public life," *American Prospect*, **13**, 35–42.

Putnam, R. (2000), *Bowling Alone: The Collapse and Revival of American Community*, New York: Simon and Schuster.

Ravasi, D. and M. Schultz (2006), "Responding to organizational identity threats: Exploring the role of organizational culture," *Academy of Management Journal*, **49** (3), 433–58.

Reay, T. (2009), "Family-business meta-identity, institutional pressures, and ability to respond to entrepreneurial opportunities," *Entrepreneurship Theory and Practice*, **33** (6), 1265–70.

Redding, G. (1991), "Culture and entrepreneurial behavior among the overseas Chinese," in B. Berger (ed.), *The Culture of Entrepreneurship*, San Francisco: ICS Press, pp. 137–56.

Reiss, D. (1982), "The working family: A researcher's view of health in the household," *American Journal of Psychiatry*, **139** (11), 1412–28.

Reynolds, J. and L. Aletraris (2006), "Pursuing preferences: The creation and resolution of work hour mismatches," *American Sociological Review*, **71** (4), 618–38.

Rothausen, T.J. (1994), "Job satisfaction and the parent worker: The role of flexibility and rewards," *Journal of Vocational Behavior*, **44** (3), 317–36.

Rothausen, T.J. (2009), "Management work–family research and work–family fit: Implications for building family capital in family business," *Family Business Review*, **22** (3), 220–34.

Rousseau, D.M. and K.A. Wade-Benzoni (1994), "Linking strategy and human resource practices: How employee and customer contracts are created," *Human Resource Management*, **33** (3), 463–89.

Royce, J. (1885), *The Religious Aspect of Philosophy*, Gloucester, MA: Harper and Row, pp. 155–6. Reprinted in 1965 by permission.

Salter, M. and B. George (2008), "Since Enron, Little Has Changed," *Wall Street Journal*, 4 December.

Sawin, K.J. and M.P. Harrigan (1995), *Measures of Family Functioning for Research and Practice*, New York: Springer.

Schein, E.H. (1983), "The role of the founder in creating organizational culture," *Organizational Dynamics*, **12** (2), 13–28.

Schoorman, F.D., R.C. Mayer, and J.H. Davis (2007), "An integrative model of organizational trust: Past, present, and future," *Academy of Management Review*, **32** (2), 244–54.

Schulze, W.S., M.H. Lubatkin, R.N. Dino, and A.K. Buchholtz (2001), "Agency relationships in family firms: Theory and evidence," *Organization Science*, **12** (2), 99–116.

Schvaneveldt, J.D. and T.R. Lee (1983), "The emergence and practice of ritual in the American family," *Family Perspective*, **17** (3), 137–43.

Scott, S.G. and V.R. Lane (2000), "A stakeholder approach to organizational identity," *Academy of Management Review*, **25** (1), 43–62.

Shapiro, A.F. and J. Gottman (2005), "Effects on marriage of a psycho-communicative-educational intervention with couples undergoing the transition to parenthood, evaluation at 1-year post-intervention," *Journal of Family Communication*, **5** (1), 1–24.

Sharma, P. and S. Manikutty (2005), "Strategic divestments in family firms: Role of family structure and community culture," *Entrepreneurship Theory & Practice*, **29** (3), 293–311.

Shepherd, D. and J.M. Haynie (2009), "Family business, identity conflict, and an expedited entrepreneurial process: A process of resolving identity conflict," *Entrepreneurship Theory and Practice*, **33** (6), 1245–64.

Smilkstein, G. (1978), "The family APGAR: A proposal for a family function test and its use by physicians," *The Journal of Family Practice*, **6** (6), 1231–9.

Sorenson, R.L. and L. Bierman (2009), "Family capital, family business, and free enterprise," *Family Business Review*, **22** (3), 193–5.

Sorenson, R.L., K.E. Goodpaster, P.R. Hedberg, and A. Yu (2009), "The family point of view, family social capital, and firm performance: An exploratory test," *Family Business Review*, **22** (3), 239–53.

Sorenson, R.L., G.T. Lumpkin, A. Yu, and K.H. Brigham (2010), "Society in embryo: Family relationships as the basis for social capital in family firms," in T. Lumpkin, A. Stewart, and J. Katz (eds), *Advances in Entrepreneurship: Firm Emergence and Growth*, Bingley, UK: Emerald Group Publishing.

Stafford, L. and D. Canary (1991), "Maintenance strategies and romantic relationship type, gender, and relational characteristics," *Journal of Social and Personal Relationships*, **8** (2), 217–42.

Stafford, K, K.A. Duncan, S.M. Danes, and M. Winter (1999), "A research model of sustainable family businesses," *Family Business Review*, **12** (3), 197–208.

Stavrou, E.T. (1999), "Succession in family businesses: Exploring the effects of demographic factors on offspring intentions to join and take over the businesses," *Journal of Small Business Management*, **37** (3),43–61.

Stewart, C.C. and S.M. Danes (2001), "The relationship between inclusion and control in resort family businesses: A developmental approach to conflict," *Journal of Family and Economic Issues*, **22** (3), 293–320.

Stone, E. (2000), "Family ground rules," in K. Galvin and P. Cooper (eds), *Making Connections: Readings in Relational Communication*, Los Angeles, CA: Roxbury.

Sundaramurthy, C. and G.E. Kreiner (2008), "Governing by managing identity boundaries: The case of family businesses," *Entrepreneurship Theory and Practice*, **32** (3), 415–36.

Sutton, K.L and R.A. Noe (2005), "Family-friendly programs and work–life integration: More myth than magic?" in E.E. Kossek and S.J. Lambert (eds), *Work and Life Integration: Organizational, Cultural, and Individual Perspectives*, Mahwah, NJ: Lawrence Erlbaum Associates, pp. 151–69.

The Family, *I Ching*, (Chinese Book of Changes) (Hexagram 37).

Thompson, C.A., L.L. Beauvais, and K.S. Lyness (1999), "When work–family benefits are not enough: The influence of work–family culture on benefit utilization, organizational attachment, and work–family conflict," *Journal of Vocational Behavior*, **54** (3), 392–415.

Tsai, W. and S. Ghoshal (1998), "Social capital and value creation: The role of intrafirm networks," *Academy of Management Journal*, **41** (4), 464–76.

Tyler, T.R. and R.M. Kramer (1996), "Whither trust?" in R.M. Kramer and T.R. Tyler (eds), *Trust in Organizations: Frontiers of Theory and Research*, Thousand Oaks: Sage, pp. 1–15.

Upton, N., E.J. Teal, and J.T. Felan (2001), "Strategic and business planning practices of fast growth family firms," *Journal of Small Business Management*, **39** (1), 60–72.

US Small Business Administration (2006), "Guide to SBA's definitions of small business," available at: http://www.sba.gov, accessed 18 October 2006.

Villanueva, J. and H.J. Sapienza (2009), "Goal tolerance, outside investors, and family firm governance," *Entrepreneurship Theory and Practice*, **33** (6), 1193–99.

Ward, J. and C.E. Aronoff (1995), "Family-owned businesses: A thing of the past or a model for the future," *Family Business Review*, **8** (2), 121–30.

Weigel, D.J. (2003), "A communication approach to the construction of commitment in the early years of marriage: A qualitative study," *Journal of Family Communication*, **3** (1), 1–19.

Williams, J. (2000), *Unbending Gender: Why Work and Family Conflict and What to Do About It*, Oxford: Oxford University Press.

Winter, M., S.M. Danes, S. Koh, K. Fredericks, and J. Paul (2004), "Tracking family businesses and their owners over time: Panel attrition, manager departure, and business demise," *Journal of Business Venturing*, **19** (4), 535–59.

Winter, W., M.A. Fitzgerald, R.K.Z. Heck, G. Haynes, and S.M. Danes (1998), "Revisiting the study of family businesses: Methodological challenges, dilemmas, and alternative approaches," *Family Business Review*, **11** (3), 257–70.

Wolin, S.J. and L.A. Bennett (1984), "Family rituals," *Family Process*, **23** (3), 401–20.

Wolin, S.J., L.A. Bennett, D.L. Noonan, and M.A. Teitelbaum (1980), "Disrupted family rituals: A factor in the intergenerational transmission of alcoholism," *Journal of Studies in Alcohol*, **41** (3), 199–214.

Zuiker, V.S., Y.G. Lee, P.D. Olson, S.M. Danes, A.N. VanGuilder-Dik, and M.J. Katras, (2003), "Business, family, and resource intermingling characteristics as predictors of cashflow problems in family-owned businesses," *Financial Counseling and Planning*, **13** (2), 65–81.

Index

Printed and bound by CPI Group (UK) Ltd, Croydon, CR0 4YY

16/04/2025

14658379-0001